S0-BYO-014

SECRETS UNDER THE BRIDGE

SECRETS UNDER THE BRIDGE

by Overton Shelmire

Henington Publishing Company
Wolfe City, Texas

© 1994 by Overton Shelmire. All rights reserved

Two Turtle Creek Village, Suite 1313
3838 Oak Lawn
Dallas, Texas 75219

ISBN   0-9641720-0-3

To Bedford...thanks for the memories

Contents

Prologue

Most of us have an early childhood experience which we remember as our very first conscious thought — the moment when we begin truly to live and join the human race as thinking beings. Before that, some invisible force guides our little bodies through all the joys, sorrows, dangers, and endless mundanities of infanthood, be it nature's marvelous instincts, caring parents, a watchful nurse, or the hand of God.

In any event, the hours spent being cuddled and nursed, enduring wet diapers and tummy aches, and all the interminable waiting never seem to register. Then, suddenly, a certain experience turns a light bulb on in our heads. It may come at the circus, a birthday party, or in the kitchen while playing with a knife, but in each of our minds there is a bridge back to the farthest thought in our past — that first memory made. Beneath that bridge lie the answers to many secrets.

I was nearly four that eventful morning in 1933 — a few days before Christmas — standing in the middle of our bathroom floor making my very first memory. The glass medicine dropper tickled my skin and made me giggle as my seven-year-old brother painted me from head to foot with Mercurochrome. When he'd finished turning me into a "redskin," Bedford stood back with the empty bottle, admiring my transformation. Then, after announcing that I would henceforth be an Indian, he took a box of soap powder off the shelf and emptied it into the bathtub full of hot water. But instead of washing me, Bedford plopped our mother's long evening gown into the billowing suds and began to scrub it furiously.

My most vivid early recollections are of growing up with Bedford, and the pages of this book are filled with our most memorable adventures together. While I had attentive, loving parents, my older brother was my role model and constant star in my life. I followed him with endless fascination, for he was the inventive Pied Piper, always dangling the carrot of curiosity in front of my nose. Bedford accepted my existence with reluctant tolerance, for I was useful to his devious purposes now and then. Nevertheless, as I dogged his every step, I was duped, cheated and made to endure episodes filled with terror and pain.

These hardships were invariably followed, however, by moments of peace and joy — such as the day he admitted that our parents hadn't really bought my puppy and me from the gypsies for 25¢ in a package deal, as he'd been telling me. That happy revelation cleared up just

Bedford Shelmire III, age 6   Overton Shelmire, age 3

about everything for the moment. Then, there was the puzzle of seeing two different department store Santas on the same afternoon. Bedford explained to my satisfaction that the one who smelled like whiskey was only Santa's helper. I felt relieved once more, for when he wasn't being my tormentor, Bedford became my trusted tutor.

As I grew older, the secrets of life became ever more complex and harder to comprehend, and my older brother ever more reluctant to offer satisfactory explanations. I began to search for my own answers at school, in my grandmother's stories, and while exploring the wonders of nature along the creek that ran by her house. There, the mysteries of the very creation of life itself were to be revealed to me later — under the old stone footbridge. And with that discovery, I would gain the independence I needed to get my revenge over Bedford, and to finally escape the magnetic orbit of his inventive mischief.

I

Off to the Shrink

Bedford was in trouble...really big trouble this time. We could hear our mother's ominous footsteps coming down the hallway, and in a moment she'd open our bathroom door and discover his latest senseless crimes. Dreading to see her reaction, he searched his fertile imagination for an alibi.

Our mother cracked open the door, expecting to find us bathing, but gasped when she spotted me standing there proud and naked, dressed only in a coat of gleaming, iridescent red. After a moment of stunned silence came the expected shriek.

"Oh no...Bedford! What have you done? Are you trying to kill your little brother?" she shouted, grabbing him by the shoulders and shaking him vigorously.

"I...I was j...just decorating Wo for Christmas, Baba," said Bedford, sounding uncharacteristically meek and humble.

"But I've told you over and over that medicine can sometimes be poison! It's going to make him sick," she said.

Our mother had received her lasting nickname, "Baba," from me, during my baby days, as I pleaded for her to take me "bye-bye" every time she approached my crib. And while I'd been named William Overton for Baba's father, my paternal grandmother had condensed those names to "Wo," feeling that my parents had hung an unnecessarily cumbersome name on one so young. Bedford now enjoyed using this moniker, as he felt that "Wo" denoted a slowness of mind and body which he thought appropriate.

Baba scooped me up in her arms and turned toward the bathtub, but she was aghast to see, floating in the water, the evening gown she'd laid out to wear that night.

"Good Heavens!" she cried. "Bedford, why did you ruin my prettiest dress? Now I can't go to the Christmas ball."

"I was getting it 'Rinso white' for you," he explained, referring to a new-formula soap he'd heard advertised on the radio.

"Well, I wish you'd scrubbed your brother instead," she said, angrily, putting me in the wash basin to sponge me off. But when my bright red glow proved indelible, Baba rushed to the hall telephone and dialed our dermatologist father at his office.

"Oh, Bed. Come home right now! Bedford has poisoned his little brother with a whole bottle of Mercurochrome!...No, Wo didn't drink it...well, when I wouldn't let Bedford help decorate the tree, 'cause he's been so bad, he put every single Christmas ball on the floor furnace and watched them explode...said he thought the shiny glitter looked pretty flying all over the floor...that is not childish technology...what if it had hit him in the eye?...Then when I sent Bedford upstairs, he decorated Wo — every inch of him — with Mercurochrome. Will Wo get mercury poisoning?"

Bedford slinked in the shadows, wondering what our dad would say.

"Quit laughing, Bed!" said Baba, admonishing her husband. "That's why Bedford does all those crazy stunts...'cause you think they're funny! And he gets his ideas from the things you do, like your great mange experiment...furthering medical science nothing, and if you're too busy with patients to come home and do something about Bedford, then I will. Goodbye!"

Hanging up in disgust, she thought back to the time her husband had brought home several moth-eaten dogs he'd borrowed from the pound. He put Bedford and me in the cage to play with them so he could satisfy his curiosity as to whether or not humans can catch the mange from animals. Both we and the dogs had a wonderful time and caught not a thing from each other.

Baba searched the telephone book, then dialed the Dallas Child Guidance Clinic.

"Hello, this is Mrs. Bedford Shelmire, Jr.. Our son, Bedford the third, needs a psychiatric examination, this afternoon if possible...all right...Dr. Ezra Perry...at three o'clock...thank you, we'll be there."

Then she hung up and turned to little Bedford, who now had a look of deep apprehension on his usually cheerful countenance. "You're going to the doctor, Bedford. Go get your coat on while I dress Wo."

"What's the doctor going to do to me?" asked Bedford.

"He's a child psychiatrist who'll ask you questions so he can get into your mind and see why you do bad things...and try to help you," she explained, icily.

Bedford went downstairs feeling scared. He would let people in his closet and in his toy chest, but he didn't want anyone getting into his mind. Then he remembered how good he'd felt just the day before when he had taken a swig of some strange liquid. Sally had been making an angel food cake and Bedford noticed the open bottle of vanilla extract she'd left sitting on the counter. It had an interesting aroma, and when he took a sip, he liked the bittersweet flavor. After he'd taken a few more sips, a funny felling had come over him — a warm, cozy sensation. Now, he yearned desperately to feel good like he had yesterday.

Bedford raced to the kitchen and pulled the vanilla extract off the shelf. He took a big swig of the flavoring and began to feel calmer. Then he took another, and another until he'd emptied the bottle. Just as he threw it in the trash, Baba summoned Bedford outside and had no trouble enticing him into our brand-new, 1934 model Buick sedan. She hit the starter, pushed and pulled the hand choke, and in a moment we were chugging through the quiet suburb of Highland Park toward Bedford's fateful — but one he no longer dreaded — appointment with Dr. Perry.

The waiting room at the Dallas Child Guidance Clinic was filled with anxious mothers and their worried offspring, waiting to see one of the child psychiatrists. The mothers scanned the room with nervous eyes, wondering if the other little patients had done something worse than their own child.

As I sat next to Baba, glowing red, Bedford's crime was pretty obvious and the other mothers gave our mom sympathetic smiles. Bedford surveyed his fellow patients. These were his kind of people-bad, just like he was.

When Dr. Perry came into the waiting room to greet us, Bedford disappeared behind the huge fish bowl that sat on a table in the corner of the room. He stared into the water with nose and mouth pressed tightly to the glass, following the goldfish with his eyes until they crossed. He swam with them in another world — a world free of parents, and little brothers who would rob him of candy, toys, attention, and affection. All the doctor could see of Bedford through the fish bowl was his tousled blond hair, looking like ocean grass, and his magnified blue eyes.

"Hello there...why you're not a fish. I'd know a real, live boy anywhere," said Dr. Perry in his friendliest, most disarming tone of voice as their eyes first met. But Bedford was deep at the bottom of the ocean in his imagination and didn't answer. Then Dr. Perry glanced over at me in astonishment.

"He's one of the reasons Bedford's here," whispered our mother, jerking Bedford from behind the aquarium like a fish just pulled out of water.

Dr. Perry took Bedford into his office to examine him. But, before long he opened the door and summoned our mother to come in.

"Mrs. Shelmire, I've been checking your son's reflexes and observing the strange way he's walking," said the doctor solemnly. "I'm sorry to have to ask you this, but has Bedford been drinking?"

"Of course not! Why, he's just seven years old," she protested.

"Well, he's the youngest problem drinker I've ever encountered. I'm certain he's under the influence of alcohol," persisted the doctor.

"But Bedford doesn't even know where our spirits are kept," said Baba.

"That's the hardest kind of drinker to stop — the sneaky ones you least expect. They'll drink anything with alcohol in it, so you've got to figure out where he's getting it," said Dr. Perry. "But his drinking doesn't explain why Bedford won't talk to me. He hasn't said a word since we came in here."

Bedford continued to study the glass-paned ant farm that sat on the table next to the doctor's couch, and remained silent.

"This is one of his ploys I want to discuss with you," she said. "When he gets into an unpleasant situation, he pretends to be deaf and dumb, and nothing will make him utter a word."

"Mrs. Shelmire, if Bedford's not here about his drinking problem, why is he here?" asked Dr. Perry.

Baba sat back with a sigh, hardly knowing where to begin the story of Bedford's recent behavioral rampage. She recounted his numerous, diabolical crimes that had led her, in desperation, to bring him to the Child Guidance Clinic. When she'd finished, the doctor remained silent for a moment, seeming mystified by all the stories of cunning, greed, and deception.

"Well, Mrs. Shelmire, I'd say first that Bedford has intelligence, imagination, and inventiveness far exceeding his years. But there's a sinister aspect to his behavior, a vein of cruelty and violence. Is there any family history of insanity or criminal record?" asked Dr. Perry.

"No, not yet, but I hope you can do something with Bedford. All the Shelmires are...very unusual," said our mother, who was convinced that the weird, eccentric genes of her husband and his family had come crashing down in this one precocious terror. "Their father treats the boys like human guinea pigs, and Bedford does the same thing to Wo. My husband keeps all sorts of poisonous plants, strange birds and animals in our backyard. It's an experimental zoo. And he looks like the Pied Piper when he walks around the garage with all those rats following him."

"Rats?" exclaimed the doctor.

"Yes, he traps them in East Texas for his typhus fever research."

"Well, Mrs. Shelmire, you have an interesting family with many problems we need to tackle. I haven't formed an opinion yet as to the degree that his genes and his environment have influenced Bedford's behavior, but it's useless to continue his examination until he's willing to talk to me. And when he is, perhaps you could bring the boy's dad in. I think I know where Bedford gets a lot of his ideas," he said, getting up to show us out of his office. "Have the boys been to see Santa yet?"

"No," said Baba. "Bedford hasn't been good enough, but I'd planned to take them to see Santa this afternoon — if he behaved himself."

"Goodbye, Bedford," said Dr. Perry. "Too bad the cat's got your tongue and you couldn't speak. I just don't know how you're going to tell Santa Claus what you want for Christmas."

Bedford looked up at Dr. Perry, finally acknowledging his presence for the first time.

"I'll tell him I want a train...and I want a plane...and I want a boat," said Bedford, practicing up for Santa.

"But Bedford...what will you tell Santa when he asks if you've been good or bad?" inquired the doctor.

Bedford frowned as he thought for a moment. "I'll tell him I'm sorry!" he said sweetly.

II

Surviving Christmas

Christmas Eve finally arrived, along with a frigid, blue norther that had raced down from the North Pole, its bitter winds blasting our house with frozen raindrops. Now the icy, low-flying clouds paused above the treetops, resting, waiting for Santa Claus and his reindeer to catch up.

"When Santa coming, Befford?" I asked as we lay in bed, watching the light from our gas stove flicker on the ceiling.

"Not until you go to sleep, 'cause if you aren't asleep when Santa gets here, he won't leave you any presents."

"How he know I not asleep?" I asked.

"Santa's got eyes in the back of his head. Now, go to sleep, Wo!"

That sounded scary. I didn't want Santa sneaking down our chimney if he had eyes in the back of his head.

"Was that reindeers?" I asked, as the wind blew a tree limb against the roof.

"No, dummy, when Santa's reindeer land, you'll hear eight thumps."

"What's eight?"

"Oh, never mind. Shut up and go to sleep."

"I can't. Santa's coming...with eyes in the back of his head."

"Well, I'll tell you a big secret about Santa Claus," said Bedford. "If he comes in and finds a kid still awake, like you are now, he takes off that great big black belt he wears and whips him with it."

I sank low in my bed as the strong north wind blew outside, playing the gutters and eaves of our two-story, shingled house like an ancient flute. Tree branches scraping against the window seemed like frantic fingers trying to come inside.

"That's the cold, hungry wind that Santa flies in on...hear it out there howling? It's looking for something warm...like you!"

I pulled the magic protective sheet over my head and remained very still, hoping the covers would keep me safe till morning.

The Shelmire home at 3813 Miramar

"Psst...pssst...wake up!" whispered Bedford at daybreak. "Let's sneak downstairs to see what Santa brought us before Baba and Daddy wake up."

I pulled the magic protective sheet from over my head and confirmed that I'd indeed survived the night. Looking out the window through the early morning light, we could see that the rooftops of other houses, the street, yards, tree limbs were all covered with a thick layer of shining ice. The scene sparkled like a ceramic city as Santa's norther continued to occupy the neighborhood with silent, penetrating authority.

We crept down the stairway and when the fireplace came into view, it was obvious that Santa Claus had accepted Bedford's "I'm sorry." Our bright red stockings, which had hung limp and empty from the fireplace mantel when we'd gone to bed, were now bulging with goodies. Beneath Bedford's stocking lay everything he'd asked for: a model airplane, an electric train, and a little metal speedboat. Santa had placed a wooden airplane, a wooden train, and a little wooden boat under mine.

As we stood there in awe, trying to decide which new treasure to touch first, Bedford was surprised to discover a present he hadn't even asked Santa for.

"Look, Wo, a woodburning set. I'll burn my name into every wooden thing I own, and make Indian campfires with the hot needle point," he exclaimed.

We emptied our stockings out onto the floor, discovering tin soldiers, peppermint canes, rubber balls, little horns, nuts, apples, and tangerines. I spotted a box of green stick candy that lay on top of Bedford's colorful pile and picked it up.

"That's my candy Santa brought me!" said Bedford, grabbing the box out of my hand and licking one of the pieces to tantalize me. "Hmmm...oh yummy. This tastes better than angel food cake icing!"

My mouth watered for a piece of that candy, 'cause nothing...nothing tasted better than angel food cake icing! When Bedford turned around to start his electric train, I grabbed a piece that had fallen on the floor, stuffed it in my mouth, and tried to swallow it before Bedford discovered his loss. But it lodged in my windpipe and I began choking. When Bedford turned around and saw my face getting beet red, unable to breathe, he rushed upstairs to wake our father.

Daddy bolted down the stairs and working quickly like the skillful doctor he was, pounded me on the back and squeezed me around the waist, trying to dislodge the candy — but to no avail. He spread my jaws and reached down my throat, trying futilely to grab the end of the obstruction. Then, I saw the room turn upside down as I was picked up by the ankles and shaken like a rag doll, feeling panic, nausea, and the desperate sensation of being suffocated.

Finally, Daddy decided to perform an emergency tracheotomy, convinced that by the time an ambulance could get here, I'd be dead or have brain damage. He carried me into the kitchen, laid me on the counter next to the sink, and told Bedford to hold my arms. I heard the rustle of steel as Daddy jerked open a drawer and saw the silhouette of a butcher knife against the glare of the ceiling light as it descended towards my neck.

"Bed, what are you doing to Wo?" screamed Baba as she ran into the kitchen.

"Hold his legs, Mabel. He's choking... ...got a stick of candy stuck in his throat...I have to cut it out," he shouted.

They pinned my struggling arms and legs down on the counter. Then I felt helpless terror when the cold tip of the knife pricked the skin of my neck as Daddy searched for the place where the candy had lodged in my windpipe. Just as he located the hard lump and began to make the incision, every reflex, every muscle, every fiber in my body suddenly rallied in a mighty convulsive cough, and up shot the green candy cylinder.

Daddy put the knife away as my lungs finally filled with welcomed breaths of air. Then he lifted me off the counter and carried me back into the living room to recover on the couch.

"Don't you know you're not supposed to take things that aren't yours?" said Bedford, lecturing me on my behavior as he resumed playing with his toys.

"Don't open that woodburning set, Bedford," said Baba as she came in to put a cold washrag on my face. "I don't know what Santa was thinking, but I'm going to put it up in my closet until you're old enough to use it."

Bedford played with his electric train and model airplane for awhile, then decided to take his speedboat upstairs and try it out in the bathtub. I asked to go watch. The little metal craft seemed harmless enough — a small candle beneath a boiler which, when heated, would emit bubbles of steam to propel the boat.

"Be careful, Bedford when you light the candle, and don't let Wo play with the matches," cautioned Baba, happy to see my curiosity begin to overcome the trauma of the near-tragedy of Christmas morning.

When we got upstairs and filled the bathtub, Bedford lit the candle. Soon, little bubbles were popping out of the tailpipe and the boat began to cruise slowly around in circles.

"This is supposed to be a speedboat, not a rowboat," complained Bedford. "Let's get some acceleration!"

He went over to the medicine cabinet, took out a bottle of Mufti cleaning fluid, then filled the compartment under the boiler and lit it. The speedboat took off, now sputtering quickly around the tub.

A few minutes later, when the new, improved fuel had all burned out, Bedford filled the compartment with Mufti once again and lit it. But as the speedboat started putt-putting around, Bedford heard our dad calling him and he abandoned ship, dashing off to engage in some other activity.

As if hypnotized, I continued to watch the little speedboat until it began to slow down, running low on fuel. With only a flicker of a flame left in the compartment, I picked up the big quart of cleaning fluid and poured it into the boat.

Suddenly, the flame flashed up the stream, burning my hands and causing me to drop the full glass bottle of Mufti. It shattered on the tile floor, burning liquid instantly covering the whole bathroom. I stood there paralyzed by fear and pain, being scorched by lapping blue flames.

When Baba heard me make a feeble plea for help, she ran upstairs to the bathroom door and looked aghast at the gulf of fire that separated us. Christmas at our house had become a holocaust. As soon as she could muster her reflexes, Baba ran to our beds and grabbed two blankets. She threw one of them on the bathroom floor, smothering the flames, and then cloaked me in the other. She put me to bed, then smeared my badly burned hands and legs with Unguentine ointment, and wrapped them in gauze.

Baba sat by my bed, wishing her doctor husband were there and wondering where he and Bedford had gone. Glancing out the window at the frozen scene, she was horrified to see Daddy slipping and sliding along the icy street in his Ford coupe, pulling Bedford on his seldom-used sled with a rope tied to the bumper. How were her sons going to survive this day, she wondered?

Just then the phone rang — her mother calling long distance to wish us all a Merry Christmas.

"Your dad and I were just wondering how your Christmas Day is going...tell us about the boys," she said.

"I don't know where to begin, Mother, but somehow we're all still alive...Wo nearly choked to death, almost had his throat slit, and I just saved him from burning to death...now Bedford's being pulled down the street by a rope tied to his dad's bumper. I'll call you back later 'cause I've got to go stop them. But I'm going to take the boys and their dad to the child psychiatrist to have their heads examined. Goodbye."

Bedford walked in a few minutes later with a satisfied smile on his ruddy face from all the extraordinary activities of this unusual Christmas Day.

"Sorry about your shipwreck, Wo, and your burns...you shouldn't pour Mufti on an open flame. But when my speedboat exploded, you should have gone down with the ship, like captains are supposed to."

Bedford was right, and I had learned another lesson from him — the hard way, as usual. Sharing a bedroom with this imaginative little sorcerer was always informative as well as exciting. Bedford was the eternal, inventive flame...I, the circling moth, due to get burned now and then. And while he could never have been misconstrued as my guardian angel, I credit him with saving my life, or at least my sanity that Christmas morning — more than making up for all the pranks he was to play on me later.

III

True Confessions

"Looks like we're the only bad kids here today, boys," said Daddy as we entered the empty waiting room of the Dallas Child Guidance Clinic. The absence of little troublemakers sitting there was evidence that the children around town had been behaving themselves in anticipation of Santa's visit.

Daddy felt right at home, for the stark lineup of heavy oak chairs and polished linoleum floor reminded him of the waiting room at his own office, which was rarely closed. But since his father, who'd shared the practice with him had died the previous year, Daddy had to close this New Year's Eve to keep the appointment with Dr. Ezra Perry — as Baba had insisted.

When the nurse showed us into Dr. Perry's office, Daddy spotted the table with the ant farm on it. Having a natural curiosity about all things, he knelt down behind it to study the ants as they scurried up and down the tunnels they'd dug in the narrow soil pressed tightly between two pieces of glass.

"Good morning," said Dr. Perry as he strode into the room. "How was everyone's Christmas?"

"Well, we survived it somehow," said Baba, her dark brown eyes narrowing as she shook her brunette head, with a frown coming over her pretty face.

The doctor looked over at Bedford, figuring the explanation must lie with him. "Wow, where'd you get that nasty cut on your forehead, Bedford?" he asked, not really expecting an answer. But Bedford no longer felt a reason to feign deafness and dumbness since the pressure would likely be on his dad this time.

"Daddy was pulling me on my sled down the street behind his car. When Baba came out and yelled at him, he ran into the curb and I slid under the car and cracked my head on the bumper."

As Dr. Perry rolled his eyes and looked around the room, he finally noticed our dad down behind the ant farm. "Why Dr. Shelmire, thank you so much for coming."

When Daddy didn't answer, being preoccupied with the activities of the ants, Bedford proceeded to recount all the horrors on Christmas Day, of which he declared himself innocent on all counts.

"Ahem, good morning, Dr. Shelmire," said Dr. Perry again, trying to get the attention of our dad who seemingly had turned deaf and dumb himself.

"Oh, just a second," Daddy finally answered. "I'm following this little tiny ant who's carrying a great big piece of leaf down one of the tunnels, and I want to see where he's taking it — maybe to the queen." A moment later Daddy stood up. "Do you realize that if you were as strong as that ant you could carry a Cadillac down the street on your back?"

"No, I really didn't," said Dr. Perry as he scrutinized Daddy. "But I'm glad to have the whole family here with everyone finally communicating for a change."

Our Dad, having been blessed with a bright, sunny disposition, was of medium height, and thin and wiry. He had sparkling hazel eyes with a prominent nose and chin. His long, thin bespectacled face had a look of gauntness because of his lack of extra flesh. No one would suspect, just looking at him, that he had played quarterback for the 1913 Texas Longhorns.

"Dr. Shelmire," the child psychiatrist began in a serious tone of voice, "I gather you have a strong influence on your son's life. Tell me something about you and your family. When you were Bedford's age, did you thrive on mischief like he does?"

"Gosh no, not me — I was too busy doing chores around the house. When my father moved my mother, three sisters and me from Louisiana to Dallas in 1894 to start his dermatology practice, he bought a frame house on Thomas Avenue that didn't have electricity, running water, or a heating system. That was years before he built our big house out in Highland Park across the creek from Armstrong School. Every afternoon I had to pump the well and carry in buckets of water for drinking, cooking, and bathing in our big copper tub on Saturday nights. Then I had to chop wood for the stoves and fireplaces, the only heat we had in the house. And there was no bathroom, only an outhouse way out in the backyard and a fence that I had to keep whitewashed. So, I didn't have any time for misbehaving," said our dad, sounding most industrious.

"But Daddy," exclaimed Bedford, "you told us about dumping all those outhouses over every Halloween, and how you had a lot more fun when they had people in 'em. And you used to steal tomatoes at the grocery store and throw 'em at the dogcatcher when he drove his wagon by."

"Me and my big mouth," moaned our dad.

"Now those sound like ideas Bedford might have come up with," said Dr. Perry, making a notation.

"Let's hear the story your mother tells about how you pulled your front teeth out," said Baba, joining in as if Daddy were a seven-year-old, also.

"Oh, I guess I did some pretty crazy stunts, too, back when I was Bedford's age," said our dad with a chuckle. "Well, a friend and I went to the circus and saw a flying aerialist who swung by his teeth from a rope. Afterwards, my friend helped me up on the chinning bar in our backyard. I tied one end of some heavy chord to my front teeth, and the other end to the bar. But I accidentally slipped off and when I bounced on the ground, the teeth were still dangling in the air. My career as a circus aerialist was over," said our dad sheepishly, as if the event had just happened.

"And Dr. Shelmire, was your father's behavior ever unusual or eccentric?" asked Dr. Perry.

"Oh, I like the story about Paw Paw and the hot water bottle," volunteered Bedford, seeming to know where all the family skeletons were kept. "He used to sleep on the train going to medical meetings. Paw Paw always took two hot water bottles to bed — one full and one empty. Everybody else had to climb out of their berths in the middle of the night to fill up their rubber bottles with warm water and go to the bathroom. But Paw Paw would just pee in the empty one so he wouldn't have to get up," exclaimed Bedford, proud of his grandfather's inventiveness.

"Hmmm...I'm beginning to see a clear pattern emerging," said Dr. Perry. "Mrs. Shelmire, tell me something about your family."

"Oh, they're just simple, small town people, peaceful and conservative. Wo is a lot like my father, while Bedford gets his misbehaving streak from his dad and old Dr. Shelmire," said Baba, summing the whole thing up neatly for Dr. Perry.

"Now, with Bedford's long record of troublemaking, tell me how he's punished," said the doctor.

"I've tried switching his legs, but it hasn't seemed to do any good," lamented our mother.

"Daddy takes his belt off and waves it around a lot, but he never hits us with it," said Bedford, tauntingly.

"That's because I feel corporal punishment should be the job of the mother, since she's always home and can see things as they happen," said Daddy, defensively. "No, my type of punishment tortures the mind, not the body. I banish the kids to bed for hours at a time when they misbehave."

"Oh, it's not so bad. I keep my pockets stuffed with things to play with," retorted Bedford, pointing to the bulging protrusions on the side of his pants. Then he emptied out a jackknife, compass, water gun, ball and jacks, Little Orphan Annie secret decoder, spinning top, and a mirror. "The mirror's so I can signal my friend next door and let him know I'm being held prisoner."

"Now let's talk about overall family relationships," said Dr. Perry, changing the subject. "Are there arguments? Does anyone get angry?"

"My husband and I have never had a cross word between us," said our mother as she and Daddy smiled at each other. "When I get mad at Bed, I just pout and don't say anything."

"What's the maddest you've ever been at him?"

"The day he took the boys to the city dump to look for a $3,000 radium needle — stuck to a piece of adhesive tape — that the nurse at his office had accidentally thrown in the trash. He told Bedford and his friends he'd give them $100 if they found it. Just imagine those poor little fellows wading through pile after pile of filthy trash. I was furious and didn't speak to Bed for days."

"The maddest I got at Daddy was when he made me stop flying the Goodyear blimp," came Bedford's unsolicited offering.

Dr. Perry didn't smile, for he'd learned by now that when Bedford claimed he'd done something, it was usually confirmed by his parents.

"That's right," said our dad, "but I didn't know he really cared that much. My best friend is the top Goodyear tire dealer in Texas and last month he finagled a ride for the boys and me on the brand-new Goodyear blimp."

"When we reached the clouds, I saw Pegasus," said Bedford, staring wide-eyed out into the distance. He went on to explain how this flying red neon horse, perched high atop the Magnolia Building — the tallest in Dallas — lit up the heavens and played with low-flying clouds, turning them pink as they brushed across its giant wings. "I just wanted to fly around it and get a closer look."

"My friend had talked the pilot into letting Bedford sit in his lap and play with the steering wheel," explained Daddy, "but when Bedford started to turn the blimp toward the Magnolia Building, I hustled him back to his seat."

"I got mad at Daddy when he took the kitties away," I said, joining in the family assault on our dad.

I explained as best I could with my limited vocabulary, that while our dad was training his hunting dogs in our backyard one day, they began to bark furiously at the stray cat who'd decided to have her kittens under our house. Daddy called off the practice, deciding that it just wouldn't do to try and convince the dogs to share a yard with a cat and five kittens. So, he picked them up and put them in his car.

"Where are you taking the kitties?" I had asked.

My dad told me he would drive them out in the country so the mother could raise her kittens in the woods. I waved goodby to them, feeling mad at Daddy, and went to sleep wishing that dogs liked cats. The next morning, I glanced under the house where the kittens had been.

There, to my surprise was the mother cat and five kittens, I explained. Our dad was amazed that the mother cat had walked mile after mile, making five round trips to bring her kittens home. He said he didn't know how she found her way, but if she wanted them here that badly, she could stay.

"Well, I've gotten pretty darn mad at these little guys, too," responded our dad, "especially the day Bedford saw a movie about William Tell and talked Wo into letting him shoot an apple off his head...promised to give Wo his bicycle if he missed. Bedford borrowed a bow and steel-tipped arrow from the older boys next door and stood back about 10 feet from Wo. He drew the bowstring back just as I drove in the driveway. When I realized what was about to happen, I honked and honked. But Bedford let the arrow fly anyway and it hit the apple dead center. I started to whip Bedford's pants off with my belt, but decided instead to send him to bed for the whole weekend so he'd have time to think about what he'd done."

"Mrs. Shelmire, you and Wo certainly live with two strong-willed, eccentric men," said Dr. Perry, shaking his finger at Bedford and Daddy. "There's a clear pattern of inherited mischief on both their parts, but no consistent, predictable pattern to their behavior. It's amazing that you two have survived all the accidents and experiments."

"Well, I am getting pretty tired of life with *three* little boys. But we're expecting another visit from the stork, and I'm praying he'll bring us a sweet little girl I can pamper and dress up."

"Not much chance of that," said Daddy. "Miramar is a street of boys — 16 of 'em with only one little girl who just moved there. No realistic, expectant mother looks for anything but a boy."

"I'm going out in the waiting room and watch the fish swim," said Bedford, tired of the conversation. He already had one more little brother than he needed and he sure didn't want to talk about getting a little sister.

"When the new baby comes, Bedford will be more jealous than ever," said Dr. Perry after he'd left, "and he'll probably require even more discipline. Dr. Shelmire, you need to be firmer with Bedford, and get more involved in corporal punishment with the boys — not just sending them to bed so they can keep on playing their games. You act more like their big brother than their father. They have too much fun with you to take you seriously when you get angry. Start using that belt instead of just waving it around. And I would caution you from doing so much experimenting with your own family, even in the 'cause of medical science.' It gives Bedford the idea that he can play doctor with Overton too, and use him as a guinea pig."

"Good points," said Daddy, excusing himself from a conversation that had become tedious, to go peer into the aquarium with Bedford.

"Mrs. Shelmire, I really don't know what to say about Bedford, and the only advice I can offer you is to give him plenty to do to keep hands and mind occupied. Buy him creative toys, like an Erector set, a Tinkertoy set, a chemistry set, a woodburning set — things to take up his spare time. If he doesn't have those kind of interesting playthings, he's going to invent his own, and heaven only knows what that might be."

"Probably something to torment his little brother with," said Baba.

"Wo, right now Bedford probably wishes you weren't around," said Dr. Perry, "and I know he picks on you unmercifully. But younger brothers have a way of growing up to be bigger and smarter than their older brother and paying them back. When that day comes, Bedford better watch out."

"Thank you, Dr. Perry," said Baba as we got up to leave. "That's reassuring."

"Oh, Mrs. Shelmire," said the doctor, lowering his voice to a whisper, "I've been meaning to ask you...about Bedford's drinking. Is there still a problem? He seems sober today."

"No, I haven't smelled any whiskey on his breath," she said. "Can't imagine how he got into it last week."

"Goodbye and Happy New Year, everyone," said Dr. Perry — probably wishing he had a drink himself — as we reached the aquarium out in the waiting room.

When we arrived home, I followed Baba upstairs as she went to check on the dress she'd planned to wear that evening. There it hung, safely in her closet, out of Bedford's sight where he wouldn't get any ideas. She'd missed the country club Christmas ball because of his overzealous cleaning of it, but she wasn't about to miss tonight's New Year's Eve party.

Baba looked up on the shelf and spotted Bedford's woodburning set that Santa had brought him for Christmas — prematurely, she'd thought. But this might be the perfect thing to occupy his time this evening when they'd be out so unusually late. She took it downstairs to the kitchen where Margaret, our plump, jolly nurse, dressed in her usual starched white uniform, was busy preparing supper for Bedford and me.

Bedford felt like Christmas had arrived all over again as he received his long-awaited, sorely-missed woodburning set. He listened intently as Baba cautioned Margaret to keep an eye on him, and not let him start a fire or poke me with the hot point of the pen-like, cork-covered, electric carving tool. As would soon become apparent, he took note of both these intriguing ideas.

By the bedtime that had been decreed by our parents, Bedford had managed to burn his initials into nearly every wooden thing he owned. As for his baseball bat, it now bore the inscription, scorched into the end, "To Bedford — Good Luck from Babe Ruth."

"Come to bed, boys," said Margaret. "It's almost eleven o'clock and I want you up in five minutes," she said, climbing the stairs.

Bedford turned on the big floor model radio in the living room and we heard some fast, bouncy music. "It's midnight in New York City, ladies and gentlemen, and this is Guy Lombardo and the Royal Canadians helping bring in 1934 with some dance music," came the voice over the speaker.

Bedford rushed into the kitchen and I followed close behind. He opened the cabinet, got out the bottle of vanilla extract, and helped himself to a couple of gulps. He wiped his mouth on his sleeve as a warm, satisfied smile came over his face.

"Happy New Year, Wo," he said.

IV

The Birds and Bees

Life around our house became more tranquil after that last visit with Dr. Perry. Baba seemed to spend most of her time daydreaming about the baby girl she hoped for, and delving through romantic books as she searched for the perfect name. Bedford's behavior showed remarkable improvement as he buried himself in thousands of newly-acquired Erector set and Tinkertoy parts, creating giant skyscrapers, super bridges, and powerful rocket ships.

Then one morning, when he'd become bored with it all, a horrible, winged monster came buzzing toward my bed, pointing its menacing stinger at me. Would the magic protective sheets I was hiding under keep me safe that morning like they always had every night? The thing was all bright yellow with big, black bands around it and, except for the mask and skullcap with drooping antennas, it looked and sounded a lot like Bedford. But, then, I'd never seen a real monster and wondered if they didn't start to look like the kid they'd just devoured — such as my big brother, maybe?

I decided to seek my bathroom sanctuary and raced through the doorway just in time, spinning around with outstretched hand to ward off the demon. I felt a sharp pain as I slammed and locked the door, catching one of my fingers in the crack and smashing it. Mortally wounded by the monster, I suffered in terror until, suddenly, I heard the voice of an angel.

"Wo, don't be afraid. It's just Bedford in his bumblebee outfit for his school program. Hurry and get dressed or we'll be late," urged our mother.

Minutes passed but I still refused to unlock the door and abandon my sanctuary. "Come out this very minute!" Baba demanded.

"No, I won't. Befford's waiting out there to hurt me," I said, somehow anticipating the many stings he would inflict on me in years to come.

No amount of coaxing would work and I refused to open the door as long as Bedford was still alive. Finally, I heard her call Daddy at his office to discuss the matter. She hung up quietly and after a suspiciously short time, beckoned enticingly through the door:

"Oh, Wo, an airplane has just landed in the backyard. The little pilot is out walking around. Hurry, he's about to get back in and fly away. Come quick or you'll miss him!"

Curiosity overwhelmed caution and I turned the lock, threw open the door, and rushed headlong into the grasp of our mom, who had a stout privet hedge branch in her hand. Sally, our cook, stood beside her, looking anxious and concerned. She had come to work for us the day I arrived home from the hospital and quickly became my second mother. Sally was good to Bedford and cared for him conscientiously, but he had his own independent way and was such an uncontrollable, devilish little fellow that she could never fully relate to him. On the other hand, I was quiet and placid, and as I responded to her warmth and kindness, we grew to love each other deeply.

Sally shared the pain as Baba switched my legs vigorously, while Bedford looked on with mock sympathy. After receiving that series of stings I raced to look in the backyard, but alas, saw no airplane or tiny pilot walking around — only my winged tricycle with little propeller, and Bedford's young friend, Mirza, dressed also as a bumblebee for the school program.

Soon we drove off for Mrs. Taylor's School. The days I spent before going to kindergarten were forgettably uneventful except when I rode along in car pools. For me, riding in cars usually meant getting carsick.

"Get off my wings!" shouted Bedford. "Baba, Wo's trying to lie down and he's squashing my wings."

"I can't help it, Befford," I groaned. "My finger hurts and I'm getting sick." The giant bumblebee suddenly flew into the front seat at the prospect of his little brother throwing up on him, and landed on the startled fellow bumblebee.

We arrived at school just in time, somehow, and took our seats in the assembly room facing a makeshift stage. I slumped limply in my chair, trying to recover as Mrs. Taylor introduced the program.

"Welcome, parents, little brothers and sisters, to the first grade program. We especially want to wish Bedford Shelmire's little brother a happy birthday."

Baba felt a secret pang as she recalled the bitterly cold day exactly four years ago in 1930, when she and our dad had driven endlessly, up bumpy streets and down rough alleys, trying to coax me into the world on his birthday. Mine would really be tomorrow, but our two one-day-apart birthdays were to be celebrated jointly tonight.

I tried to smile as Bedford and Mirza flapped their wings and did pirouettes in a mock birthday celebration. The other children on the stage tittered as they stood there awkwardly — costumed, in addition to the bumblebees, as birds, trees, flowers, and butterflies.

Bedford Shelmire and Mirza Ámirkhan dressed in
their bumblebee costumes

"Today we have prepared a program about nature's seasons — spring, summer, fall, and winter. It's a program about some of Mother Nature's exciting little things — flowers, trees, butterflies, birds and bees," Mrs. Taylor announced.

Our mom blushed and felt uncomfortable at the impropriety of Mrs. Taylor's mention of "birds and bees" but she was relieved when none of the "little things" on the stage seemed to acknowledge the accidental sequencing of those words by Mrs. Taylor. The program went on as exuberantly and chaotically as could be expected with excited children in exotic, homemade costumes. Butterflies tried to land in trees, the bumblebees stung the birds, and flowers bloomed accidentally while winter snow in the form of Lux flakes floated down over the trees. In the end, the program was fun-for-all, free-for-all, and enjoyed by everyone, including me — if not as enlightening as Mrs. Taylor had planned.

That afternoon as I climbed the back porch steps behind Daddy, a great mystery suddenly occurred to me. If this huge giant walking up ahead was only one day older than I, then why was he so much bigger? I was still pondering the answer to this secret as Bedford and I sat in the kitchen, with the finger I'd smashed in the bathroom door still throbbing.

"Show me how old you are," Bedford said in a conciliatory gesture.

I held up my first three fingers, just as I had for nearly a year.

"Now, how old will you be tomorrow?" he asked.

I added the bandaged fourth finger to the display, with my newly-felt pride at being four the next day somewhat diminished by what my older brother had caused to happen to me. Then I asked Bedford to explain why our dad was so much bigger and stronger than I, given our day-apart birthdays.

"Eating birthday cake makes you bigger and eating spinach makes you stronger," he said. "When you've eaten 40 cakes and all the spinach Sally gives you, you'll be as big and strong as he is."

"I want some spinach now to grow big, Befford," I pleaded.

"Oh you do, eh? Okay," he said, as he went to the pantry, opened a can of spinach and heated it on the stove. Then he stood back with a satisfied smile on his face and watched me eat the whole thing.

"Happy birthday to you, happy birthday to you, happy birthday, dear Daddy, happy birthday, dear Wo," everyone sang a little later.

The chandelier was turned off as nurse Margaret entered carrying a huge chocolate cake for Daddy with many brightly burning candles, followed by a proud Sally, the cook, and an angel food cake with five candles on top, including my one to grown on. I stood in awe. What had been a normal, uneventful family gathering a moment before had suddenly become a wondrous pageant as the candles bathed the room with a mysterious, flickering light, and the faces of the celebrants became alive with the glow of anticipation.

We blew with all our mights, circling the candles until the very last one flickered out, and did I need my "one to grow on!" I felt so small. How would I ever be able to blow out 41 candles like Daddy had? And why hadn't the spinach begun to work, I wondered? The lights came back on and a haze of smoke arose from each candle where a moment before had been a bright, flickering flame. The spell was broken. Presents were opened, ice cream and cake served. I took one bite of angel food cake...and threw up all over the floor.

"What in the world?" exclaimed Baba. "Looks like somebody's fed Wo a whole can of spinach, and you know how he hates the stuff!"

"Bedford, I'll just bet you had something to do with this," said Daddy, loosening his belt.

By next morning, I had fully recovered from the overdose of spinach and was all set to enjoy my real birthday. But terror can strike at any moment, from any direction when you are four and living with a "fiend" who spends much of his time turning the most harmless tool or toy into a device of torment and destruction. Bedford chased me into the bathroom once again — this time with the hot point of his wood-burning set and, having finally gotten his little brother out of his hair, descended into the basement to make an Indian campfire. Baba had instructed me never to lock the bathroom door under any circumstances, but in frantic desperation, I had forgotten and turned the bolt with all my might.

After spending what seemed an eternity in my refuge, I heard a commotion downstairs as smoke started pouring under the bathroom door. Baba soon began pounding on it and shouting:

"Wo, come out quickly — the house is on fire! I really mean it! Out this very minute!"

The smoke told me that this time I had no choice. I squeezed the round thumb-bolt with all my might, but since I hadn't had any spinach that morning "to make me grow big and strong," it wouldn't budge. I panicked, afraid Baba wouldn't believe me. But finally, convinced that the lock was really stuck, Baba notified Daddy at his office, then telephoned the Highland Park Fire Department to come put out the fire burning in our basement. I heard the station bell clang, coming from two blocks away, the fire truck motor crank up, and the siren wail.

Moments later, the big, shiny red machine rolled up, and out jumped three firemen in heavy, black rubber boots, coats, and helmets. A crowd began to gather from up and down the street as the firemen lifted a gigantic ladder up to my bathroom window sill. Two of them raced down to the basement with extinguishers while the third began to climb up toward me. I was now frozen with fear — instead of a switch in his hand, he was carrying a huge axe. He reached the top, glanced at me through the screen, then ripped it off and threw it to the ground. He stuck a tremendous black boot in the window and climbed in, using the toilet as a step. Shouts came from below that the smoky, but minor fire was now completely out. The huge fireman managed to unbolt the door, much to my relief, rather than chop it down. Then he picked me up and carried me in one huge arm downstairs, past Baba who was on the telephone, and out the front door. I felt proud and triumphant as the assembled crowd of neighbors watched with relief and amusement.

"You weren't supposed to lock the door anymore," muttered Bedford, envious of all the attention I was getting on my birthday, and trying to look innocent.

"Befford started the fire," I said, pointing the bandaged finger at my horrified big brother. "He lighted a Indian campfire in the basement."

All eyes turned on Bedford, with the concentrated power of a death ray. He looked up at the big, angry-looking fireman, a sheepish smile coming over his face.

"I'm sorry," he said meekly.

V

Defying Gravity

Winter soon departed, spring blossomed, then summer showed up — along with a new baby brother named David. But when fall arrived, babies of a far different sort arrived at our house.

Two baby alligators cruised contentedly in the freshly-dug pond as Baba watched from her bedroom window, getting angrier by the minute. She had never been able to raise flowers, and now Daddy had gone and dug a mudhole right in the middle of her backyard lawn and filled it with water and alligators.

Planners had laid out our deep Highland Park lot with plenty of space for — in addition to the house — ample lawn, flower beds, vegetable garden, garage, tool room, servant's quarters, clothes lines, animal yard, and hen house. If something had to give in the constant battle of backyard elements, invariably it was Baba's zinnias, petunias, and pansies that suffered. She'd long dreamed of having beautiful flower beds. Instead, boys, dogs, cats, chickens, and now alligators overran her yard. But soon, she would enjoy the lush plants and lovely blooms of Cuba.

Her frustrations and disappointments ran deeper than a lack of flowers, however. Our father shared few of her interests. On weekends when Daddy wasn't working in his poison ivy garden, or trapping rats in the East Texas oil field for his typhus fever research, he would disappear to the country club in his quest for the elusive round of par golf. He never took her to concerts, the opera, or ballet. If she went with friends, he'd pout at being left alone or perform some outlandish experiment. He attended church with her only on Easter Sundays. The minister, ending his sermon, would invariable peer down at our dad and say:

"To those of you we won't be seeing until next Easter, I want to wish you a Merry Christmas!"

Despite their different interests, Daddy had really been a good husband in the ways that counted most. He was devoted to his family, and provided for our every need in his frugal way. Baba, though, needed fulfillment and yearned for fun, gaiety, dancing — elements that had long been lacking in her life. Tomorrow she and Daddy would board a cruise ship in Galveston and sail to exciting, colorful, romantic Havana where he would attend a dermatology meeting. Nothing was going to stop her.

She had been saddled with small children almost since she'd come to Dallas. Nevertheless, she would miss her three boys — most of all baby David, asleep in his crib — and wondered how she could tell us she was leaving. But she would, tonight, and she'd hold and rock each of us.

"Still mad about the alligators?" we overheard Daddy ask.

"Yes, and the swamp you made of my yard," she replied.

"Don't worry, we'll just keep the little 'gators for awhile, then let them go at White Rock Lake."

"Before they grow too big, I hope," said Baba. "Why'd you have to go and get two alligators anyway? The only person who's had more animals in his backyard than you was Noah, and at least he had some-place to keep them."

"Noah was running a salvage operation — I'm doing research," he answered.

Despite all his eccentricities, our mother simply adored this funny, wonderful, unabashedly selfish man and couldn't be married to anyone else.

That night our parents put us to bed with tender goodbyes, but in the wee hours of the morning, Bedford and I awoke with burning welts appearing on our faces and bodies. Daddy diagnosed two cases of chicken pox. Baba put aside her tremendous feelings of disappointment, for the moment, to care for us. When she'd seen Daddy off for his meeting in Havana, and all was finally quiet, she then had time to sit down for a good cry.

Baba brought us lots of ginger ale and chicken soup and tried to make us forget our discomfort by playing records. After a few days, our fevers subsided and our burning, aching pocks began to itch.

"Don't scratch your faces," Baba warned, "or you'll make scars."

To keep our hands occupied, she brought me a "Little Orphan Annie" book, and a "Dick Tracy" book for Bedford.

"Bum book Befford," I said, as I tossed mine on the floor. Annie's eyes just weren't right.

He put his book down too, growing restless after having his tremen-dous energy subdued by his illness. This was the moment Baba dreaded, for she knew that being cooped up with Bedford while sharing the chicken pox would hardly be a convalescence for me. What would he pull this time? She was afraid to take her eyes off him, yet had to leave the house for an appointment.

"Why don't you and Wo make something with your hands so you won't scratch your faces? Here's some paper and scissors and a ball of cord. Try this 'cat's cradle,'" she said as she demonstrated.

Surely Bedford couldn't get into too much trouble doing that, she thought as she drove away. When she had gone, Bedford got several volumes of the *Book of Knowledge* encyclopedia down and we turned through the exciting pages of inventions, trying to find something more challenging to make.

"We could build an automobile, or a diving helmet, or a radio station if we had the right parts; we'll build 'em someday," he said confidently. "I know what we can make with the parts we've got — a parachute. Dick Tracy says 'He who conquers gravity will rule the earth.' Let's build a parachute so we can at least defy gravity."

"What is grav-i-ty?" I asked.

"Well," Bedford thought, "it's like how stingy you are with your toys...you hold on tight to them and never want to let them go. That's how the earth is, and we are its toys, along with animals, houses, trains — everything. It holds us all tight 'cause it's selfish, like you."

He took a sheet off my bed and tied pieces of cord to it, then tied the other ends of the cord to a harness he'd made out of canvas suitcase straps. Soon he had the makeshift parachute packed and ripcord adjusted.

"Ready to jump, Wo?" he asked.

"Why don't you jump first?" I said.

"Because, I'm the inventor and have to observe and record the results."

"If I jump, will I get hurt?"

"No you won't; that's the whole point of a parachute — to defy gravity."

Reluctantly, I agreed to be the test pilot and he strapped the parachute over my itching back and boosted me up on top of our high toy cabinet in baby brother David's nursery. I looked down nervously from the terrifying height.

"Jump, Wo, jump, and don't forget to pull the ripcord," prodded Bedford. "And don't worry — I packed that chute myself."

Baby David cooed happily in his crib as I jumped, and struggled with the ripcord. I crashed on the floor in a heap with the unopened parachute. When I regained my composure, Bedford was squirting tube after tube of model airplane glue onto a cut up pillowslip and spreading it over the cloth with a ruler.

"What are you doing now, Befford?"

"Oh, you're feeling better...and not so mad anymore? Sorry about your crash, but that was pilot error; you waited too long to pull the ripcord. We need a longer jump to give the chute time to open. You could stand in this window and you could jump out and..."

"No, no, I'm not going to do it," I shouted. "But...what is that you're making?"

"I'm making a second parachute. When the glue dries, you'll have this small chute to help the main chute open when you jump."

"Me jump?" I asked in mock protest, beginning to find his inventions and powers of suggestion irresistible.

"Sure, and you can help me dry the glue. Stick your head in the chute and blow till it's dry," said the inventor.

After I'd blown and breathed the glue vapor for several minutes, I emerged on a cloud — in a dope-headed daze.

"I feel like I'm flying, Befford."

"I think you're ready for the big jump," he said, sensing a rare opportunity.

He helped me stagger over to the second-story window and had to keep me from falling out as he strapped on the parachute.

"I'll just tie this little chute on and the big one should open like a dream. That'll do it. Good luck...ready...jump!" shouted Bedford.

I leaped out the window in my drunken stupor, fully expecting to fly, rather than fall. But fall I did, and fast — right past the kitchen window. Sally, standing at the sink, saw me go hurtling by, followed by some cord, a bedsheet, and a billowing pillowslip. The main chute finally opened, simultaneous to my crashing into a patch of grass between the basement steps and the pit of startled baby alligators.

"It opened — my parachute worked!" shouted Bedford from the upstairs window, with exuberance that epitomized man's inhumanity to man.

Sally rushed out, exemplifying love and devotion as she administered to my crumpled body with her characteristic tenderness. Having been relaxed "on the vapors" when I crashed, I suffered no broken bones. As soon as I could focus my eyes, Sally and Baba appeared, hovering over my bed like multi-colored angels.

Baby David, who'd been watching the whole parachute fiasco, stood wide-eyed in his crib. Suddenly, without warning, he rolled over the side rail and landed headfirst in his dirty diaper can, screaming and crying, his protruding legs churning. Oh no, thought our horrified mother as she ran into his room. Could she have another Bedford on her hands? Why did she have four little boys, including her husband, and no soft, sweet little girl to dress and relate to? Who would she trade — Bedford? Me ? David? No, she'd keep her boys, but out of David's room...and out of parachutes.

VI

Peeking at the Centennial

The prisoner trembled as the warden, priest, and guards entered his cell.

"It's time to go," said the warden. "Do you have anything to say?"

"I'm innocent...I didn't do it...I was framed," pleaded the wild-eyed man.

"That's what they all say," whispered Bedford, unconvinced, as we sat on the front row of the live "crime show" at the 1936 Texas Centennial Exposition in Dallas. We had been strolling along the Fair Park midway with our parents one hot June morning when a barker got our attention:

"Ladies and gentlemen, Warden Lewis E. Lawes of Sing-Sing Prison proudly presents his crime prevention exhibition, with actual behind-the-scenes facts on crime in America — its causes, prevention, detection, and punishment. See 1000 amazing features from inside prison walls — only 40¢ for adults and 15¢ for children."

Baba and Daddy chose to watch ice skating at the Black Forest beer garden instead, but Bedford lured me in with him to see lots of guns, a gangster getaway car, and maybe even Dick Tracy. Now the priest began a solemn chant as the condemned murderer prepared to walk the "last mile" to the electric chair — across the stage right in front of us.

"The Lord is my shepherd, I shall not want. He maketh me to lie down in green pastures..."

That sounded nice to me, but the prisoner still looked worried and wouldn't go. The guards pulled him out right in front of us on the stage. Struggling for a moment, his legs buckled and he had to be carried by the arms.

"Yea, though I walk through the valley of the shadow of death, I will fear no evil..." the priest droned on.

"I don't want to die!" screamed the terrified prisoner. "All right, I confess — I did it. But, I didn't mean to kill the old lady. It was an accident. I'm sorry...I'm not ready to die...I'm sorry!"

"He said he was sorry," I whispered.

Everything would be all right now. Saying "I'm sorry" had always worked for Bedford. But, the guards continued to drag him into a room where a huge wooden chair with leather straps stood. They buckled the frantic man in the chair and placed a wired metal saucer on top of his head.

"Surely goodness and mercy shall follow me all the days of my life, and I shall dwell in the house of the Lord, forever," the priest concluded.

"Okay, ya dirty coppers — I'm glad I killed her. She had it coming and so do you. Go rot in hell," said the unrepentant murderer with his last gasp.

A man in a black suit standing outside threw a big switch and fire crackled and spewed over the wires and into the air as the prisoner jolted and jerked. His head fell over and he remained still. A smoky haze rose from the limp form as a doctor listened to the man's chest and pronounced him dead.

"Wow, did you see how they fried that killer!" exclaimed Bedford. "That's what's gonna happen to you, Wo, if you don't behave."

The guards unstrapped the body and carried it off on a stretcher. They might as well have come to get me too, as I sat stunned and frozen in horror from the grotesque episode I'd just witnessed — the play seemed all too real to me. Just then, Warden Lawes came on stage, looking down at us somberly.

"You have seen the 'last mile' walked as it actually happens night after night, throughout the country. This should convince the criminally inclined that crime does not pay. We have shown the cold, grim side and proved that crime can never declare a dividend for its speculator — that there is a cause for crime and there is a cure. If not, there is the inevitable detection and finally...punishment," the warden concluded.

That punishment sure had been a lot worse than a switching, I thought. My legs felt wobbly as we followed the audience around to various displays of weapons, early prison tortures, the new lie detector, and methods of counterfeiting.

"I could make coins with my electric lead-molding set," whispered Bedford sheepishly, as if his intent to break the law had already made it a fact. "It's pretty hard to make ends meet on 25¢ a week."

On our way out we passed the gang lord's big car, so black and shiny we could see our reflections as we circled its armored body, giving it the veneration due a spaceship just landed from Mars.

"I'll make a car like that," said Bedford. "I could take the gasoline motor off Baba's washing machine, only I don't know where to pick up bulletproof glass, a disappearing license plate, and a smoke screen device."

"Well, how was gangster land, men?" asked Daddy as we walked back out on the midway.

"Great," said Bedford, as I remained speechless. "We got lots of good ideas."

"I just hope they're on the right side of the law," said Baba.

The midway was a magnet for the Depression-weary Centennial crowds. Milling through concessions, hunting thrills and amusement, gasping at the sights, they halted to heed the barkers.

"Right this way, ladies and gentlemen. Come see Midget City, a Lilliputian community where one hundred midgets live and work together."

We entered a serene village with strange little people just my size, and peered into their tiny city hall, store, bank, and restaurant. All seemed peaceful and pleasant in this little community where everyone stayed small, forever. There were no guns, no gangster cars, no electric chairs. I was finally beginning to feel happy and comfortable again as we walked back to the midway.

"Can we ride that Ferris wheel?" I asked. It looked scary but everyone twirling around on it seemed to be having such a good time.

"Not now," came the answer as we approached a large, white mountain of snow with a cave-like entrance. Daddy began reading a big poster:

SEE LITTLE AMERICA FIRST — A REPLICA OF THE MOST AMAZING CITY EVER BUILT, THE WORLD'S FARTHEST SOUTH COLONY, THE ANTARCTIC BASE FROM WHICH ADMIRAL RICHARD E. BYRD AND HIS DAUNTLESS MEN SPENT MANY MONTHS, PUSHING BACK THE LAST FRONTIER, DISCOVERING NEW LANDS AMID UNTOLD HARDSHIPS AND PERIL.

The frigid atmosphere inside the icy cave had the musty, pungent odor of furs, leather, and dogs.

"Feel the air-conditioning, Wo? It's a new invention where a machine cools the air," said Bedford. "Bet I could make one like it."

We stopped to look at a dozen Alaskan husky sled dogs, enjoying their leisure after having served the expedition so faithfully and well. They looked majestic and wise, as if they each had an adventure story to tell. Bedford rushed ahead to visit the radio room, having noticed the two, tall poles with an antenna wire strung between them on top of the snow mountain outside.

"I'm going to build a radio station someday," he promised, studying the microphone, needles, and knobs.

We gazed at the expedition's big Ford trimotor airplane, resting on enormous landing skis, its huge wingspan barely fitting within the snow cave. Bedford looked up at it, wide-eyed and silent. I kept waiting for the expected pronouncement. Finally he made it.

"I'm going to build a...model of this plane," he said, having finally met his match and the limits of his ambition and resources.

"Are we going to ride the Ferris wheel now?" I asked Baba.

"No, we need to hurry to make the five o'clock Calvacade of Texas Pageant."

We walked behind the Cotton Bowl stadium and entered another grandstand, made of wood, that faced an enormous stage as wide as a football field. On it were mountains, canyons, forests, plains, and roads and trails across which the processions would move. The Cavalcade was a mammoth, dramatic spectacle, a re-enactment of the highlights of 400 years of Texas history, beginning with the discovery of the area by the Spanish in 1519. The extravaganza had huge prairie schooners, oxcarts, stagecoaches, a full-size ship, longhorn cattle, Indian tepees, and soldiers with rifles and cannons.

We watched in awe and wonder as hundreds of men, women, and children took part in presenting the store of dramatic events under the flags of Spain, France and Mexico...to Texas' independence as a Republic in 1836...to a state of the Union in 1846...on to the Confederacy, and finally re-uniting with the other states of our great country after the Civil War.

Startling sights and thrills seemed endless that September afternoon at the Centennial, but the biggest surprise came as we turned the corner onto the midway. There, before us, loomed a great ship, the *SS Normadie* rising out of the pavement, with portholes on the sides and big anchors hanging off its bows. It seemed to be sailing right out of a quaint city called Paris, with high roofs, tall chimneys, and window boxes filled with flowers. We walked the gangplank, climbed to the restaurant on the top deck, and sat down for supper. A French sailor took our order, but they didn't have anything I asked for. During one of the long waits between courses, Baba and Daddy left the table to visit friends.

We sat next to a railing with a flat deck beyond, and a sign:

DANGER — KEEP OUT — NO PERSONS
BEYOND THIS POINT

But we could hear music, clapping, and whistles, and see the flash of silver-white light as darkness approached. I knew what Bedford was going to do. Suddenly he bolted over the rail, and I followed. Reaching the other side of the deck, we got down on our hands and knees and looked over the edge. Our eyes were filled with golden hair, painted faces, and bare, white skin — lovely arms, legs, and bosoms everywhere! We watched with breathless excitement, bedazzled by the flash of colorful, sequined gowns being put on and pulled off.

Bedford and I were peering into the costume changing tent of the French Review and the top had been rolled back for ventilation that hot evening, exposing the dancers and all their charms to our prying eyes. Finally, Baba broke the spell as she motioned for us to come back to the table.

Darkness had arrived as we walked off the gangplank of the *SS Normandie*, and the lights of the midway blinked and blazed. The rotating Ferris wheel reminded me of the lighted parasols in the French Review. But now the hour had grown too late for a ride and once again, I would have to be patient.

The next day I helped my Sally dry the Sunday lunch dishes and told her of all I'd seen at the Centennial.

"There was a village of little tiny people...a big ship sailing out of town...a cold cave with an airplane in it...naked girls in a tent...and a man in the electric chair, and..."

"You saw what?" asked Sally, disbelievingly. "What an imagination you have, Honey, but you kids always think you see a lot more than you really do. What did you like best?"

"I liked the Ferris wheel, but I didn't get to ride it."

"Say, tomorrow's Colored Day at the Centennial and my day off, so I'm going out. Let's ask your mother if you can go with me, and we'll ride the Ferris wheel as many times as you like."

The next morning we boarded a streetcar for my very first trolley ride. Baba had given us the price of admission, plus a crisp new $5 bill to last us all day on the countless pleasures the Centennial had to offer. Sally flipped a small metal plate over the window that read "white," to "colored." Then she put me in the seat in front of her where the plate was flipped to "white."

"Why can't I sit next to you, Sally?" I asked.

"You have to sit where it says 'white,' and I have to sit where it says 'colored'— it's the law."

The motorman looked back approvingly, and pushed and pulled his lever to start and stop along the tracks. I spent most of the trip to Fair Park flipping the plate back and forth from "white" to "colored" to "white," breaking the law, unconsciously, with every other flip.

We entered the main gate and headed straight for the Ferris wheel.

The sign read "TICKETS — 5¢." Sally handed the $5 bill to a rough-looking woman in the ticket booth, but received only 90¢ change.

"I gave you a $5 bill," said Sally sweetly, "but you only gave me change for a dollar."

"No you didn't," said the woman gruffly; "you only gave me a one."

"It was a five. The lady I work for gave it to me this morning," said Sally, pleadingly.

"No, it was just a dollar," said the woman with finality in her voice; then she looked away and ignored us.

Sally stood there quietly for a long time, staring out far beyond the fairgrounds. She had always been able to solve problems with patience and waiting, but not this time. She didn't know what to do...there was nothing she could do. We just kept standing there, waiting for something to happen, but it didn't and I hurt for her. We walked away without riding the Ferris wheel; Sally was just too proud, and I understood.

We strolled along, enjoying the sights and sounds. Finally we sat down by the lagoon to decide how we'd spend the 90¢ we had left. There would be nickel Dr. Peppers at 10, 2, and 4 o'clock as the advertising signs suggested, and hamburgers at noon for a dime. That would leave us just enough to do the funhouse, the crystal maze, hall of crazy mirrors, and to give the claw machine a couple of cranks.

Finally, when we had plunked down our last dime for two drinks, we explored the numerous free attractions. We saw a marionette show, a rope-walking goat, the hum-a-tune man with his strange, waffle-looking instrument, and the animal pavilions.

Late in the afternoon, Sally got out the Ferris wheel tickets and decided not to deprive me of my ride just because her pride had been hurt when we were cheated. Walking proudly past the horrid woman in the booth, we gave our tickets to a fat, sweaty, cigar-smoking man in an undershirt. He closed the wooden gate over our seat and the big wheel began to turn. It surprised me when we rotated backwards, and I feared I would slip off the bench as I watched the ground fall swiftly away.

I felt the blood rush to my feet and closed my eyes as we reached the top, but the butterflies in my tummy became so intense as we began to descend that I had to open them again. The fear of falling changed, on the second revolution, to the thrill of flying high above the milling throng.

When we'd made a few revolutions and the time came to get off, the fat man let us go around again, and again, and again, for what seemed like an hour or so — much to our delight. Perhaps he knew what had happened?

All seemed right in the world as Sally and I sauntered along the main esplanade, hand-in-hand, admiring the murals and giant sculptures of stone. It was twilight and the huge searchlights began to shoot up from the Hall of State in a fan pattern, looking like quills of fire. Music wafted from the pylons that had winged horses on them, as spray from the fountains drifted in pastel-tinted clouds. And, the most beautiful spectacle of the Centennial, the esplanade, was free.

When we arrived home, I told Bedford of all our adventures, but he offered little sympathy over the theft of our $5 bill — he was deeply engrossed in the construction of his model of the Antarctic expedition's Ford trimotor airplane.

A few days later, the epic Texas Centennial Exposition came to a successful close. As the multitude of exhibits and rides were being dismantled, the huge airplane disappeared mysteriously one night from the replica of Admiral Byrd's Antarctic base, never again to be seen.

"How about that!" said Bedford, looking at the newspaper story with a picture of the empty snow cave. "First you and Sally get robbed, then Admiral Byrd has his plane swiped — right under the nose of Warden Lawes and his 'crime show.' Now who says crime doesn't pay?"

VII

Crossing the Bridge

"Hurry up, Wo, or you'll be late your first day of school, " urged Baba one September morning after the Centennial summer had sizzled by.

My fingers grasped the ends of the shoelaces — fumbling to make them loop around, over, under, and through each other — but no manipulation...no arrangement...no forcing of the laces would work.

"Mabel, he's having trouble because you let him start off doing things left-handed," admonished Daddy.

"No, he's just retarded," said Bedford. "Here, Wo, I know a simpler way to tie your shoelaces. Try this...first, wrap the laces around each other. Then, make a big loop out of each end. Now, wrap the loops around each other and pull them tight. Get 'em tied and I'll walk you to school so I can monitor the knots."

I did as he said and suddenly, as if by magic, a beautiful bow appeared on top of my shoe. In a moment, Bedford and I were striding down the street toward school with my two proudly-tied shoelaces leading the way. But by the time we reached the charming stone footbridge that spanned the creek near my grandmother's house, they were both untied and dragging behind; nothing lasts forever, it seemed.

I leaned down to tie my shoes and could see the reflection of Armstrong School in the water beneath the bridge. I would cross this stone arch every morning to unlock the secrets of education, but there were deeper secrets waiting for me below — secrets of the very creation of life itself, and the bridge would keep them for me there. For now, school beckoned.

"I can't tie my shoes, Bedford. I forgot how," I pleaded.

"Okay, dummy, I'll tie 'em for you, but this is the last time," he said.

He got down to fix them, then dashed off for home. I waved goodbye to him in appreciation, as a teacher standing at the nearby school entrance motioned for me to come in. I turned to run for the door, but my feet wouldn't work — Bedford had tied my shoelaces together, and I fell flat on my face.

Overton Shelmire at age 6 in 1936.

Vowing to kill my big brother when I got home, I struggled to untie the knot, but it was tied too tightly. The mystified teacher had to come over and do it for me while other students snickered at my strange misfortune as they ran across the bridge on their way to school.

"Good morning, children. I'm Miss Cowser, your first grade teacher," said the small, cheerful lady when I finally arrived at class. "Now that you're seated, let's discuss all the rules you must observe in my room."

She went over being on time and staying in our seats; washing our hands and not talking in class; sharing things and putting them back in their place; not playing in our desk inkwells or eating paste.

"Tomorrow we'll brush up on the letters of the alphabet and start to make words," said Miss Cowser. "Then we'll put the words together to make sentences. If we make the words our friends, they will tell us stories. Next, we'll begin learning arithmetic. Lots of fun-filled adventures lie ahead with words and numbers!"

When the first day orientation was over, Baba waited for me back at the bridge. "Now, Wo, you'll be walking by your grandmother's house when you pass over this bridge on your way home. Stop by and visit Maw Maw as often as you can. She and your Aunt Olive get lonesome. They'd love to see you and hear about school."

I could see the reflection of my grandmother's red-tile-roofed, Mediterranean style home under the bridge. Every afternoon I would cross over to hear the secrets of my family heritage unlocked by her stories. The other answers I would need to extend my own branch of our family tree would wait for me there — beneath the bridge.

I didn't stop by Maw Maw's house that afternoon, however. Seeking revenge for the humiliation he'd caused me on the bridge, I raced home ahead of Baba and up to Bedford's closet. I fiddled and fumbled with the elusive square knot until I finally mastered it, and when Bedford returned home from his own school orientation, he found all his shoelaces tied together in jumbled mats of tight knots, each topped with a perfect bow.

"You little screwball, I never should have taught you how to tie your shoes. I'm sure not teaching you anything else, ever, and I don't want you taking part in my experiments or inventions from now on!" he raged.

"Fine with me. I always get hurt when I do and I don't want to be your brother anymore," I said, storming out and vowing never to assist him again.

My school days passed quickly by with so many new challenges: making the numbers count, mixing different colors, playing new games, and learning to read and write — finally conquering *Dick and Jane*. But going home after school was lonely. Miramar may have been a street of boys, but there was no one my age to play with — they were all older. And Daddy worked late at the office, while Baba was away most afternoons with her volunteer work, club activities, and bridge games.

My former brother and I ignored each other as if we were invisible to one another, our paths crossing only at suppertime. Bedford buried himself eagerly in his schoolwork, and I wondered if he would ever experiment or invent anything again. Then, one afternoon, he appeared with some heavy brown sacks. I feigned lack of interest as he pulled down the attic stair, ascended with his mysterious packages, and pulled the stair up behind him. What was Bedford doing up there, I wondered, as the minutes, then hours ticked by?

The next afternoon, having decided to find out for myself before he got home, I got up on a chair, grabbed the chain, and pulled the attic stair down. Perusing the crowded, dimly-lit room, I saw stacks of boxes, piles of magazines, a rack of shotguns, rods full of out-of-season clothes, and a five-gallon jug of corn whiskey Daddy and his friends had made during Prohibition days. I kept my distance, remembering how Baba had poured a Christmas bottle for Hawkins, our yardman, but it had exploded on her closet shelf, drenching her wardrobe.

Rounding some large packing boxes, I came upon the work counter Baba used to wrap Christmas presents. Now, Bedford had loaded it with jars of white and yellow powder, mixing bowls, a scale, pieces of heavy cord soaking in a smelly liquid, and blocks of burnt wood he'd been scraping into a fine powder. In the middle of it all was his electric train remote control, with the end of its long wire wrapped around one of the pieces of cord. Here was Bedford's secret laboratory! On the floor, next to the empty brown sacks, lay a list of words that Bedford had written and checked off. Recognizing the letters but unable to make out the strange, new words, I stuffed the piece of paper in my pocket and crept back downstairs before Bedford could catch me.

Next morning, I took the list to school to see if my classmates recognized any of the words, but they'd not seen a single one of them in *Dick and Jane*. I didn't show Miss Cowser for fear she'd think I was dumb. But after school, I crossed the bridge to Maw Maw's house.

"I'm glad you came to see me, Wo, but I'll only let you stay for a few minutes because you need to go play in the fresh air and sunshine," said my grandmother, who was old and thin with snow-white hair put up on top of her head in a high bun.

"What do these big words mean, Maw Maw?" I asked, handing her the list. "I want to know what Bedford's making up in the attic."

Her bright blue eyes sparkled over her half-glasses as she began to read. "Let's see, it says 'ingredients: sulphur; potassium nitrate — saltpeter; charcoal — finely ground.' Oh, I know what he's making, 'cause your father was always experimenting with chemicals, too...used to make his own firecrackers. It's gunpowder. Bedford sure takes after his dad.

"Now the next words on Bedford's list are...'fuse — heavy cord saturated in sparkler powder solution; jacket — use foot-long Christmas wrap tube; explosive — two pounds of gunpowder; detonator — electric train transformer.' Why, Bedford's not making firecrackers — he's building a bomb! Oh, your poor mother. Bedford's up to no good again. I'd better call her right now."

"Our folks are gone and Margaret's off this afternoon. Is Bedford going to blow the house up, Maw, Maw?" I asked, apprehensively.

"Wo, listen to me," she said. "I want you to run home like the wind. Go up in the attic, get all Bedford's powders and flush 'em down the toilet before he gets home."

I knew just what to do. Flushing was Baba's ultimate solution to any wrongful possession, such as my between-meal candies, Bedford's cups of vanilla extract, and Daddy's foresworn cigarettes. A quick flush and those things vanished forever before our eyes. Now, nothing appealed to me more than the thought of flushing Bedford's dangerous experiment down the toilet.

I streaked home as fast as my legs would carry me and climbed to the attic. Scurrying between the boxes, I suddenly crashed into the five-gallon jug of Daddy's corn whiskey, turning it over. The volatile liquid sloshed back and forth in the bottle as I lay there, mortified, afraid it would explode and blow the roof off the house and me with it. Finally, the potent brew settled down and I found the strength in my knees to get up off the floor and continue my mission.

Reaching the counter, I grabbed the various jars and bowls of white, yellow, and black powder and emptied them into one of the paper sacks. Just then I heard footsteps on the attic stair. Bedford had arrived home. Having delayed too long, I hid behind one of the big boxes as Bedford made his way to the laboratory. Discovering his loss, he became so angry that I decided I'd better make a dash for the stair and toilet below. But Bedford caught up with me and grabbed my shirt, causing me to drop the sack.

"Where are you going with my chemicals?" he shouted, with clenched fists raised over my head. "I'm going to kill you!"

"Maw Maw said you were making a bomb and told me to flush all your stuff down the toilet," I said.

Bedford stopped in this tracks, paralyzed. He couldn't kill me now. There was a witness — his grandmother knew about his bomb.

"Why do grandmothers always know everything?" he lamented, looking down at the silver-gray mixture that had spilled out on the wood floor.

"Wait a minute, Wo, that stuff doesn't look too bad. Here, I'm gonna test it."

He put a pinch on a plate and struck a match. POWEE...! went the mixture as flame and smoke shot up to the attic rafters.

"Wo — you've done it, you mixed the gunpowder just right! You're not as dumb as I thought, so I'm gonna let you help me with the blast."

"I don't want to — you're going to blow up the house," I answered.

"I am not. Listen, Wo, today you have the opportunity to participate in a momentous scientific experiment — the first-ever detonation of a bomb by remote control from a safe distance away, using the spark of an electric train transformer to ignite the fuse. But we'll have to blast this afternoon before Maw Maw squeals on us."

"No, I said I'd never help you again with an experiment."

"Okay, Wo, but I was gonna let you be the fusilier and your name would have been in all the history books," he said.

"What's a fusilier?" I asked.

"Help me carry things to the backyard and I'll show you," he said, sweeping the spilled gunpowder back in the sack. He went to the counter, plugged up a Christmas wrap tube, filled it full of gunpowder, then inserted a fuse.

"Hurry, while everyone's gone except Sally. She's in the basement doing the laundry and will never hear a thing with that gasoline Maytag motor going. Wo, get the electric train remote control, the spool of wire, and follow me," instructed the inventor.

Bedford walked off, cradling the huge bomb in his arms like a sacred icon. Burning with fascinated curiosity, I picked up the control and wire and set out behind him. Reaching the backyard, Bedford dug a deep pit right in the middle of Baba's Bermuda grass lawn.

"Daddy always gets in trouble when he digs holes in Baba's grass," I reminded Bedford.

"That's okay, Wo. When we get through patching it back, only the worms will know there's been a blast."

He placed the bomb in the hole, wrapped the end of the wire tightly around the fuse, then unwound the spool of wire into the nearby garage. He plugged in the cord of the train control, closed the swinging garage doors, and positioned himself beneath a window where he could set off his bomb and observe the blast. I crouched down behind him, fingers in ears, and held my breath.

Bedford turned the detonator dial slowly from one to ten, then cheered wildly as a puff of smoke rose above the pit. But he grew silent as the smoke stopped as quickly as it had begun.

"Fusilier — front and center!" he shouted. "Here's the chance to do your job. Run out there and look down in the hole to see if the fuse has gone out."

"But I'll get hurt if the bomb goes off," I said.

"No, no, no, that's what remote control detonation is all about. The bomb won't explode till I set it off from in here. Now run like the wind," he shouted, shoving me out and slamming the garage door.

It seemed I'd been running like the wind all afternoon, I thought as I reached the pit and dropped to the ground, still fearful.

"Go ahead, Wo. Put your head in that hole and take a real quick look," prompted Bedford from the garage.

I wanted to run the other way, but I'd been entrusted with an important job, and it had to be done. I peeked cautiously over the edge of the abyss. There, now cradled in the black earth lay Bedford's majestic bomb, covered with bright, shiny red paper. I paused and stared in hypnotic fascination at this explosion-waiting-to-happen that was wrapped up like a Christmas gift.

"Hurry up, Wo, have you gone to sleep?" shouted the impatient inventor. "How about the fuse?"

"It's gone out," I reported, seeing that part of the fuse had burned away, then it had gone out where it touched the damp earth.

"Then re-connect the wire to the fuse," directed Bedford from the garage.

"I can't get the pieces to stay together," I said.

"Then tie the wire and fuse together in a bow knot. You can do that, and hurry before someone comes along. I'm starting the count now...one...two...three..." he said, turning the dial on the power trans-former.

I struggled to tie the string and wire together, but my perspiring fingers were trembling and the fuse burned my skin.

"Wo, if you're having so much trouble tying a knot, why don't you just pretend they're my shoelaces. That should do it...four...five...six..."

"That did it!" I proudly announced a moment later, admiring my beautiful bow that sat on top of the bomb.

"Okay, fusilier, to the rear, double time...seven...eight...nine and holding..." Bedford shouted.

I watched in frozen horror as the bow suddenly began to sizzle and sparkle. Just as I finally made it to my feet and turned to run for the garage, the bomb exploded with a mighty...KABOOM...knocking me down and covering me with clods of dirt and grass.

"Hooray, hooray!" shouted Bedford as he emerged from the garage, rolling up the coil of wire. "Are you all right Wo?"

"I think I'm dead. Why'd you blow me up?"

"That wasn't my fault. There shouldn't have been a detonation till the dial hit ten. Must've been a power surge in the main lines, so you can complain to the power company. Now, c'mon, let's get this hole filled up and the grass patched," said Bedford as he began to shovel dirt back in the hole.

"Never, never, never, never. I'll never ever help you do anything again," I vowed as I lay there face down.

"Oh no, " moaned Bedford, suddenly. "Here comes that snoopy Mrs. Dill driving down her driveway. Now we're sunk."

Mrs. Dill, the next-door neighbor, pulled up in front of her garage, got out, and peered at our strange proceedings over the low hedge that separated our two yards.

"Bedford Shelmire, why did you dig that big hole right in the middle of your mother's lawn? You're as bad as your father. Oh, your poor mother. She's got two of you just alike. And look at Wo, playing in the dirt like a pig. Why, he's filthy!"

"Wo's in mourning," said Bedford.

"In mourning over what?" asked Mrs. Dill.

"Our cat, George, died and we're burying him," answered Bedford.

"I don't remember y'all having any cat named George," said Mrs. Dill.

"Oh, he didn't stay home much. He was usually off cattin' around," explained Bedford.

"But why's smoke coming out of the hole?" asked Mrs. Dill.

"Oh..er...why we cremated George. That's what he wanted."

Just then Sally appeared, walking up the basement stair with a load of wet sheets to hang on the laundry line. When she saw our solemn faces next to the freshly-dug hole, she came over to the graveside, bowed her head, and began humming a spiritual. Sally was our most loyal, dependable mourner. She had seen so many dogs, cats, birds, lizards, guinea pigs, chicks, turtles, and...alligators come and go over the years, that now, whenever she saw our sad faces next to a freshly-dug hole, she automatically walked over and mourned — no questions asked.

I had no trouble maintaining a sorrowful countenance that day. My ears still rang and I felt nauseated from the blast. Mrs. Dill, on seeing the pathetic scene, bowed her head out of respect for the dead and walked into her house without saying another word.

When the "funeral" was over and Bedford had filled the hole and replaced the last clump of grass, he walked by the back steps where I'd been recuperating and observing the cleanup operation.

"Wo, I'm on my way to smooth things over with Maw Maw. I'll cross my fingers and tell her we've been having a funeral for George all afternoon. And if she doesn't believe me...well, she can just ask Mrs. Dill."

Late that afternoon, Daddy drove in from East Texas where he'd been trapping rats for his research on the sudden epidemic of typhus fever in that part of the state.

"Daddy, Daddy, did you bring us a surprise?" I asked, hugging his knees.

"Oh, I'm sorry, Wo, I forgot," he said apologetically, having been preoccupied with his work — as usual. While we got lots of presents at Christmas and on birthdays, he seldom thought to stop by a store to bring us small day-to-day surprises.

Daddy carried the cages of rats into the garage, which he used as his laboratory, unaware of Bedford's own scientific triumph that had taken place there earlier in the afternoon. He emerged with a shovel and a couple of the rats that had expired in transit, dug a deep hole in Baba's flower bed, and deposited them as I looked on sadly. Then, just as Bedford returned from Maw Maw's, Baba drove up with David from a visit with her parents in Central Texas.

"Well, how was school, and rat trapping?" asked Baba after giving everyone a big hug.

"Fine," answered Daddy first, seeming to have more to tell than Bedford or me. "Caught a bunch, but had to stay up most of the night working the traps by the light of those oil well gas flares. The derricks are getting thicker than pine trees over there. Several farmers came up to me offering to lease their land, but I don't know anything about drilling for oil. Think I'll stick to medicine."

"Sure, I'd rather have a garage full of rats any day than those smelly old barrels of oil," joked Baba, but her smile faded as she looked around her yard. "Someone's been digging in my flower bed, and I think I know who."

"Had to bury a couple of rats," said Daddy, sheepishly.

"And just look at that place in the middle of the yard where the grass is growing in all different directions," she moaned.

"We buried a cat there," said Bedford, crossing his fingers. "I'm sure Mrs. Dill will be telling you all about the beautiful funeral."

"But why can't you two bury your dead in the alley?" pleaded Baba.

"'Cause the backyard makes such a pretty cemetery," explained Bedford.

After everyone else had gone into the house, I stood between the two graves, trying to sort out all the confusing events of the day. Just then Mrs. Dill walked back up to the hedge.

"Wo, I saw you and your dad having another funeral. Who'd you bury this time?"

"Daddy brought lots and lots of big rats home and two of 'em died," I explained.

"Oh good heavens, between Bedford's crazy inventions and your dad's worthless experiments, those two are going to put your poor mother in her grave," she said, walking off.

But, then, how was Mrs. Dill to know that the American Medical Association would soon award a silver medal to our dad when his research — using guinea pigs as patients — established the blood-sucking rat mite as the principal source for the spread of typhus fever? Or why should she suspect from Bedford's antics that a decade later he'd become a doctor, himself, on only his 21st birthday — a new record for his medical school.

As the days and weeks passed, the bomb incident became lost in my memories of so many of Bedford's other inventive surprises. But I missed being involved with them, as they'd offered a break in the after-school boredom and loneliness. Baba became busier than ever with volunteer work and Daddy seemed totally consumed with his medical practice and research.

Then one day, he returned after being overdue from the East Texas oil boomtown of Henderson where he'd gone to trap more rats, since several new cases of typhus fever had been reported there. Bedford and I waited in the backyard as he got out of his car, looking tired and haggard, and felt him tremble as he hugged us tightly.

"Yesterday afternoon as I set my traps in the woods...I heard a loud..."BOOM" in the distance, and the ground shook," he said softly with a far-away look in his eyes. "When I drove back to the town where I was staying, people there told me there'd been a terrible explosion at a big, new school building in nearby New London. Before long, ambulances began arriving, bringing injured children to the local hospital. I went there and stayed all night, helping out."

"Did some older boys explode a bomb?" I asked.

"Of course not dummy, be quiet," said Bedford.

Daddy went on to explain that a lot of natural gas had leaked out into the basement under the school —— waiting there like a time bomb — from a pipe leading to an oil field. Ten minutes before school was to have been let out, a teacher in shop class flipped a switch to turn on an electric sander. It made a spark that set off the blast which ripped the building apart and blew off the roof. They pulled the dead and injured children out of the rubble all night. The total count was 294 children and teachers killed.

"I feel so lucky not to be one of those fathers...such a horrible tragedy," he said, hiding a tear. "Oh, I almost forgot, I brought you boys a surprise, and next time I go trapping, I'll do it on a weekend so you can go with me."

He handed each of us a big box of bubblegum, my very favorite treat in all the world. I'd never seen so many pieces. That night, facing nightmares about those dead children in New London, I went to bed with the box of bubblegum cradled in my arms. Now I had a lifetime supply, and my Daddy had brought it to me.

The next morning began cold and gray as our entire student body at school assembled in shock and sadness outside by the flagpole. The stars and stripes hung at half mast as we mourned and prayed for the students and teachers who'd been killed by the explosion. In a thunderous instant, the small, oil-rich East Texas town of New London had become the object of world-wide pity.

"Messages of sympathy are streaming in from everywhere," said Mr. Earle, our principal. "Here's one from Adolph Hitler, the German chancellor, addressed to President Roosevelt:

> *'On the occasion of the terrible explosion at New London, Texas, which took so many young lives, I want to assure your excellency of my and the German people's sincere sympathy.'"*

"He must be a nice man," I whispered to Miss Cowser, squeezing her hand tightly.

VIII

Washing Away My Sins

"Watson, come here. I want you," called Bedford from our room upstairs.

Silence ensued.

"Watson!" screamed Bedford. "Come up here right now. I need you."

More silence ensued.

Bedford stormed downstairs into the living room. "Wo, what do you think would have happened if the real Watson had acted like you when Alexander Graham Bell called him? Well, there wouldn't be any telephone, that's what."

"I'm decorating the Christmas tree and David is helping me," I said.

"You call that decorating? You're putting the icicles on upside down."

"David likes 'em pointing up," I explained.

"Well, how do you expect me to test my new long distance telephone by myself?"

"I don't know, but I'm not helping. Besides, Baba's going to be home in a minute and take us downtown to see Santa Claus. I'm going to ask for a bicycle."

"You haven't been good enough, so Santa's gonna fill up your stocking with switches and ashes," he said, pointing to the middle stocking of three that hung from the fireplace mantel.

"But I acted real good all week," I protested, having done my very best to please my teacher, parents, God, and Santa Claus in no particular order.

"That won't cut it. Santa looks at your sins for the whole year. You gotta be good every single day to get a bike," said my omniscient older brother.

But just what had my sins been? I'd always tried to walk the tightrope between good and evil, but somewhere along the line I must have stepped off. I thought back: I'd thrown one of Bedford's rotten eggs at the dogcatcher — maybe a sin. When the crazy lady on the corner chased us out of her yard, I pulled up some of her flowers and delivered them to her in a gift box — probably a sin, too. There was the morning I played hooky from Sunday school and made Baba cry. She had told me how she'd promised God at my christening she would see that I got a good Episcopalian upbringing and attended church regularly. I'd made her turn that promise into a lie — surely my worst sin of all.

"What can I do now, Bedford, to make Santa Claus forgive my sins?" I asked.

"I'll think of something, " he said, confidently. "You can start by holding the other end of my telephone. Santa gets real mad at kids that don't help their big brothers."

"But some big brothers say there's not really a Santa Claus," I said.

"Of course there's a Santa Claus, and he's gonna bring you your bicycle if you act right," said Bedford reassuringly, not wanting to lose his rosy-cheeked ally. "Don't everybody's parents and grandparents say he's real and send his picture to each other on little cards? They're older and smarter than we, and besides, we're going downtown so you can see him for yourself and try to get out of the mess you're in."

Just then Baba came home to take us downtown to see Santa. As I rushed outside, heading for the garage, I passed Mrs. Dill.

"Good morning, Wo. Where are you going in such a hurry?" she asked.

"To see Santa Claus. I'm gonna ask him for a bike," I answered.

"And I suppose that Bedford will probably be wanting a flame-thrower this year?" she said.

When Bedford, David, and I walked into the department store with Baba, we were greeted by a myriad of joyous, new wonders: bright, sparkling sights; crisp, tinkling sounds; warm, radiant smiles; rich, pungent aromas. When you are seven years old, you see, hear, feel, and smell them all. It was Christmastime 1937 and the store was filled with busy, last-minute shoppers, all intent, it seemed to me, on making the children they were with deliriously happy on Christmas Day.

As we approached a small, cascading fountain in the center of the store, an intense, sweet smell greeted us. Women were touching their fingertips to the fragrant pool and dabbing the liquid behind their ears.

"That's magical Christmas water, Wo. Put it all over you and it'll wash away your sins. Then Santa Claus won't know anything about 'em," said Bedford.

Unable to resist his powers of suggestion and thinking of that bicycle I wanted so badly, I dipped both hands in and splashed it over my face, neck, and arms. As we headed toward the elevators, everyone we passed turned to stare at me. We boarded the toyland express, operated by one of Santa's helpers — a girl dressed in a red Santa outfit trimmed in white ermine, with black belt and boots. The lights went out and we began to soar toward toyland to the sound of jingling bells.

"Wow, some little girl sure smells good," said the pretty operator in the darkness. "She won't need to ask Santa for any perfume this Christmas 'cause she must have a great big bottle already."

When the elevator stopped and the lights came on, my beet-red face made it obvious that I was the fragrant passenger. The sweet cloud and the stares followed me all around toyland, thanks to Bedford; the "water" had been cheap cologne.

Finally, we saw Santa Claus sitting in an enormous gold chair and my heart pounded with excitement. He reeked with a smell like Daddy's whiskey each time he belched out a cheerful "ho, ho, ho." But a look of bewilderment came over his face when I sat down on his knee and he smelled me. I had intended to tell him I wanted a shiny, new bicycle, but we were both speechless.

I got up from the standoff feeling anxious and uncertain about the power of those magical waters. David's turn came next and he looked up with an adoring, trusting grin at red-faced, bleary-eyed Santa.

"Is that really Santa Claus?" I asked Bedford. "He sure doesn't act like it."

"Well, Santa Claus is like God in a way," said Bedford. "Sometimes he does strange things that are hard to understand...things that make us wonder if he's real. But we go on asking him to give us stuff, hoping he is."

When we got home, I went to ask Margaret, our nurse. She confirmed, in her gentle, thoughtful way my suspicions that Santa just might not exist.

"He is a wonderful spirit, as real as your own hopes and dreams can make him," she explained.

Rather than taking something away from me, she offered a new concept of hope and faith in another benevolent spirit — her Savior, Jesus Christ.

That afternoon, the real highlight of the Christmas season came when we went to see Bedford play the part of Tiny Tim in his school's production of Dickens' *A Christmas Carol.* Baba had a tattered costume made for him and Bedford did a sensational job of making himself up, creating a sallow, deeply-lined face with darkened sockets around his eyes to make them look weak and tired, disguising their bright blue color. With English cap and blond hair, he looked just as Dickens had described Tiny Tim. He used his skinny frame to best advantage, looking sickly and starving as he limped out of the house on a crutch that cold, foggy afternoon.

We drove over to pick up a couple of his fellow students, then headed out Preston Road toward Texas Country Day School. When we pulled into a filling station, the boys decided to put on a small play of their own. The attendant wiping the windshields noticed that sitting between two robust, attentive schoolboys was a fragile, pathetic little creature with a shawl over his shoulders.

As he wiped from window to window, the attendant couldn't keep his eyes off "Tiny Tim" whose own black-circled eyes were glazed and drooping like a dying baby bird. Suddenly, the boy went into a rigor; his eyes rolled up into his head, and he fell over motionless into one boy's lap. When his shocked friends failed to revive this lifeless form, they covered the pale, ravaged little face with the shawl, then fell sobbing into each other's arms.

The startled attendant tapped on the front windshield to let Baba know of the tragedy taking place on the back seat. She was preoccupied, listening to Christmas carols on the radio, and merely smiled, nodded, and wished him a Merry Christmas as we drove away.

I had observed the drama from the front seat, trying to look serious while bursting with laughter on the inside. I had made another new discovery: my big brother could be hilarious, and when he made me laugh, I forgot all the tricks he'd ever played on me.

During the play when Tiny Tim died, my eyes welled with tears. How curious that was, I thought, since I'd wished him dead so many times before. Then, when he came alive again and chirped "God bless us every one" to ecstatic applause as the curtain fell, I realized I had a very special brother, after all. I would follow him to the ends of the earth, and on the way, barely miss falling off the edge — countless times.

IX

The Magic Lantern

"What are you doing up in *my* pear tree?" asked the pretty little blonde, who appeared to be just my age.

It was a bright, sunny day the following spring, with nature bursting out all over — not the sort of day for an unpleasantness, but here one came.

"I didn't know it was *your* pear tree," I snapped.

"Yes it is, and that's *my* house," she announced, pointing to the big two-story red brick home.

"Well, I climbed up *your* tree to help my brother string his telephone wire to the window over there," I said, purposefully.

"That's *my* big brother's window," she said.

"My" seemed to be the biggest word in her vocabulary, and now I knew why Bedford didn't like girls. I tried to ignore her, but then she began to speak sweetly...enticingly.

"I'm Carolyn, and I've never climbed a tree before. Is it scary up there?" she asked, her big, blue eyes opened wide.

"No, it's fun. Here, grab my hand and I'll give you a pull. Don't worry — I won't let you fall."

Soon we were both sitting in the broad crook among the pear blossoms, as the warm spring breeze fluttered the petals and Carolyn fluttered my heart. But just as we were getting acquainted, Bedford walked out of the house and motioned for me to hurry home with him so we could try out his new long distance telephone system. I climbed down, feeling sorry I had to leave Carolyn up in the tree, wondering how she'd get herself down. Arriving home, Bedford pulled out a huge seashell and attached it to the end of the long copper wire we'd just stretched through the trees.

"It's my new shellphone," Bedford announced proudly, "made from a conch shell that our great-grandfather Shelmire used as a horn to call the field hands for lunch on his plantation. I found two of 'em in the attic. See the hole in the end? If you press your lips on it tightly and blow real hard, it makes a loud blast that can be heard for miles. And if you put it up to your ear, you can hear the roar of the ocean still echoing inside."

I lifted the shell to my ear and, to my astonishment, heard the distant thundering surf.

"I figure if we can hear the ocean that far away, we ought to be able to pick up Bill Burford in the next block with those shells, using copper wire instead of string. He's waiting on the other shellphone, so let's make a call. Hello, Bill, this is long distance. Come in Bill...come in Bill!" shouted Bedford into the wide, pink mouth of the conch shell. "What's the matter, Bill, I can't hear you?"

A look of disappointment came over Bedford's face as he got no response, and could hear only the roar of the ocean. In frustration, he put the shell to his lips and blew with all his might. "AH-HOOOOOOMMM..." went the shell. I thought my eardrums would burst before the sound stopped echoing around the room. As I started to run out, there came a faint, "ahhoooooommm" from the shell.

"That's Bill blowing back at us," said Bedford, savoring this hollow victory; his long distance telephone had not performed quite as planned. While it could carry the grand blast of the lowly conch shell, it was unable to transmit the feeble sound of the human voice.

Bedford honked once more and there came back over the wire a strange series of multiple blasts and pauses of differing lengths.

"Bill's trying to send a message, but I have to figure out the code and that's gonna take some time," said the disgruntled inventor.

The next afternoon I decided to go see Carolyn, happy to have a new friend despite the fact that she was a girl. To avoid Bedford's taunting, I took the forbidden alley where I'd been told not to walk going to and from school. As I followed the muddy ruts, insects buzzed, birds chirped, and blooming wildflowers filled my nose with their sweet scents. I stopped to pick a bouquet for Carolyn, then wondered why I had.

Months before as I walked past an open kitchen window on my way home from school, I had heard a man's voice speaking over a crackling radio — a king in a far-away land who was giving up his crown for the woman he loved. That was nice of the king to give his crown to his brother I'd thought, but why give it up for a woman? Still remembering the incident with wonder, I couldn't realize that the "why" of the king's crown and the "why" of Carolyn's bouquet shared a common denominator.

When my muddy shoes and I arrived at Carolyn's house, it seemed she'd been expecting me, or at least someone. There were three exquisite mud pies laid out on a table.

"Oh I'm so glad you came to have dessert, and thank you for the pretty flowers. Now, this is apple pie, this is chocolate, and the middle one's cherry. Which kind do you want?" she asked, preparing to cut a large hunk for me. Her blue eyes filled with anticipation, but I could only anticipate a mouthful of dirt.

"I'm not very hungry 'cause my front tooth hurts. It's about to fall out."

"I'm sorry. Maybe some other time. I'll just save the pies for you," promised Carolyn.

School ended June first, that magical day we were allowed to take our shoes off. By September, our soles would be as tough as shoe leather. Today, though, the grass felt sharp and prickly under our tender feet.

At twilight, I followed Bedford down the rough, hot sidewalk to the Burford house. He carried a glass jar that he and Bill aimed to fill with lightning bugs. But after catching a few, they became bored and handed the jar to me and my new best friend, Carolyn. Soon, the creek bed across the street began to sparkle with aerial activity. We ran over and started grabbing fireflies and "pouring" them into the jar, quickly filling it with the luminous little blinkers.

We waded into the cool water and the slippery rocks felt good under our feet. Standing there ankle-deep, just below the enchanted bridge, we held the jar between us and gazed into it as if it were a crystal ball. Carolyn's cheeks were bathed in an eerie light as the sky grew dark and the fireflies darted and sparkled overhead and all around us. We traded whispered secrets about older brothers, coming trips, and summer joys.

"It's dark, Wo. I have to go home now," she said, breaking the spell.

"Don't worry, Carolyn. I'll walk you home with this magic lantern," I promised, as we set off on our perilous journey — a few steps across the street to her house.

Before saying good night, we opened the jar. Then Carolyn and I and all the pretty lightning bugs flew off in different directions. The magic lantern of wonder and friendship was, once again, just an empty jar. We catch experiences, like fireflies, when we can. Then, we must turn them loose — and remember.

"No, you can't go play with Carolyn today, Wo...or with any of your friends...not for the rest of the summer," said Daddy. "And you'll have to stay out of the sunshine and away from the swimming pool."

I felt devastated. Why couldn't I go see Carolyn, and what was summer without friends, sunshine, and swimming? Daddy gathered Baba, Bedford, David, and me together to explain.

"There's an epidemic of polio — infantile paralysis — that's just hit Dallas and the rest of the state. It's a terrible disease that cripples children your ages, and sometimes adults — you've seen how President Roosevelt has to wear steel braces on his legs and live in a wheel chair. There's no way to prevent polio except to avoid contact with other children during the hot summer months, especially in swimming pools. So, I want you boys to stay home...indoors...all summer long...do you understand?" We did, but couldn't imagine how we'd survive.

As the days of boredom and deprivation passed torturously by, Bedford occupied his time trying to master the Morse code on his shellphone with Bill.

"Honk Honk Honk...Honk...Honk...Honk...Honk Honk Honk. Do you know what that means?" he asked. "It's S.O.S. or 'save our ship.' That's important to know if you're out in the middle of the ocean and your ship's sinking — like the Titanic did."

"Oh really?" I said, hoping I could remember, should that particular situation ever arise. "But Bedford, why don't you just call up Bill on the hall telephone?"

"Oh no, then everybody in the house would hear our secrets. Do you want to learn some more letters?"

"No thank you. My ears hurt 'cause you've been honking all week."

The incessant honks of the shellphone did not go unnoticed by Mrs. Dill next door. Unable to get her afternoon nap because of Bedford's noise, she grew increasingly agitated and cranky late at night. And since she was taking Spanish lessons for a trip to Mexico and needed to hear the language spoken, she tuned in a Mexican station every night, placing her radio on the window sill opposite our bedroom window and turning the volume up. It was the battle of the decibels, and I was caught in the cross fire, unable to go to sleep each night until the wee, small hours.

We couldn't complain, though, for there was an unwritten law granting complete freedom of the airways among neighbors. In the sweltering days before air-conditioning, it was necessary for everyone to raise their windows and ignore the noise of others, for catching the cooling south breeze was all that mattered when the temperature hit 100 degrees. If it wafted in with the sounds of Freddy practicing his saxophone, Mrs. Stetzel beating her rugs, Mr. Crush cursing his wife, or...Mrs. Dill playing her radio, so be it. Listening to one's radio at any hour, day or night, was everyone's sacred right and Mrs. Dill took full advantage of this unwritten neighborhood code.

When, finally, the Spanish language stations signed off the air, and just as Bedford and I figured we'd get some peace and quiet, Mrs. Dill would turn the dial to radio station S-A-V-E-D, broadcasting from just across the Mexican border.

"Turn your radios up real loud and listen to the word of God," shouted the Bible-thumping, hellfire-and-brimstone preacher at top volume. Night after night, he went into tirades about that demon rum and the wages of sin, filling our ears with his frightful pronouncements of gloom and doom.

"Wow, Bedford, hell sure sounds scary. Do you think I'll have to go there?"

"Wo, you may still have time to straighten up. And you sure better, or you'll end up down below where sinners slave in a fiery furnace while the devil pokes 'em with his pitchfork," said Bedford, only too happy to repeat the terrifying picture of hell the border preacher had painted so convincingly. "But didn't you hear the preacher say he'd square things with God for you if you'd send him a dollar?"

"I don't have a dollar, but I still want to go to heaven. Margaret says it's nice up there."

"Well, I don't know," said Bedford, staring up at the ceiling. "There's not much to do in heaven, unless you like to sing and play the harp and just sit around on a cloud. As for me, I tried being good all the time, but it was just too hard. And I'm not sure heaven's gonna be all that much fun, anyway."

"If I go to heaven, how long do I have to stay there?" I asked. Here I was, trapped in this summer hell with Bedford, and now the prospect of heaven didn't seem much better.

"I don't know. Go ask Margaret. She reads the Bible every day. Now, go to sleep!"

Margaret, always looking for an opportunity to give me a spiritual lecture, was delighted when I asked her to enlighten me next morning. The simple, loving theology expounded by our Seventh Day Adventist nurse covered virtually every facet of my life on earth as well as my future in heaven or hell with unquestionable answers and conclusive predictions.

"Am I going to heaven? How long do I have to stay there? Where do I go after that?" I asked.

"Nowhere. You never leave heaven. You stay there forever," she answered with finality.

"How long is forever?" I asked.

"Forever means ever...and ever...and ever — you don't ever leave heaven."

I found the thought of having to stay in one place forever...and ever...and ever absolutely terrifying. I couldn't sleep at night, staying awake long after Bedford, worrying about it. I decided to be good enough to go to heaven, but bad enough so I wouldn't have to stay there forever — vowing to walk the tightrope between good and evil for the rest of my life.

On the mornings after Mrs. Dill's Mexican radio stations had kept us awake half the night, we tried sleeping late, but to no avail. Seeming needless of sleep herself, she turned her radio on to a series of 15-minute soap operas, obviously bent on murdering Bedford and me with her big Philco.

Aunt Jenny's Real Life Stories came on the air first early each morning, as her "nephew," Ted, the radio announcer would drop in on his "Aunt" Jenny. After she'd served him a piece of her wonderful pie, invariably baked with Crisco, she'd tell him a poignant story of love lost or found; of love requited or unrequited. And as I shared the emotions, the joys, the tears of Aunt Jenny's lovers, I longed for Carolyn and her mud pies — invariably baked with creek water.

When Bedford had heard all the soap opera hugging, kissing, and cooing he could stand, he'd haul out of bed, wind up the Victrola, and put on his favorite record — *Frankie and Johnnie*. It was America's classical gutter song about the two lovers who'd sworn to be true to each other, "as true as the stars above." But Frankie caught Johnnie with another woman one night and got her revenge.

> *Frankie threw back her kimono,*
> *She took out her little forty-four.*
> *Root-a-toot, three times she shot,*
> *right through that hardwood floor.*
> *She shot her man, 'cause he done her wrong.*

This was Bedford's kind of soap opera — a simple, permanent, no-nonsense solution to a lover's quarrel... "No tears, no sighs, no long goodbyes," he'd say as the record ended. Day after day he changed the Victrola needle, cranked up the phonograph, and played *Frankie & Johnnie* — over and over and over again. By noon each day, every radio in the neighborhood blared songs by Pappy O'Daniel, the Stamps-Baxter Quartet, or the Light Crust Doughboys. But whatever room I was in, upstairs or down, the sound of "He was her man, but he done her wrong" rose above the din.

By mid-afternoon each day, the fierce west sun had scorched that side of our house and raised the temperature in our room to around 110 degrees. The noise and heat were relentless — my ears besieged by the babel of radios, my body wrapped in a blanket of hot air. Hour after hour, day after day, I dreamed of plunging into the deep, quiet, cool depths of the nearby Highland Park swimming pool. But it, like heaven, would just have to wait.

Then one afternoon Bedford came banging up the stairs with a new creation that was his answer to the heatwave. "It's my new air-conditioning machine," he announced, placing it in the opening of the up-raised window opposite the Dill's house. He'd made a primitive "swamp cooler" out of a large rectangular fan, over the front of which he'd tied an excelsior pad from a packing box. At the top of the fan he'd attached a water trough with holes punched to allow the water to trickle down through the excelsior and be collected in a pan at the bottom. The hot air would supposedly be cooled as it was blown through the wet pad.

"Wo, just feel how cool it is in here. The temperature's down to 100°, " he said proudly after a couple of hours.

"It feels hotter to me," I said, beading with perspiration as the machine blew damp, muggy air into the room.

While the roar of the fan finally drowned out Mrs. Dill's radio, the constant trickle of water began to fray my nerves after a few days. The sheets became soggy, the walls and ceiling dripped with humidity — Bedford had made a rain forest out of our room.

One morning as I lay in bed mesmerized by the humidity and relentless dripping of Bedford's "swamp cooler" — which was something akin to a Chinese water torture — I heard the faint sound of honking on the shellphone which lay on the table next to my ear.

"Bedford, there must be a ship sinking somewhere. I heard an S.O.S."

"No, dummy, that's Bill sending a distress signal," he said, grabbing the phone. He and Bill hadn't communicated in a couple of weeks because it had been too hot to honk at each other and besides, they'd run fresh out of secrets — till now. Bedford listened intently, decoding a startling message.

"They're moving," he said. "Bill and his family are moving away — this morning."

I ran to a front window and peered down the street to the next block. My heart sank as I saw two huge moving vans in front of Carolyn's house with men loading furniture and boxes. I watched the proceedings all morning, feeling sick inside that my friend was moving away and I wouldn't even get to say goodbye to her. By mid-afternoon Bedford and I found ourselves home alone when Margaret took David to the doctor and Sally went out to her room for a nap.

Suddenly, I decided to run down the street, tell Carolyn goodbye, and come right back before anyone missed me. I hopped and limped down the street with my tender feet broiling on the hot sidewalk, hollow-eyed from lack of sleep, and pale as a ghost from lack of sunshine. But by the time I arrived at the house, the moving vans had pulled away from the curb and were rounding the corner right behind the Burfords in their car. Miramar was once again — a street of boys.

I walked slowly past Carolyn's pear tree, the white blossoms long gone, and looked sadly in the windows of the deserted house. But on the back porch there was a table and on top of it sat the conch shell with a note for Bedford, and the three mud pies — uneaten. She had saved them for me after all!

Returning home along the rough, hot sidewalk, I compulsively went out of my way so I could gaze at the oft-dreamed-of swimming pool. There it was, nestled in the park under giant cedar elms.

When a tan, smiling lifeguard opened an iron gate and beckoned to me, I followed him inside the fence as if he were St. Peter and his golden gate, whom Margaret had spoken of so often. Suddenly, I felt peace, contentment, and serenity. The summer of pain and turmoil was behind me. Looking around, I saw no other children, only a few older people swimming laps, happy to have the place to themselves.

Thinking myself safe from polio, I dove into the welcoming pool and swam to the bottom. I held my breath for a minute that seemed an eternity, floating in the cool, caressing emerald water — a balm for body and soul. Here was silence — absolute blessed peace and quiet. Feeling I'd been reborn, I wondered how sitting on a cloud in heaven could be any better than this. And here was a heaven where I didn't have to stay forever — I could come and go as I pleased.

As the summer came to an end, the polio epidemic diminished as quickly as it had begun and the day finally arrived when we had to put our shoes back on and start the second grade. I was glad to see my classmates again, but the one bright sparkle in my life was missing — my pretty, after-school playmate. So, when Bedford said that Carolyn's mother had called — on the hall phone this time — to invite me to Carolyn's seventh birthday party at the Burford mansion where they'd moved, my heart jumped with joy.

"Will other boys be there too?" I asked, apprehensively.

"Sure, Wo, there'll be lots of other boys," promised Bedford.

A few days later, Baba drove me south along Turtle Creek Boulevard until we pulled up in front of a huge palace. I got out in my freshly-starched suit with present in hand and looked up in amazement at the strange, Italian-Moorish facade with a domed tower. I rang the bell and a uniformed butler ushered me into the vast entry hall.

"Miss Carolyn and her friends are playing games on the terrace and you may join them there," he said with great pomp. "Just walk outside through the living room and you'll find them."

I tiptoed timidly past the enormous fireplace and under the ornate coffered ceiling of a room that would one day become the dining room of the Mansion on Turtle Creek Hotel. I peered through the French doors and my heart went pitter-patter when I saw Carolyn. But then, to my horror, 20 more little girls came into view as they scurried across the terrace after her. I had been the only boy invited to the party! Bedford, who'd never been overly liberal with the truth where I was concerned, had duped me once again.

I ran in panic back to the front door, but Baba had already driven away. What would I do now? How would one boy play with a bunch of girls? What games do girls play, I wondered? Walking back into the living room, I felt bewildered and alone. When I saw Carolyn and her friends coming into the mansion, I hid behind the couch.

The girls played pinning the tail on the donkey, then came a treasure hunt, giving each guest a chance to explore the mansion as they looked for prizes. The fever of the hunt sent several little girls sprawling in their pretty pressed frocks to look under the furniture and I was discovered.

"Wo, what are you doing behind my couch?" asked Carolyn, smiling this time.

Then all the giggling, paper-capped girls dragged me out from behind the couch and over to the birthday table — which was strewn with presents and favors — to eat ice cream and ANGEL FOOD CAKE!

At first I felt humiliated, but after a few minutes I felt comfortable...I felt welcome...I felt popular. They were all glad I'd come, especially Carolyn. I had never been alone with a group of girls, but it wasn't so bad after all. I began to realize that little girls looked better, smelled sweeter, and acted nicer than little boys.

"Can I walk down the creek and visit Carolyn again, sometime?" I asked Baba as we drove home.

"Oh no, Wo. It's too far. But if you're ever invited back, I'll drive you there."

I never saw Carolyn again, but my appetite had been whetted for bright curls, twinkling eyes, whirling skirts, dancing feet, and girlish giggles. A spark, like the fireflies in the creek, had been ignited in my heart by Carolyn and her bevy of beauties on that warm October afternoon.

But alas, my memory of Carolyn's pretty face, blonde hair, and blue eyes would be blurred over the coming years by countless impostors.

X

Counting on Service

The sleepy, Central Texas town of Hillsboro, located halfway between Dallas and Marlin, saw no action during the Civil War. Most of the fighting in the Lone Star State took place hundreds of miles away along the Gulf Coast at Sabine Pass, at Galveston, and at Brownsville. There was plenty of action every time our family pulled up to the gas pumps of Grimes Garage on our way to Marlin.

Three supercharged little boys would bound from the big Buick with emotions, bladders, and parents ready to explode any minute. Then the countdown would begin for the chance to win soda pops. A sign on the wall promised:

FREE COLD DRINKS FOR THE CARLOAD
IF CUSTOMER FAILS TO RECEIVE SERVICE
WITHIN 60 SECONDS.

We would count for 30 or 40 seconds and no one seemed to be working there. Then, suddenly, from garage doors and from behind other autos, charged an army of four or five young men dressed in khaki uniforms, wearing black rubber bow ties. The first one attacked the gas tank, after inquiring whether we wished regular or Ethyl gasoline. The others skirmished with the tires, water, battery, oil, windshields, and chrome.

This time, as usual, our side lost. Disappointed, and now more desperate than ever, we raced into the restroom, fighting for position. When we came out, our parents were sipping Coca-Colas and we plunked down three nickels for a Delaware Punch, a Nehi lime, and a Cream Soda, instead. Refreshed, we climbed into our Buick, with auto and occupants now prepared for the second half of our Marlin journey to spend Thanksgiving with Grand Bunch and Grand Daddy.

"We'll have Thanksgiving lunch tomorrow at Papa Battle's house," said our Dad. "Your great-grandfather is one of the few Confederate Civil War veterans still living!"

"Baba took us to see *Birth of a Nation* when you were gone last summer, to show us what the Old South and the Civil War were like," said Bedford. "I thought it was real good, but Wo never understood what was going on. The movie was silent, and the story was written up on the screen. He can't read that fast."

"Well, he can practice the next time we pass some Burma Shave signs," laughed Daddy.

Sure enough, a few minutes later a new set of Burma Shave signs appeared, one sign at a time, on the horizon. I began reading as fast as I could:

TO GET AWAY
FROM HAIRY APES
LADIES JUMP
FROM FIRE ESCAPES
BURMA SHAVE

I had read the advertisement so convincingly that Bedford vowed to use that brand of lather soap faithfully when his time came to shave.

Finally, we drove into Marlin and arrived at the home of our grandparents, located next to Marlin High School. Soon, we were climbing one of the fire escape slides that hung on the side of the school building. These tall, rusting steel chutes provided the most exhilarating activity this small, tranquil town had to offer, and attracted us to them as if we had been magnetized. Every time we came to visit, Bedford and Cousin Posh Oltorf spent hours climbing slowly up, and then thundering down — over and over and over again until their rust-stained pants had holes in them.

Although Posh was a couple of years older than Bedford, they had compatible, quick wits and a friendship based on mutual interests in adventure, inventions, and family history, all of us having descended from our great family patriarch, Churchill Jones. In 1853, Jones moved to Texas with his large family and settled at the Falls of the Brazos River near Marlin. He had sent his son and slaves ahead to carve a cotton plantation from 28,000 acres of wilderness he had purchased for 50¢ an acre. Jones' daughter, Sarah, and husband came in the wagon caravan with their baby girl, Sue, who would grow up to marry our great-grand-father, Thomas E. Battle.

"Hurry, Wo. Climb on up," shouted Bedford. "You can do it. Just don't look down."

Bedford and Posh had already reached the top of the slide and stood on the platform outside a third-story window of the old brick building. I grasped the rims of the steep metal chute and struggled to keep my feet from slipping out from under me. My fingers ached as they gripped the sharp steel edges, these fire escapes having been designed to slide down, rather than climb up. Slowly...painfully...victoriously...I reached the platform at the top for the very first time.

"Congratulations, Wo," said Posh. "Now, while you try to get up the nerve to slide back down, you can admire this great view."

We looked toward the sinking sun. Beneath it we could see Posh's Uncle Zeke in the distance, sitting in front of his filling station, waiting for the infrequent customers with empty gas tanks to pull up to his pumps. Just beyond were the tombstones and mourning live oaks of Calvary Cemetery, where so many of our relatives enjoyed "eternal rest." In the next block from the school, we looked down on Posh's rambling old home where he lived with his mother and Uncle Zeke. In front stood a giant live oak tree, where we would sway on the limbs and listen to Posh tell stories.

Just below us was the story-and-a-half Victorian home of our grandparents, Maude Battle Bunch and William Overton Bunch. It was a picket-fenced, oak-tree-shaded oasis in the midst of a town block of Marlin Public School buildings, which surrounded it on three sides. The sparse Bermuda grass lawn, where horned toads roamed, was kept sticker-free for our bare feet in the summer by our grandfather's meticulous, caring efforts.

"Are you ready for the 'big slide,' yet, Wo?" asked Bedford.

"No, it's too scary," I said. The steep chute looked three miles long.

"Well, you can't blame him," said Posh. "You can see all the way to the 'ole Brazos River from way up here."

Until about a hundred years before, Indians had camped around the Falls of the Brazos River and hunted all over the area. They had been dispersed by the Texas Rangers when the white settlers came in, Posh explained.

Suddenly, we saw a tall, thin bicycle rider wearing a straw hat, with a metal clip around his pant leg, approaching. It was our grandfather, taking a short cut home from work through the school yard.

"Let's all slide down and surprise him," suggested Bedford. "We'll pretend we're Indians. Wo, jump in my lap and we'll be one big brave."

I hopped on and we took a thrilling plunge down the long slide with Posh right behind. We landed at the bottom, making Indian war whoops just as a startled Grand Daddy Bunch passed by on his bike. We circled our victim, doing a war dance and waving imaginary tomahawks, then attacked from three sides — quickly subduing rider and horse.

"I surrender, I surrender! Please leave me my scalp," pleaded the defeated calvaryman. "It doesn't have many hairs left on it."

"No, we just want your horse," said Bedford. He and Posh then took possession of the captured "steed" and rode away. I took the relieved, smiling prisoner by the hand and led him off toward his fort — and supper.

Our grandparents' house had a cheerful countenance on the outside when its trellis-shaded porches were covered with trumpet vine, honeysuckle, and morning glories. At the same time, the house seemed to brood inwardly no matter the weather or season.

Dark brown woodwork dominated the interior — tall columns, fireplace mantel, wainscots and cornices. The dining room table had a cloth crocheted by Grand Bunch to help her get through the boredom of a life she felt was beneath both her dignity and expectations. On the walls hung her own oil paintings — the captured, far-away, romantic landscapes of her dreams.

The columned library alcove contained Grand Daddy's prize collection of books of literature, poetry, the classics, encyclopedias, dictionaries, books on art, music, and nature. These volumes enabled him to climb into the hearts and minds of men leading far more adventurous lives than his own, as the owner of a dry goods store. In the eyes of his loving daughter and grandsons, however, he was a knight of old in shining armor, the epitome of the true, cultured Southern gentleman.

"Grand Daddy sure has lots of books," I said. "Wonder if he has any 'bout *Dick and Jane*?"

"'Course not," said Bedford, back from his bike ride. "He couldn't go to school after his folks died, and he had to teach himself everything with serious books like these, not silly little picture books like you read."

After supper, I climbed the stairs to the solitary attic bedroom, thinking of my grandfather's sad, lonely, friendless orphan days.

The welcomed morning finally came, bringing a bright, shiny, crisp Marlin Thanksgiving Day, filled with promise, until....

"Why can't I go with you, Bedford? I won't be any trouble," I pleaded.

"Baba, Wo's trying to follow me down the street to Posh's house. We've been invited by Reverend Goddard to go with him and explore the Indian mounds out by the Falls of the Brazos. We don't want Wo with us 'cause we talk about things he shouldn't hear."

"Like what in the world?" she asked, a little apprehensive of the answer.

"Posh tells me stories about our family, and the Reverend talks about what happened to the settlers around here long ago. Some of it gets pretty spooky."

"Now, Bedford, it's Thanksgiving, the day we count our blessings, and give thanks for our great big, wonderful family and all God has given us. You can be nice to Wo and take him with you this one day. There's no one else his age for him to play with. Besides, there are lots of only-children, like I was, that don't have any brothers or sisters to be thankful for today."

"How'd they get so lucky?" muttered Bedford, as he rushed out of the house with me in hot pursuit.

A block down the street, Posh waited for Bedford and Reverend Goddard on one of the low limbs of the giant live oak tree. Behind the tree stood the rambling old one-story, early Texas home, its long, comfortable veranda now occupied by a couple of snoozing cats. Next to it stood a cage containing a nervous monkey. I walked over and peered in at it.

"Oh, that's Jake," said Posh. "He belongs to my Uncle Zeke. Here, I'll let him out. He loves to climb the big oak tree. That's why he doesn't run away. That tree is said to be over a thousand years old and the Indians used to have powwows around it during their hunts and wars."

"How do you get Jake back in his cage?" asked Bedford.

"If we can't catch him, we hand Jake a banana with knock-out drops," answered Posh.

Jake jumped out of the cage and stalked across the yard on all fours. Suddenly, he bounded to the veranda, grabbed a startled cat, and climbed with it underarm all the way to the tree top.

"What's Jake doing to the kitty?" I asked, as the cat let out a blood-curdling shriek.

"He's loving it," explained Posh. "Jake's the only monkey in Central Texas, and cats are the only thing warm and cuddly he can find to squeeze. When he captures a cat, he rushes to the top of the tree every time. The cat has to make up its mind whether it wants to be loved or dropped, but that's not much of a choice."

We climbed back up on a long, serpentine limb that swung up and down with us like a huge see-saw, keeping an eye on Jake and his victim. Reverend Goddard finally turned the corner in his old Plymouth sedan and pulled up under the great tree.

"Posh, I see Jake's up to his old tricks," said the clergyman.

The Right Reverend F. Percy Goddard was an ardent amateur archeologist and expert on the history of Indians in the area. While his life's work was saving the souls of his fellow man, exploring their earthly remains was his hobby. For him, the answers to the secrets of life and the hereafter lay not only straight up and straight down, but all around.

We hopped in the car, and our search for answers and arrowheads began. We drove down the hill and turned into Uncle Zeke's rickety old filling station, which looked as deserted and empty as the glass cylinders that sat on top of the two gasoline pumps. Reverend Goddard pulled up in front of the regular pump and I began to count. I reached 60, but there was no sign of service or free drinks.

"Are you sure your Uncle Zeke's open today, Posh?" asked Reverend Goddard.

"He's open every day of the year. He bought this old station just so he wouldn't have to stay home and get bored. He likes to sit here and watch the cars go by," said Posh.

I counted 60 again and just as before, nothing happened. Finally, the men's room door opened, and out limped Uncle Zeke. He greeted us warmly as he dragged one leg over to the Ethyl pump.

"Fill me up with regular, will you, Zeke?" asked the Reverend.

"I'm all out," Zeke said, pumping Ethyl gasoline up into the glass cylinder by cranking a long handle back and forth. When it was finally filled with a dozen gallons of the sloshing amber liquid, Zeke squeezed the handle and the gasoline began filling our gas tank. He gave the rear windshield a half-hearted swipe with a greasy rag, then turned to watch the liquid descend.

"Can you catch the front windshield, Zeke, and check the water and oil?" asked Reverend Goddard.

"My boy Pete's off today for Thanksgiving, Reverend. Come back by tomorrow and he'll take care of it. My leg's giving me the devil."

"Why does Uncle Zeke limp?" I asked.

"When he was a little boy," whispered Posh, "he fell off his pony and broke his leg. Uncle Zeke didn't tell his mother how bad it really was 'cause he was afraid she wouldn't let him ride anymore. He kept his secret; the bone didn't heal and the leg quit growin'...been a cripple ever since."

"Zeke," Reverend Goddard called out. "I just passed your house and your monkey has a cat up in the top of the tree again."

Zeke nodded and continued watching the gasoline.

"I was just wondering...will Jake bother all the cats?" asked the Reverend.

"Oh, yeah," replied Uncle Zeke, sitting down on a stool beside the gas pump.

"You mean, not just female cats, but he takes male cats up there too?"

"I think so," answered Uncle Zeke, preoccupied. A long silence followed.

"Well, what difference does it make...it's all wrong anyway," the man of the cloth pontificated.

"That'll be a buck-fifty for the gas, Reverend."

"Do we get our free drinks now?" I asked.

"Sure you do, Wo," said Uncle Zeke, not realizing he had lost a race. "But you'll have to drink them here or leave two cents apiece deposit. If I let every relative in town have a drink and the bottle, too, I'd be out of business in no time."

"Zeke," said Reverend Goddard, handing him the money, "I did a service at Calvary Cemetery yesterday and I noticed an interesting tombstone next to some of your Bartlett markers — a marble statue of a telephone linesman climbing up a pole, the man having been electrocuted in the line of duty. I wondered if he'd been any of your kin?"

"No, but that's sure a dangerous precedent, Reverend. If our family had tombstones like that, they'd all be shaped like sex symbols or whiskey bottles," said Uncle Zeke.

Then he put the money in his pocket and sat back down to watch the world pass by, a little bit at a time.

"Zeke's Service Station," said Reverend Goddard wistfully, shaking his head as we drove away. "Worst service...and best conversation in town!"

XI

Getting Over the Hump

Cotton was now king here in the Indian's former hunting domain, explained Reverend Goddard as he drove us over mile after mile of fertile cotton fields that had once been part of Churchill Jones' mighty plantation.

"Look, Bedford. It's the old family graveyard," said Posh, pointing to a red brick wall that stood under a group of huge post oak trees. "There's a treasure buried in there someplace."

"Glad we brought shovels," said Bedford.

"Take it easy, boys," said Reverend Goddard. "We're going to dig up Indian relics, not your ancestors lying in that graveyard."

Churchill Jones brought with him to Texas his wife, eight children, five sisters, and their respective families. As soon as he had built several log houses for them, and cabins for his 100 slaves, he turned his attention to building their future accommodations, including a family cemetery like the one they'd left in Virginia. It had a handsome brick wall around it, with two beautiful, hand-wrought iron gates from New Orleans.

Churchill Jones profited greatly from his Texas venture. Rumor was that he had buried a chest of gold coins during the Civil War. After his death, the legend persisted. Time and again the family graveyard had been pitted with holes dug by treasure hunters. So far they had been unsuccessful, but Bedford had not yet had his turn.

Reverend Goddard drove on past the cemetery wall and parked at the edge of a gentle mound, where Indians had once lived, worked, and died. He opened the trunk, and amongst the picks, shovels, and trowels was a box of treasures he'd collected on digging expeditions at numerous Indian camp sites. There were flint knives, tomahawks, and hand axes; exquisite bird points, net sinkers, and spear points; pottery fragments and grinding stones.

We took our shovels and began turning the rich Brazos River bottom soil. After a half-hour of digging, it had yielded only a few fragments of clay pots and broken flint arrowheads. Then Bedford's shovel struck something large and white.

"Look, it's a skull," shouted Bedford, holding up the grotesque thing he'd just dug out of the Indian mound. Reverend Goddard put his shovel down and walked over to examine it.

"Let's see," said the amateur archeologist. "This skull belonged to a big Indian brave...probably died in a battle with the white man — see that bullet hole in the top? Dig deeper in the ground and you may find <u>his</u> treasure. The Indians buried their dead with weapons, utensils, and tools they would need in the happy hunting grounds."

"Weren't these hunting grounds happy?" I asked.

"They should have been," he answered. "The forests were full of game, the streams full of fish, and the land fertile, but the Indians spent most of their time fighting over those rich treasures with other tribes and the white man. So, they needed a happier place to go when they died — like heaven."

After a few moments of furious digging, Bedford uncovered several animal horns.

"I'll bet that Indian was a big chief, and these were his buffalo horns," theorized Bedford.

"Goodness me...it must be Buffalo Hump, the great Comanche Chief," said Reverend Goddard — winking at Posh. "Bless that old Indian's soul. It was around here that he led his braves in their last big battle with the Texas Rangers. The Comanches went on the warpath and the Rangers were sent here to stop them. Chief Buffalo Hump led a final charge on horseback, wearing a huge headdress of buffalo horns. The Rangers were outnumbered, but they had the new Colt six-shooters, giving each man the firepower of six. They all took aim at Buffalo Hump. When he fell, the battle was over and the Indians left forever."

"Can I take Chief Buffalo Hump home for an experiment?" asked Bedford, clutching the skull to his chest.

"We'll take it to study," the Reverend answered, "then I'll rebury it next week before Indian spirits get mad and go on the warpath against us palefaces again."

Just then, a neighboring farm boy walked up. We'd become friends while picking cotton the previous summer, and he was anxious to join in the digging. Together we gripped Reverend Goddard's last shovel, and were turning the soil laboriously when we unearthed a flint toma-hawk — undoubtedly the prize possession of the "Chief."

"Just look what you boys found yourselves!" exclaimed Reverend Goddard. "Since you dug it up together, I don't know who it belongs to. The best way to decide is for each of you to guess a number between one and ten. I'll tell Bedford the number and whoever guesses closest to it gets the tomahawk."

Then he whispered the number in Bedford's ear. While the Reverend looked down to inspect the ancient flint piece, Bedford strolled by me nonchalantly and whispered — "eight."

"Eight," I parroted before I had time to realize the dishonesty of what Bedford had caused me to do. The unsuspecting clergyman handed me the tomahawk when the other boy guessed three. I ran to the car with my new prize possession to hide in shame. I'd done a terrible thing. I had cheated. I began to wonder — if hell is the opposite of heaven, what is the opposite of "happy hunting grounds?" I would surely be punished in one of those two "unhappy" places.

Before long, Reverend Goddard walked off to investigate another Indian mound. Bedford and Posh raced with their shovels to the cemetery wall and climbed quickly over the iron gates which had rusted shut. Why were they going into that spooky-looking place...to dig for the buried treasure — without me? I hopped out of the car and headed for the foreboding brick wall.

The bright, sunny day suddenly turned to twilight as I peered through the gates. The graveyard was covered with a ceiling of thick, intertwined tree limbs and matted brambles. There, stood numerous stone burial vaults and tombstones. Each one seemed to be vying for my attention, trying to convince me that while Churchill Jones and his family might be gone, they were surely not forgotten! The overgrown state of the once-proud cemetery was a testimonial to a family disunified by size, distance, passing generations, and money.

As I stood there dusting off the names, dates, and epitaphs with my eyes, I could hear the boys talking. I climbed over and crept through the graveyard until I discovered them standing in front of Churchill Jones' large crypt. I crouched behind a tombstone and listened.

"They say that angry Indian spirits keep moving the buried treasure around so no one can find it. They're supposed to come back every Thanksgiving," said Posh.

Bedford was silent and motionless for a moment. Then he looked up, down, and all around. He picked up his shovel, and, as if in a trance, walked to a remote corner of the graveyard, and began digging.

"Why'd you want to dig way over here?" asked Posh.

"'Cause I have a hunch," said Bedford, confidently. "If the Indian spirits come back every Thanksgiving to move the gold, they must have hidden it exactly...where the only ray of sunshine...that comes into the graveyard...on Thanksgiving Day...at precisely 11 A.M....hits the ground. And this is the spot, here in the corner. See that beam of sunlight?"

"Well, that's as good a guess as any, I suppose," said Posh, joining in with his shovel. "But wait a minute. Why would they want to show us where it is?"

"Because we've got their chief sitting on the running board of Reverend Goddard's Plymouth," said Bedford. "He's our hostage. They want us to find the treasure 'cause it's the ransom. In a minute you're gonna hear the jingle of gold coins as my shovel hits that chest."

But the next sound they heard came from me. As I tiptoed over a grave behind them, the earth suddenly gave way beneath my feet. I let out a yell as I imagined frantic hands clutching at my ankles. The Indian spirits were going to punish me for the cheating I'd done with the tomahawk we had stolen.

Bedford and Posh, startled from their digging, turned around to see me being swallowed up by a grave. They leaped over the gate with a quick bound, as my legs turned, literally, to clay. When the boys had reached safety on the other side of the wall, they called back for me to look down to see if the treasure was there in the hole with me. I didn't know if the grave harbored an ancestor, an Indian, or simply an animal burrow, and I wasn't about to find out.

When I'd finally scrambled over the old rusted gates, I asked Bedford why he didn't go back and check for buried treasure.

"Oh, I don't figure it's worth the trouble," he said meekly, when he'd regained his voice. "I'm sure the thieves have picked over every possible spot where treasure could be hidden."

As we pulled away from the graveyard, Bedford and Posh lamented the fact that Chief Buffalo Hump's braves didn't seem to want him back very badly. But Reverend Goddard was deep in thought, for while Bedford and Posh had been digging for buried coins, he'd been searching, instead, for treasures of the human spirit. Chief Buffalo Hump sat on the shelf under the rear car window, leering at me over my shoulder. He seemed to be saying that while his Indian braves had missed getting me this time, I just might not be so lucky the next.

XII

Giving Thanks

As we drove back through Marlin, Bedford held the skull out the window while the chief nodded to the startled townsfolk like a visiting monarch.

"All right, everybody — let's all welcome Chief Buffalo Hump and his braves on their annual warpath," Bedford shouted.

"Put that thing away," said Reverend Goddard as we passed his Episcopal Church. "People might think I'm delving in witchcraft. I don't fit their standard image of a minister, anyway."

We drove on through this prosperous, small town past stately, Greek-columned homes. Posh seemed to have an extraordinary tale to tell about the occupants of each house, personalities who gave Marlin its own special mystique. There were stories of pioneering persistence, extraordinary eccentricity, flamboyant entertainment, of fortunes and reputations made and lost.

Finally, we pulled up in front of Papa Battle's towering Victorian home, which commanded a full corner of the entire town block on which his homestead was situated. The picturesque roof line, with its "gingerbread" woodwork and golden eagle atop the weathervane, climbed up into the crisp fall sky. We grabbed the skull and tomahawk, thanked Reverend Goddard, and ran around the house, straight for the barn.

There we found our dark friend, John Battle Jones, sitting on a stool beside a cow. He was wearing blue overalls, starched white shirt, and thick, leather work boots. His curly, snow-white hair looked as if it had turned to cotton.

"Hi, John!" we shouted, rushing to throw our arms around him from every direction. "How are you?"

"Hidy boys. I'm fine, jes' fine," he answered. "Say, where'd y'all git dat skull?"

"We've been out at the Churchill Jones cemetery diggin' up relics with Reverend Goddard," said Bedford.

"Well, yo white relics buried in dat graveyard gonna bust dey haids on all dem branches when dey tries to fly up to heaven. Jes' look at de hole in de top o' dis one."

Bedford and John Battle Jones in 1929

"That's not one of our 'relics,'" said Bedford. "It's Chief Buffalo Hump and he got shot with a Colt six-shooter."

"Dat's tough, real tough," shrugged John. "But it sho is nice o' you to invite an Injun to Thanksgivin' lunch like dem Pilgrims did."

"What are you doing, John?" I asked.

"I'm milkin' dis ole cow so's you'll have somethin' good to drink wid dat Thanksgivin' turkey Mary's cookin."

He took aim and gave each of us a surprise squirt of warm milk. Then he emptied his bucket into a large, round can and carried it to the kitchen. After that, we followed him, as if he were a black pied piper, to the gazebo where he churned some cream into butter. John churned and talked and talked and churned.

"Yessir, I carried to de train station de trunk o' each o' Mr. Battle's five daughters when dey went off ta school, includin' yo grandma, Miss Maude," he said to Bedford and me, "an Miss Sing, Miss Mabel, Miss Susie, an Miss Pauline. Den, when dey married, I carried all dere trunks as dey started off on dey honeymoons. Now I carries some of de grandchirren's trunks when dey goes off ta college."

John Battle Jones, who'd been born into slavery on Churchill Jones' Falls Plantation during the Civil War, had now worked for Papa Battle and his family for over half a century. He had learned to read and write by watching and listening to the Battle daughters do their homework in the kitchen. At all weddings the family provided a place for John and called his name as often as that of any other person as the family pulled presents from under the Christmas tree.

John, with his gentle, humorous nature, nursed and baby-sat the children of several generations. Once, when Posh was a toddler, John took Posh's tiny, white hand into his own black one. It amused John to see the little boy rub his hand as if to remove the blackness he imagined had rubbed off on it.

"People comes in lots o' duffunt colahs, Posh, but dat don' make wut a person is inside; beauty is only skin deep, but ugly is bone deep," John had said.

When John finally finished churning and telling stories, he carried the milk and butter from the gazebo to the kitchen, where Mary, the cook, was putting finishing touches on the Thanksgiving turkey.

Family members began to assemble in the large, paneled dining room: our parents, grandparents, cousins, great-aunts and great-uncles, more relatives than I ever dreamed of. All the chairs at the big dining table quickly filled.

I sat between cousins Berry and his younger brother, Chuck, who'd been named, ponderously, Churchill Jones Brazelton after his great-great-grandfather.

Papa Battle shuffled in, adjusted his hearing aid, and the old Civil War veteran greeted each of us warmly. His white hair hung straight where he had parted it neatly. His eyelids drooped, it seemed to me, from having seen so much.

"Wo," he asked, "how are you going to eat Thanksgiving turkey with your chin on the table?"

Papa Battle sent Cousins Rose and Rosalis for the thick family Bible, and as soon as I was perched on top of it, he said the blessing. The huge turkey was brought to the table with dressing and cranberry sauce. Then Mary brought me a glass of milk. Papa Battle noticed me making a face as I tasted it.

"What's the matter with the milk?" he asked.

"It doesn't taste good. I don't like milk that comes from a cow. I like milk that comes from a bottle," I explained.

By late afternoon the last piece of pumpkin pie had been consumed, and last family story told. On the way home, Posh invited Bedford to spend the night with him. Not wanting to be left out, I wrangled an impromptu invitation from his mother, who overruled Bedford's protest.

"Oh, there'll be plenty of room for all three of you in Churchill Jones' great big old bed," she added, much to Bedford's chagrin. "And I think it'll survive the night. Once, when a tornado blew their house down, the Jones family saved themselves by hiding beneath its sturdy timbers."

Arriving at Posh's house, we felt stuffed and tired and soon it was time for bed.

"Now listen, Wo — we didn't invite you here, so go to sleep and don't be any trouble," warned Bedford.

I accepted the small amount of room allocated to me in the antique bed and tried to remain very still — until I had to get up.

"Why didn't you go pee before you got in bed?" asked Bedford.

"I forgot."

Getting back in, I tried to lay still, but finally had to turn over.

"Keep your cold fanny away from me," said Bedford. "Your feet are like ice. Don't touch me."

"I can't help it, Bedford. I just can't go to sleep," I said, staring up at the huge, velvet-draped canopy over us.

"Try counting sheep — that'll do it. Imagine a sheep jumping over a fence...then, another and another. Count them as they go by and see what happens. Count as many as you can, as long as you can."

"I'm through," I said after a few moments of peace for Bedford and Posh.

"You're what?" he asked.

"I already got to 20...that's all the sheep there are," I said.

Posh, now sharing Bedford's aggravation began to tell a bizarre and harrowing story he'd just conjured up.

"Say Bedford, did you know that Great-Great-Grandpa Churchill Jones died mysteriously in this very bed, thirty years to the day after Chief Buffalo Hump's braves were defeated. They found him smothered to death under this very same canopy you see hanging over our heads. It was as if someone had pulled it down, but no one had entered the room. A single feather lay on top of his dresser."

"Maybe the spirits of the dead Indians did it," said Bedford, picking up on Posh's strategy. "They were mad about cotton being planted over their tribal graves."

I looked over on Churchill Jones' dresser. There sat Chief Buffalo Hump's skull, grinning ominously.

"I don't think I like sleeping in this bed," I said. "I'll just rest on the floor."

Their ploy had worked perfectly. Remembering the story of how the Jones family had saved themselves from the tornado, I crawled under the sturdy oak bed, with my head sticking out from under it and resting on my pillow which I'd put behind the big rocking chair. Bedford and Posh could hardly hide their glee, and I could hear them whispering until I dropped off to sleep under the warm rug I'd pulled up over me. Aunt Madeline came in to check on us, sat down in the rocker, and leaned back to stretch. I let out a yell as the rocker came down on my head, cutting a large, bleeding gash.

"Look — Wo's been scalped," said Bedford, groggy and terrified when he saw the blood streaming down my face. Chief Buffalo Hump and his scalping band of Indian spirits had gotten their revenge.

It was late when Aunt Madeline led me up the street to my grand-parent's home, wounded in body and spirit, with my dome wrapped in a bandage. Though safe, I still feared the spirits of the Indian braves, so I pulled the covers high over my head. There were some things I could always count on — like the magical power of protective bed sheets.

XIII

Lee's Last Lieutenant

I awakened to the thumping of an Indian tom-tom as the bedroom door squeaked open. My head throbbed when I sat up in bed and tried to focus my eyes. The gruesome, gray skull peered in the doorway at me. It was dancing to the beat of the drum and, except for the feather sticking out of the hole in the top, it looked and sounded a lot like my older brother. Of course, I knew it was, and I recognized the sound as the red drum that Santa had brought David for Christmas. Besides, the ghostly spirits had ridden out on the first rays of sunshine that streamed in my room, having been foiled by the magic protective sheets — like phantoms always are.

"Get out of here, Bedford, and take that dumb skull with you," I said. "I'm not scared anymore."

"Good morning, little Wo. How does it feel without a scalp?" jeered Bedford. "Now people can look in and see that your head's empty. Posh and I are leaving for Duke & Ayres in fifteen minutes. Baba said we're s'posed to take you with us, so hurry up if you just have to go."

Another bright, sunny day of Marlin adventure lay ahead, starting with a walk downtown to spend the quarters Baba had given us, at the "five and dime" store.

"Take something made of glass," said Posh, waiting for us in the front yard. "I'll show you how to stain it amber in the public fountain."

Bedford knew just where to find a white china nude figurine that had been stashed away in a far corner of the attic. I thought for a moment, then raced to our car and took Baba's glass ash tray from the glove compartment. She had learned to smoke cigarettes from Daddy, but would keep her "un-ladylike" habit a secret from her father for the rest of his life. We put the things in a paper grocery sack, along with our strange assortment of Indian relics, and headed downtown.

After walking a few blocks we came to the public fountain in downtown Marlin, where steaming, hot mineral water gushed gratuitously through spouts and poured into foul-smelling pools of amber water. Mostly old people occupied the numerous benches under the open, arched pavilion. They stared with bleary, empty eyes at the falling water, wishing its energy could be theirs.

"They come here to tune their anatomies and get rejuvenated by drinking the mineral water," said Posh. "It doesn't seem to work on them though, the way they look, but it works real good on glass."

These waters, and the Marlin Baths and Clinic, had given Marlin a national reputation as a health spa. People came from far and wide, seeking the water's magical powers.

"The New York Yankees used to make Marlin their spring training camp," explained Posh. "They won all those pennants with our hot baths and mineral water!"

The multitude of glazed eyes began to squint and try to focus as we emptied the sack. Bedford placed the skull and tomahawk on the edge of the pool. Then he put the ashtray and nude figurine between them, as if he were conducting some sort of strange pagan ritual.

"Put the nude in the water and swish her around like this," said Posh, dunking the ash tray in the steaming, rusty-looking liquid. After a few minutes, he took the ash tray out of the water and we admired nature's wonderful transformation. What had been clear glass was now a sparkling, iridescent amber.

Bedford picked up the china nude and immersed her legs for a few minutes with the concentration of a scientist, taking particular care not to wet any of her anatomy above the legs. Then he turned her upside down and dipped the nude carefully in the pool, stopping exactly where the water met the middle of her bosoms.

Reverend Goddard walked by on his way to the church, just as Bedford turned his dripping figurine upright. The china nude had acquired a glorious bronze tan, except for her lily-white one-piece bathing suit band around the waist. Her nudeness was now shockingly lifelike. Curious passersbye stopped and stared. Some of the old-timers, whose eyes had now come to life, giggled and elbowed each other in the ribs.

"Marlin may not be ready for such worldly art just yet, Bedford." said Reverend Goddard.

"Well, Chief Buffalo Hump is ready to go back to the 'happy hunting grounds.' Here...we were bringing him to you," said Bedford.

"And I want him to have his tomahawk back. He might need it," I said, handing Reverend Goddard the stone.

"I'm sure that old Indian's soul will be happy to get it back, wherever he is," said the Reverend.

Then he put the skull and tomahawk in the sack and walked on. Buffalo Hump's spirit had now departed and so did we, leaving the old-timers entertained, if nothing else.

In the next block we came to the First State Bank. Through the window we could see Papa Battle in a meeting. He waved at us as we walked by his Ford coupe that John kept cleaned, polished, and tuned to perfection. Papa Battle had driven himself to work so John could help Mary straighten up after Thanksgiving. Our great-grandfather had retired in 1907 at the age of 61. After staying home for a few days, he realized that idleness was not for him. He founded the bank and had not missed a day's work in 30 years. Now, at 91, he was the oldest bank president in the nation.

A few minutes later we were prowling the aisles of the Duke & Ayres "five and dime" store, carefully considering our purchases. It appeared to us a wondrous bazaar, with a thousand items from which to choose, and one thoughtful purchase could provide days of entertainment. What would I buy today — a gun that shoots caps, or water, or rubber darts; ball & jacks, or a jackknife; telescope or a kaleidoscope; lead soldiers or a rubber hunting knife; a spinning yo-yo or a spinning top; a checkerboard or a paddleboard? The possibilities seemed endless, the purchasing power of the quarter enormous.

Bedford selected a ready-assembled, balsa wood airplane model with a thick, rubber band motor. When he got home, he would wind the wooden propeller exactly 175 times and launch the plane dramatically from high atop the steel slide — over and over again. Posh thoughtfully purchased a bud vase that he intended to stain amber as a present for Aunt Madeline. I decided on a beautiful tin sword and scabbard with leather strap — the weapon of a general.

Around the corner stood Grand Daddy's dry goods store, with bolts of fabric, shoes, and hats displayed in the show windows. We found no shiny black Ford parked in front, but our grandfather's bright blue bicycle stood proudly on the sidewalk. Grand Daddy, busy with a customer, invited us to entertain ourselves by riding the ladder next to the wall that rolled on wheels. Besides being fun to ride, the ladder provided access to the upper storage shelves that were too high to reach.

"Just look at your piece of glass, Wo," exclaimed Grand Daddy, finally. "It's such a beautiful color. What is that?"

Bedford had hidden the nude bathing beauty in his shirt, but I'd been too late putting the amber ashtray behind my back. Now I was afraid I'd given away Baba's secret. I also feared he would think I'd been smoking.

"Oh, it's a berry bowl," I said, crossing my fingers.

"Well, it looks like an ashtray to me," said Grand Daddy. "I don't believe in smoking, especially for women — it's very un-ladylike. As for children, it is strictly forbidden. You boys haven't been smoking, have you?"

We shook our heads in feigned innocence, remembering all those grapevine smoke rings we had puffed into the air the day we'd arrived.

"Daddy smokes, but he quits all the time," I said. "Last week he threw some cigarettes in the toilet before he went to sleep. The next morning he fished 'em out, dried 'em in the sun, and smoked 'em. Isn't that funny?"

Grand Daddy Bunch looked indignant at this story of strong tobacco and human weakness. Then he noticed my bright, shiny new sword and smiled.

"Your uniform is not complete, soldier. We can't have you serving the South with a bandaged head. We'll just make you a hat."

He took the *Marlin Daily Democrat* and folded it into a magnificent triangular military hat that would have rivaled Napoleon's. I marched proudly out of the store and we returned to the magical fountain. As soon as Posh had finished tinting the bud vase, he and Bedford disappeared down a side street. Left alone, I decided to go see Papa Battle and John.

My great-grandfather had just driven home from the bank and was sitting on his front porch when I arrived. The former Confederate cavalryman stood up slowly and saluted as I climbed the steps, wearing the paper hat; dragging my tin sword.

"I'm glad you came to see me, soldier," he said, pulling up an extra rocking chair. "What army are you from? I'm not sure I recognize the uniform."

"I'm a Confederate soldier," I said.

"Well, I used to be one, too," said the old soldier. "I left school and joined my father's cavalry unit when I was fifteen, and my uniform didn't look much better than yours. Say, how're you doing at your school? Are you making good grades?"

"I like the second grade. Mrs. Newton is nice, and she likes me. She wrote a note for me to take home to Baba that I'm doing real good," I said.

"Well just a moment, and I'll show you a letter that my teacher wrote home to my daddy about me," he said, as he shuffled inside to his desk.

In a moment, he returned with a dried flower and an old letter he'd saved, which we read together:

> *Washington College, Lexington, Virginia. June 28, 1870...*
> *Dear Judge Battle, I have the pleasure of communicating to you*
> *the action of the faculty of Washington College commending*
> *your son, Thomas E. Battle, for his regular attendance on*
> *college duties, his industry and improvement in his studies*
> *during the late session...with best wishes for his future welfare,*
> *I am, respectfully, R.E. Lee, President.*

"General Lee died shortly after writing this letter, and since I had been a Confederate soldier before attending Washington College, I marched proudly at the head of his funeral procession in the soldier's Escort of Honor. Few of the General's lieutenants could reach the funeral because of high floodwaters around Lexington, Virginia. So, I helped remove all the flowers from the casket as it was placed in the vault — including this dried one — feeling like I really was one of his lieutenants. I suppose, in a way, I was the last soldier to serve our great Robert E. Lee," said the old man as I listened attentively.

"I'm sorry the North won the war," I said.

"Neither side really wins a war, Wo. When a church that took a hundred years for a peaceful army to build is destroyed, both sides lose. When a youth is killed, a widow, orphan, or cripple made to suffer, all humanity loses. Now, Wo, a time will come when you'll need to stand up to a bully to avoid a fight. Sometimes there is no other choice, but, most every fight that ever happened could have, and should have been avoided, especially the Civil War, where brother fought brother."

"I fight my brother all the time," I confessed, as I saluted Papa Battle. Then I ran out back to look for John.

A few months later, Papa Battle finally missed a day's work. As he lay in bed, he asked that a cot be placed next to him so that John Battle Jones, his devoted servant and friend, could be nearby when the end came.

After Papa Battle died and everyone had left the old place, John would drive the Ford coupe — that my great-grandfather had willed him — around back of the house and park under the grove of oak trees. There he would sit, waiting for family members to summon him for odd jobs.

While he waited, John would remember the sounds of laughter and tears of the past. He would dream and re-live all the proud, bygone days he had spent — serving Lee's last lieutenant.

XIV

The Blue Norther

At Christmastime, Santa came and went, forgetting to bring his cold norther — and my bicycle. But then, three weeks later on my birthday, both arrived.

There it stood, right in the middle of the living room floor, beckoning to me. "Come feel my fenders, rub my frame...hold my handles, crank my chain," it seemed to say. Only a handful of spectacles had stirred such an emotional response in me until then: the wonder of watching a baby chick peck its way out of an egg; the amazement at hearing music from a spinning wax disc come out of a wooden box; the excitement when discovering the treasure of toys Santa had left beneath my Christmas stocking. But gazing at my very first bicycle became the matchless thrill that evoked the entire gamut of my emotions.

I stood there in awe, stunned by the most splendid sight I'd ever seen. It had been painted green to match my eyes, like everything else I owned: toothbrush, cap, lunch box, clothes, cup and flashlight, to keep them from getting mixed up with Bedford's blue and David's brown things. Green was my stamp of possession.

It had glistening chrome, shiny white sidewalls, and sparkling spokes that radiated out in every direction, like so many future adventures on which my new bike would whisk me away. That proud, new possession represented fun, freedom, status, and most of all — growing up.

"Just look at that big, springy seat and long handlebars," said Bedford. "Don't forget who taught you to ride a bike, Wo. I might want to borrow it sometime."

"And I won't forget how I crashed when you pushed too fast," I said.

"That was strictly rider error!" chided Bedford.

This being my eighth big special birthday, Baba reluctantly agreed to let me take my new prize to school this bright, warm January, 1938 day. A rapid change in the weather had been forecast, however, and she worried about me riding home.

"Hurry on to school, but stay on the sidewalks except when you walk your bike across Beverly Drive," she instructed. "When you reach your grandmother's house, Aunt Olive will open her garage and you should park it in there, then walk across the bridge to school."

I memorized these orders of the day like a cavalry scout, and off I rode into a bright, new world of two-wheeled mobility. Heads turned from all directions as I rang my bell to warn the little satchel-carrying pedestrians that Overton Shelmire was coming through, riding his brand-new Columbia bicycle on a mission of utmost urgency with secret orders strapped — in textbook form — to the luggage carrier. My leather aviator's helmet and flight goggles, pulled down over my eyes, made it obvious that I meant business.

As I got off to walk across Beverly Drive, motorists slowed in deference to one who owned such a beautiful possession. He really must be somebody, they thought...I thought. After that, I slowed down only to pull my knickers up over my skinny legs so they wouldn't get caught in the chain. When I arrived at Maw Maw's, Aunt Olive was standing in front of the garage, ready to take my steed into the stable. Armstrong School, looking like a distant military outpost, loomed just across the bridge.

"Happy Birthday, Wo. Look at that beautiful new bicycle!" said Aunt Olive, as Maw Maw waved congratulations from her upstairs window. "Your mother called and asked me to let you park your bike here where it'll be safe. She may have to pick you up after school because there's a blue norther rolling in. That sky looks as ominous as it did eight years ago this very day, when you were born."

I had been so intent on my mission that I hadn't noticed that the northern sky had become a deep, slate blue — a striking backdrop for Aunt Olive's perfectly-kept gray hair and hazel eyes. Daddy's unmarried sister, the "old maid" of the Shelmire family, swung the garage doors open and I rolled my bike inside. I put the kickstand down and took a last glance at it sitting there, looking magnificent in the dim light as we closed the doors.

"Now you run along to school and put as much knowledge into that aviator's cap as it'll hold," said Aunt Olive. "I don't want my school tax money to be wasted."

I wrapped my arms around her waist. Her hips felt soft and her tummy warmed my cheek as the cold wind began to blow, breaking the stillness of the air. As I reached the crest of the bridge and turned to wave, a frigid gale hit my hand and the bare tree limbs above began to thrash. It was a chill more piercing than any I'd ever experienced before. Leaning down to pull my knickers up, I suddenly felt sick, and my head began perspiring beneath my cap. A mood, as ominous as a blue norther, came over me.

I walked down the bridge toward school feeling like anything but a birthday boy. How could I feel so bad, I wondered, when I'd just gotten that beautiful, new bike? I made it to class and smiled faintly at pretty

Phyllis Murphey across the aisle. Then I filled my brain with facts as long as I could, until my head got dizzy, hot, heavy, and slumped over on the desk. The teacher became alarmed as she felt my forehead. She sent me to the school nurse, who took my temperature, then called my mother.

As we drove home through the somber, gray chill, I was glad my bike stood safe and sound at Maw Maw's house. Baba put me to bed with a raging fever. While she went to call Daddy, the penetrating blue norther sneaked into my room and began crushing my chest. I tried to call her but couldn't make a sound. Struggling to breathe, shivering cold, and afraid, I pulled the covers up over me. Would the magic protective sheets save me this time, like they always had?

An eternity later, a pinpoint of light appeared at the end of a tunnel, growing larger and larger. Something red came toward me...a skeleton of blood...my blood...dancing up to me. Then the scarlet tracery of bones melted into nothing and it became dark again.

"Any change, Doctor?" asked Baba, drained of prayers and energy after sitting by my side day and night through my three-day-long coma.

"Now, I don't want you to get too encouraged; your son's still in grave condition. He opened his eyes for a moment when I pricked his finger to draw some blood," said the doctor.

I had double pneumonia and since antibiotics did not yet exist, the chances of my survival were slim. Daddy waited in his easy chair through those long, sleepless nights, lamenting the fact that although he was a doctor, as a dermatologist he couldn't help with my treatment. Bedford had buried his head in books to keep his mind occupied and his feelings under control. David, at first annoyed at being uprooted from his room so that it could become a private hospital for me, had discovered my toy chest and played merrily with its unguarded contents.

Sally and Margaret kept the household going and cared for the rest of us, confident with the inner strength of their deep, religious faith. They were convinced that whatever happened, I would have the arms of God around me. Daddy was jealous of their strong, comforting convictions. While he had concluded long ago that the mystery of life exceeded his understanding, he was no atheist. Attuned to the scriptures of nature, he loved his fellow man, followed the golden rule, and worshiped all creation.

When Margaret came in to sit by my side through the night, Baba hugged and kissed me softly, then left the room. I felt warm at last. The invading blue norther had rolled on to do its conquering some place else.

The air blew fresh and cool like springtime, but it smelled of rubber and made a hissing noise. As my eyes began to focus, I could see I was in some sort of transparent tent. Margaret sat outside, her large, white uniform illuminated by the dim night-light. She turned her radio to some soft, Sunday night music, then left the room for a few minutes.

Suddenly, I heard an outburst of noise on the station, of a man speaking at such a rapid, staccato pace that I could hardly understand him. His words sounded hard and clipped, and he spoke in a terse, nasal voice. It was Walter Winchell, speaking to me and 50 million other Americans.

> *Good Evening, Mr. and Mrs. America — from border to border and coast to coast, and all the ships at sea — let's go to press!*

The sound of a telegraph ticker pecking out Morse code followed. Then came his news report. Before signing off, Winchell gave his usual Sunday evening accolade to take the sting off his biting commentary:

> *Last night I went to the Stork Club, ladies and gentlemen. I saw the singing star of the Princeton Triangle Club, T. Berry Brazelton, who recently introduced that new hit song, 'East of the Sun and West of the Moon' — written for him by a college classmate. While his friends sipped mixed drinks at the bar, Berry drank a big glass of milk. Now there's a young American who has his principles and is not afraid to keep them. Congratulations to you, Berry, for taking care of that fine voice. And orchids to you, Mrs. Brazelton, back in Waco, Texas, for raising such a fine, clean-cut young man! Now, until next Sunday...*

The nation had stopped what it was doing to listen to Walter Winchell; I'd stopped hallucinating...and he was talking about my own Cousin Berry!

When Margaret came back in the room, she looked startled to see my lips move; I was trying to make myself heard. She ran downstairs to tell my parents. In a moment they rushed in, lifted the oxygen tent, and put their ears close to my mouth.

"Baba...Daddy!" I wheezed. "The man on...the radio said...Cousin Berry drank a glass of milk...at the Stork Club last night and...he sent orchids to Aunt Pauline."

I would remain in bed, convalescing, for another month — long days of boredom, depression, and worry. Had I been forgotten by my friends at school? Would I ever catch up with them in my studies?

The morning finally arrived when Baba drove me back to Armstrong School — on February 14. We got there early, and when I walked in the classroom, there on my desk sat a big box covered with pink and white crepe paper and red hearts, with a letter slot in the top.

When I took off the lid, I felt bedazzled at the breathtaking sight of a pile of colorful valentines, one from each of my classmates. Some were homemade, with lacy hearts glued on in three-dimension. Others had been store-bought, with their serious or silly messages inside.

I savored each and every one before putting them all back in the slot of my sentimental treasure chest. I was remembered...I was missed...I was loved. The one that meant the most was a handmade valentine from Phyllis Murphey:

> *Roses are red, violets are blue,*
> *When it's raining, I think of you —*
> > *drip.*
>
> *Your friend, Phyllis*

How thrilling! She had never been romantic toward me before.

I felt butterflies in my stomach that afternoon when school was out and I walked across the bridge toward Aunt Olive's garage to pick up my bicycle. It seemed like a vault containing a king's treasure as I swung open the doors and my eyes adjusted to the dim light. There the bike sat in all its splendor, with its shiny chrome and bright green paint glistening through a thick layer of dust. I wiped it off with loving care, wondering if I could still ride a bicycle and hoping my legs would be strong enough to crank the pedals.

When I got on and wobbled out into the fresh air and sunshine, I had a feeling of exhilaration and freedom I hadn't experienced since my birthday, a resurgence of my spirit and strength. At last it had come — the reconciliation of my total love affair with life.

I found myself pedaling toward Phyllis Murphey's house. My heart fluttered as I spotted her sitting prettily in a swing that hung from the giant hackberry tree in her front yard. I laid my bike down in her driveway and rushed over to join her on the swing.

"Thank you for the pretty valentine," I said. "It made me feel a lot better."

"You're welcome. I'm glad you got well and came back to school...we missed you," she told me.

My heart was bursting with affection and I wished I could put it into words, but I decided to carve our initials into the tree instead. There it was, finally — *O.S. + P.M.*, the sentiment surrounded by a carved heart.

As we sat there admiring my handiwork, we heard a sickening crunch of metal. Her father had backed over my bicycle with his car. I ran to the driveway and looked down, unbelieving, at the bent frame, crumpled fenders, and broken spokes.

Love has its sorrows...and its costs, I had discovered.

XV

The War of the Words

Bedford put down the knife and stepped back like Dr. Frankenstein, studying his sinister-looking creation. A flickering candle inside the jack-o-lantern caused its fierce eyes and crooked mouth to glow as if a demon dwelled within. As I stood there admiring it, the big, carved pumpkin seemed to personify all the fiendish ideas Bedford's fertile mind had ever conjured up.

Suddenly, Bedford disappeared out the back door, leaving me to dispose of the slimy, smelly, gooey insides of the pumpkin. Walking to the alley, I avoided the neighbor's black cat, lest it cross my path and bring bad luck. A deep haze had caused an eerie light for all that Indian summer afternoon. Now, with darkness approaching, the air was chilled and leaves swirled around the yard as if puffed by a phantom. Halloween — 1938, just the sort of evening for alien creatures to visit the earth, a perfect night for a war of the worlds.

Warily emptying the trash, I noticed Bedford and Richard, the boy next door, digging with a shovel.

"What are you looking for?" I asked. "Is something buried down there...or...someone?"

The boys didn't answer. They were carefully scooping handfuls of dirt as if they expected to find buried treasure. Just enough twilight remained when they finished for me to see the dozen rotten eggs they'd buried two weeks before.

"These are Halloween stink bombs, to throw at the houses of mean people we don't like," explained Bedford. "Come help us carry them to the garage."

As he handed several to me, I dropped one and it splattered across the toe of my leather shoe, emitting an insidious, nauseating smell. We carried the Halloween arsenal to the garage; then Richard went home to listen to Charlie McCarthy, like almost everyone else across the country. I rushed into the house, plunked down in front of the big living room radio and turned the dial to the Sunday night Mercury Theater instead.

"Wonder why they're playing that dance music?" said Bedford as he came puffing in. "It's past time for the program to start."

Just then a news announcer interrupted, saying that several explosions had been observed on the planet Mars, and that flaming gas was moving toward the earth with enormous velocity.

"Sounds like we're in for some bad weather," quipped Bedford.

An interlude of dance music followed. "Darn it, they keep interrupting the program with music," complained Bedford as he switched the dial to give the Edgar Bergen and Charlie McCarthy show a try. Charlie was singing:

> *A-haunting we will go, a-haunting we will go.*
> *Hey, Charlie,* said Bergen, *the word is hunting.*
> *Well, not on Halloween, it ain't,* replied Charlie.

Bedford turned the dial back to where the Mercury Theater was supposed to be. Just then, the music stopped and an announcer came on the air with a bulletin: a huge flaming object, believed to be a meteorite, had fallen on a farm near Grover's Mill, New Jersey. A farmer who had witnessed the arrival of the unusual visitor to his backyard was being interviewed:

> *I poked my head out the window and seen a sort of greenish streak, then bingo — somethin' smacked the ground...knocked me clean off my chair.*

Hundreds of curious onlookers crowded the scene to take a look at the huge, green cylinder. Suddenly, it began to open up. The terrified on-the-scenes announcer described in horror what happened next:

> *Something is crawling out of the top, something or someone as large as a bear. Its face, ladies and gentlemen, is indescribable. I can hardly force myself to keep looking at it, it's so awful-looking. Its eyes are black, and the mouth is sort of V-shaped, with saliva dripping from its quivering lips.*

"Wow, Bedford, this story is just like last week's program, the one you missed about a horrible-looking blind boy who lived on a farm," I said. "His folks never took him into town 'cause he was so ugly, no one could stand to see him."

"Be quiet, Wo," said Bedford, on pins and needles. "I'm trying to listen!"

"Then this farm boy met a girl..."

"SHUT UP!" yelled Bedford.

Baba rushed into the room to referee the problem and turned her nose up in the air, sniffing.

"What's that horrible smell, Wo?" She was looking at my left shoe, which was covered with rotten egg and resembled a glazed brownie. "I can't imagine what you stepped in to smell like that. Go clean it off!"

When I came back in the house, dance music was playing again and Bedford had a somber look on his face.

"Wo, it's awful what I just found out. Those strange beings who landed on the New Jersey farm are the scouts of an invading army from the planet Mars."

"Oh?" I said, with mild concern. I had just finished cleaning my shoe and here was a brand-new problem to deal with.

"We don't know much about 'em, or what they're doing here on earth," said Bedford.

"That's what the ugly, blind farm boy said on last week's program. He was lonely and miserable and didn't know why he was living on this earth," I said, as Bedford tried to ignore me. "The blind boy was allowed to wander only a little ways from his farmhouse, keeping his hand on the fence rail so he could find his way back. One day he felt another hand. It was a girl. She took her hand away, but she was the first person who wasn't afraid of him, who would talk to him. They met there every day and talked and talked and talked about all sorts of things."

"Don't you understand, you dope? The Martians have landed. They're melting everything and everyone in sight with heat-ray guns. The radio announcer at the scene just got zapped," said Bedford, trying to convince me that the terrifying story was true.

As we sat riveted to the radio, the station reported that there seemed to be some difficulty with their field transmission, and until the problem could be cleared up, they would bring us dance music from New York City.

"What's all that on the radio?" came Daddy's voice from the sun parlor.

"Oh, nothing much," said Bedford. "Martians have landed in New Jersey, that's all."

"Hmm...that sounds like dance music to me," said Daddy. "The Martians must be doing the rhumba."

A few minutes later, a grim-voiced announcer interrupted the musical interlude to give the latest details of the invasion: the army and air force had been unable to stop the Martians and their huge tripod machines, who were now advancing rapidly toward New York City. We continued to soak up every electrifying word that came out of the radio, to be gripped by every hair-raising event that unfolded as the Martians continued their relentless march. Then a hoarse-voiced broadcaster reported from his vantage point on a Manhattan rooftop:

Warning! Poisonous black smoke pouring into city — gas masks useless...urge population to flee. The enemy is now in sight...everyone's running...the smoke's reached Times Square.

People are falling like flies. Now the smoke's crossing Sixth Avenue...100 yards...it's 50 feet...

A brief coughing, then silence. When, finally, the Martians were overcome by the earth's bacteria, we sat there stunned and emotionally drained by the powerful drama we'd just heard.

The star of the Mercury Theater came back on with an announcement, little realizing that he and his fellow players had just convinced the radio audience that the planet had been invaded by Martians — sending thousands of New Yorkers driving off into the hills.

This is Orson Welles, ladies and gentlemen, and that was just our radio version of dressing up in a sheet and jumping out of a bush and saying 'Boo!' If your doorbell rings and nobody's there, that was no Martian — it's Halloween.

"That was good!" I said, "but I like how last week's program ended better. One day the horrible-looking blind boy stayed too long talking to the girl — the one that didn't mind his looks. He was afraid he'd be late to supper, so he asked the girl what time the big town clock said. She answered, 'I don't know, I can't see.' He'd discovered why she hadn't run away from him — she was blind like he was! They walked home holding hands, telling each other they were beautiful."

"Well, Wo," said Bedford, "just what was so great about your program? I don't get the point. That was a pointless story."

I thought for a moment but could simply not put my feelings into words. Then Baba spoke from the sun parlor.

"Bedford's wrong, Wo. That was a *poignant* story."

"Yeah, Bedford," I repeated, "it was a poignant story, not pointless."

"I guess so," he said, finally admitting that my play may have had a redeeming quality he hadn't noticed.

I didn't know the meaning of the word "poignant," but I was certain that her word summed up what I couldn't express about the story. I had won this "war of the words" with Bedford!

XVI

Making a Face

"I saw that! All right, Wo, you've had it now! Upstairs this minute," shouted our dad. "I told you not to throw any more peas at the table."

"Bedford threw some at me first. Didn't you see him?" I protested.

"I saw you, and I've told you both: no throwing food! Go upstairs to my closet, get out a belt, and take it to your bathroom. Don't come out until I get there, and don't go into your room, first."

"Oh, Dr. Shelmire, let him stay and eat his gingerbread," pleaded Sally, walking in with my favorite dessert. "He just loves it with my cream sauce."

"No, I'm simply not going to put up with throwing food at Sunday lunch," he answered, "and Wo, I don't want you eating with your left hand. It's bad manners and I'm going to break you of it. Next time you come to this table, I want you to keep your left hand at your side. Understand?"

Bedford grinned contentedly, like the Cheshire cat, as I got up and walked slowly out of the room. David was unconcerned and continued to stir his peas, mashed potatoes, and meat together in a messy swirl. Why do big brothers always start things, and are too smart to get caught, I wondered? Little brothers have to take the blame, while baby brothers get away with anything they want to do. Why did our dad always get so cross and nervous with us when Baba would go off to visit her parents, leaving him to "hold the fort?" He would complain about the food, laundry, housecleaning, and most of all, our behavior.

Today was worse. He was threatening to whip me with his belt. I climbed the stairs with a surge of self-pity and opened Daddy's closet. I studied his belts. Which would hurt less, the thin black belt or the thick brown one? I had been switched by Baba with a privet hedge limb, but never whipped with a belt, so how could I be sure I'd make the right choice?

I decided to chance the thin one and took it dutifully into my bathroom. I closed the door and began the interminable wait for punishment. The silence was deafening and I could almost hear my heart pounding as I counted off the seconds, minutes, then hours. Finally I heard footsteps on the stairway and a knock on the door. I opened it to face my fate, but it was Bedford.

"Sorry you're getting a whipping," he said. "You shouldn't wind up your pitch like Dizzy Dean when you throw stuff at the table. Look. Flick it sidearm...like this, see? Then nothing shows above the table."

"I'll remember that," I said, feeling little consolation.

A couple of hours passed as I awaited punishment. Daddy climbed the stairs occasionally, only to go right back down, procrastinating. Once Sally stopped him at the foot of the stairs and pleaded with him to let her inflict the whipping, promising to do it with vigor.

"I know how hard you'll whip him, Sally; 'bout as hard as a wet noodle," he said.

The telephone rang, and soon a knock sounded on the bathroom door. The fateful moment had arrived, I thought, and I trembled as I opened it.

"We'll have to put off your punishment," said Daddy, sheepishly. "I just got a call from your 'Uncle' Clark. He's going to stay with us for awhile, and his plane arrived early from Chicago. He'll be using this bathroom, so take your bath early. I don't want you back in here. I have to go out to the airport to pick him up now. I'll deal with you later."

Once again my Dad had avoided committing corporal punishment, just as he always had, and always would. I was being made to bathe this Sunday afternoon at a time when I usually sat glued to the radio, listening to *The Shadow*. As soon as I heard Daddy drive away, I went into my room and tip-toed out with the table model radio, passing Bedford who was deeply engrossed in a book. I plugged the radio in and placed it on the edge of the tub that was filled with hot, soapy water.

I slipped under the comforting suds and turned the dial to *The Shadow*, just in time to hear the sinister voice of Orson Welles sneering and laughing:

> *Who knows what evil lurks in the minds of men? The Shadow knows....Hm Hmm Ha Ha Ha Ha.*

I soaked, relaxed, and relished my unexpected reprieve as the Shadow, whose mystical, hypnotic powers learned in the East rendered him invisible, solved yet another complicated crime. I lay there for a long time, dreaming what I might do with the power to make myself invisible.

At dusk I would listen to another of Welles' Mercury Theater productions. While they were always entertaining, there would never by anything like those two great horror stories: about the ugly, blind farm boy, and those hideous Martians stomping across the New Jersey farmland.

I tried to imagine their faces as I reached for the radio. I'd lost track of time. Perhaps the Mercury Theater had already begun. The radio teetered on the edge of the tub as I turned the dial. Suddenly, the door burst open. Shocked and surprised, I tried to focus my eyes. There, above me stood a monster with a hideous face. Could this be a Martian, or the ugly farm boy from the Mercury Theater, grown up and come to visit? He had deeply-pocked, colorless skin devoid of eyebrows or lips, and a shapeless hole where a mouth should have been. His ears were misshapen and the veins on the side of his neck and temples seemed as big as garden hoses.

"What are you doing? Are you Crazy? Don't touch that radio!" yelled the monster with a loud and terrible voice. His face flushed and his hands trembled as he gasped for breath.

He grabbed the radio, jerking the plug out of the wall, and clasped it to his chest with both arms. He walked to the window for a moment, speechless, his gaunt visage staring out into the distance. Then he looked down, knowing he had terrified me.

"Do you know what would have happened if that radio had fallen off the tub into the water? It was just about to. Know what electrocution is?" he asked.

The word sparked the energy in my mind that suddenly grew into a vision of a man lurching and lunging at Warden Lawes' crime show, a prisoner being executed by a sudden surge of electricity.

"Yes, sir," I said grimly, finally realizing what might have happened.

"You could have been killed. I have some friends in Chicago who had a little girl just your age," he said, as I realized this was Uncle Clark. "She took a radio into the bathroom and it fell into the tub and electrocuted her. That's why I was so upset when I saw you about to do the same thing. Now, scram out of here; it's my turn to get a bath."

When Baba drove in from Marlin and came into my bedroom to check on me that Sunday night, she could sense my fear of the man who had possibly just saved my life.

"He's had lots and lots of cancers on his face," she explained. "Uncle Clark made a terrible mistake. He experimented with a new invention he didn't know anything about. It gave him the awful disease that's eaten his skin away."

Baba went on to tell how Daddy, attending medical school in Vienna, had become close friends with a handsome young South Dakotan named Clark Finnerud. Later, Dr. Finnerud studied under a prominent Chicago dermatologist. As one of his office duties, he gave patients with stubborn diseases of the skin, such as cancer, exposures of radiation from the doctor's new X-ray machine. Observing the healing effects of X-ray on other skin problems, he had a nurse give his own acute facial acne strong exposures from the X-ray machine after work.

He continued the treatment for months when he experienced no discomfort, and noticed decided improvement of his cursed malady. The stronger the treatment, the clearer his complexion became. The X-ray machine at that time was a relatively new and unproven invention whose sinister potential for radiation burn lay lurking beneath apparent beneficial qualities. Clark Finnerud never suspected he was condemning his face to break down with countless, disfiguring skin cancers in years to come.

When that terrible time came, he turned to his trusted former classmate and dermatologist friend from Dallas to operate on the rapidly multiplying cancer sores. Each year, following their annual reunion at a medical meeting, Daddy would cut out the cancers that had accumulated since the previous meeting. After a few years of the annual carnage, Clark Finnerud's face had become a crazy quilt of scar tissue from countless gouges, incisions, and stitches.

"Uncle Clark is here so your father can make him a new face this time," said Baba.

Now I understood why our dad had been so agitated and cross with us. Tomorrow he would begin to perform a heartbreaking series of operations on the face of his dear friend.

The next afternoon when Uncle Clark came home from the Medical Arts Building with our father — his face pitted with numerous, bleeding holes — he went straight to his room. I could see him through a crack in the door as I passed. Daddy had helped another doctor make a long tube of skin, sliced from Uncle Clark's shoulder, with the skin connected at each end. What looked like a suitcase handle of his own skin, arched on top of his shoulder.

When Uncle Clark came in a few days later, his head hung to the side — one end of the tube had been sewn to his cheek. The other end was still attached to his shoulder to maintain the blood supply. After another couple of days of Uncle Clark's torturous confinement, Daddy and the other doctor cut the piece of smooth shoulder skin loose and grafted it over Uncle Clark's pitted cheek and chin. The doctors repeated this procedure for a few weeks until new skin covered Uncle Clark's entire face. I looked at him now with the same revulsion; his face glistened in a horrifying patchwork of reddened skin grafts.

Bedford spent those weeks in obsessed fascination, closely following each new step of the operation. He visited with Uncle Clark every evening, asking questions and telling him about plans for his own experiments, inventions, and for becoming a doctor, too. Bedford looked upon Uncle Clark's battered countenance with the reverence due a scientist injured while performing a noble experiment, and with the respect accorded a scarred student swordsman from Heidelberg.

The day finally came for Clark Finnerud to head north toward home to nurse the wounds on his face and soul at his beloved retreat, his log house on Blue Lake in Northern Wisconsin. There, he had planned to hide from the world with his wife Gertrude by his side, if and when his face finally became unacceptable for the public to look upon. But now he had a new face... and new hope.

We all drove out to the Love Field Airport terminal. Inside the rotunda a gigantic terrazzo map of the United States covered the floor. Bedford and I raced to see who'd be first to stand directly on Dallas. Suddenly, Uncle Clark grabbed us by the waists and tucked us under his arms. Where were we going with this monster, I wondered?

"I'm taking you back with me to Blue Lake," he said as our feet touched down on the smooth, gray terrazzo of Wisconsin. His voice finally rang with a bright optimism I hadn't heard before as he tried to smile through his frozen, expressionless features.

"All right for you, Clark," said Daddy. "If you're determined to have us, we'll all come to Blue Lake after the summer dermatology meeting in Chicago. I'll check your stitches, but it sure is going to be one expensive house call!"

XVII

Lost in Space

"The train's coming," said Bedford as he put his ear on the tracks, listening for vibrations.

After anxiously awaiting this moment for weeks, the time had come for us to board the *Texas Rocket* for Chicago. Bedford placed a penny on one of the gleaming steel rails that would carry us there and back.

"Just watch the wheels of the train mash this penny into a flat sheet of copper," he said.

Then he went back into the Highland Park station. I had a nickel, so I placed it on one of the rails. Daddy waited inside with three cameras: a large Argus for Bedford, a middle-sized Kodak for me, and a small, fake water gun camera for David who used it to squirt Bedford in the ear. When I told Bedford I was trying an experiment of my own — putting a nickel on the track instead of a penny — he rushed to the station window and poised his camera on the sill.

"What are you doing?" I asked.

"I want a shot of the derailment," he said.

"What's a derailment?" I asked.

"It's a train wreck, dummy. A kid put a nickel on the track in West Virginia last month, and 300 people got killed when the train rolled down the mountain."

I tried to rush out to retrieve the nickel, but Baba caught me as the puffing locomotive appeared down the track. I hid my eyes when the train — pushed ahead by enormous steel wheels connected to huge rods that plunged in and out of cylinders — approached the coins on the track. To my great relief, there was no derailment — only the engineer and the coal man waving to us, seemingly unaware of the danger they had just survived. The porter took the bags, the conductor yelled "All aboard," the motorman waved outside his caboose, and the train started chugging over my flattened nickel.

The sun was setting as we crossed the Red River into Oklahoma. We ate in the diner, and I wondered how the white-uniformed waiter kept from spilling everything.

"Your grandfather and I rode these same tracks to Chicago back in 1902," said Daddy. "He went to see the new invention, X-ray, and took me along. I was just your age, Wo."

"What is X-ray?" I asked, "Was that what did such terrible things to Uncle Clark?"

"X-ray shows a picture of the skeletal structure inside you," answered Bedford. "You know, like when you buy Buster Brown shoes and the X-ray machine you look down into shows you the bones in your foot. You can see if the shoe fits by wiggling your toes."

I realized how I'd used X-ray lots of times and wondered now if my toes might curl up someday and fall off.

"Your grandfather bought an X-ray machine when we got back to Dallas, and after he used and tested it, he wrote a warning to his colleagues that I wish Uncle Clark could have read before ruining his face," said Daddy pensively. "He said that while X-ray was a great, new invention for treating cancer, the remedy might do more harm than good until X-ray's characteristics were fully understood."

Uncle Clark met our train in Chicago the next morning, his face looking even more horrible than I had remembered. He took Bedford and me sightseeing, while our dad attended his medical meeting and Baba shopped with David.

Everywhere we went, people knew Clark Finnerud. He had a large circle of friends and numerous, devoted patients in his successful Chicago practice of dermatology. Taxi drivers, policemen, waiters, and salespeople greeted him with warmth and affection. Even strangers said hello, responding to the smiling eyes of this happy, gregarious extrovert who was undaunted by his physical appearance.

While Uncle Clark looked like an ugly, scary person, everyone seemed to sense that inside he was a sweet, gentle, friendly man. As old, black John Battle Jones might have said, his ugliness was only skin deep, but the beauty of his soul was "bone deep."

"Now it's time for you to see what this old world is all about!" said Uncle Clark as we climbed the entrance steps to the Field Museum of Natural History.

Inside, Uncle Clark led us through exhibits of stuffed animals of every kind: birds, bears, reptiles, and fish. Rooms displayed the various races of mankind: cavemen, Pygmies, Indians, Eskimos; peoples of Africa, Australia, Mexico, China. We saw a shrunken human head, a totem pole, the skeleton of a great dinosaur, and the two-ton meteorite that had been "captured" by the earth's gravity.

Finally, we stopped to catch our breath and use the restroom. Being anxious to see more of the wonderful displays, I ran back out of the restroom first.

"Stand in the hallway where the guard can keep an eye on you," Uncle Clark called after me.

I tried to do as he had instructed, but forgot when a distant doorway — filled with bright colors, exotic shapes, and rich textures — beckoned to me irresistibly. "Archeology of Egypt" read the sign above the door. "Egypt." The word itself seemed cryptic, secretive. Here was a room full of mystery, power, and secrets! Aunt May and Uncle Bowie lived on a ranch outside a town called Egypt, Texas, where there were only a few ordinary-looking people and houses, a general store, and a filling station. This sure didn't look anything like that Egypt!

There were huge statues of strange-looking people; wall paintings of such vitality that the figures seemed to jump off the wall; pictures and models of buildings of unimaginable size and solidity. On display, were dazzling jewelry, sumptuous furniture, ornate royal trappings — so many items of unspeakable grandeur and beauty, and everywhere the glint of gold!

The entire scene looked like an episode from "Buck Rogers, Space-man," my comic strip hero who traveled the cosmos in his rocket ship in the year 2400, exploring new, fantastic worlds and civilizations. I noticed a sign next to some statues that read 2400 B.C.. Whatever B.C. meant, the year seemed a long time off from 1939. Maybe these statues represented space people from the future? Indeed, some of the space people lay in futuristic boxes, wrapped tightly in space suits, looking as if they were ready to blast off on long, interplanetary journeys.

Huge statues of the "future people" towered over my head, staring down from all directions with vivid, enameled eyes that seemed to pierce through me like X-rays. They were curiously dressed, much like the people I'd seen in the Buck Rogers comic strip, wearing ornate necklaces and bracelets, and strange-looking space helmets. The Egyptian women were voluptuous in their brightly-colored gowns, the men swarthy and athletic-looking — quite a contrast to the other museum visitors who were studying the displays with me. Those men wore dull business suits, their physical features hidden by shapeless sleeves and pants. Knotted ties choked their necks, and they'd laced their feet in tight leather shoes. The women visitors wore shapeless dresses, and while they colored their cheeks and lips red, none looked as beautiful as the women from the future who lined their eyes with green paint and wore gold ringlets in their braided hair.

Forgetting Uncle Clark and Bedford who were searching for me in another direction, I wandered through the room looking in awe at pictures and models of the space people's buildings — huge, columned temples and tremendous, square pyramids that looked larger, more solid than even the skyscrapers of Chicago. Great, tall, pointed obelisks must have been their spaceships?

A square, stone building stood at the end of the room — a tomb, dated 2700 B.C.. Picture-writing — hieroglyphics — that used picture symbols rather than letters of the alphabet and words, covered the tomb walls. This should be the writing of the future, I thought; it seemed so much easier to use than having to learn to spell and pronounce difficult words. Reading the picture-writing stories on the wall, I wandered slowly inside the dimly-lit burial chamber and noticed a lighted button and sign reading:

> *PRESS BUTTON TO SEE WORLD'S LARGEST SINGLE X-RAY FILM, A BRILLIANT LIFE-SIZE PICTURE OF THE SKELETON OF A MUMMY FROM 2800 B.C., MADE IN THE MUSEUM'S DIVISION OF ROENTGENOLOGY USING A NEW, UNIQUE X-RAY TECHNIQUE THAT COULD NOT BE USED ON LIVING TISSUE BECAUSE OF ITS CAUSTIC EFFECT.*

Bedford had once said what a mummy was, but I'd forgotten — something scary, though. I stood there afraid to press the button; the X-ray used on the mummy might be the same kind that had burned up Uncle Clark's face. Suddenly a hand thrust by me through the darkness, and a long, thin finger pushed the button. A bright, blazing, full-size X-ray picture of a mummy's skeleton suddenly appeared. Then came a deep voice with a foreign accent.

"Do you see? The third rib of the mummy has been cut out!"

Looking around, I saw a tall, dark man wearing a turban and started to run in terror, but his strong hand gripped my arm.

"Don't be afraid, young man. I'm a doctor, and I've been studying the remarkable operation an Egyptian doctor performed on this mummy over 4,000 years ago. I don't want you to miss seeing it."

"But aren't these space people from the future?" I asked.

"Hm...I wonder," answered the strange, shadowy man. "The pharaohs did seem to come suddenly from out of nowhere to the banks of the Nile River, bringing with them remarkable new inventions and ideas to the earth."

"Bedford invents things," I said.

"Who's Bedford?" he asked.

"He's my big brother. I think he came from another planet."

"Well, perhaps the pharaohs did, too? They invented the first paper — to put their picture-writing on, the 365-day calendar, and the basic methods of surgery. They built the largest, most solid buildings known to humankind and," he paused, "the first religion in the world with a hereafter, the 'other world' to go to, as they called it.

"Then the pharaohs disappeared from the face of the earth with their great civilization, just as quickly as they had appeared. When their tombs were opened, most of the pharaohs were gone — grave robbers, it is said. When it was your Jesus' tomb that was found empty, they say he went to a 'better place.' Perhaps the pharaohs, too, went to their 'other world.'

"And when they left, they took the answers to many secrets. You know, little man, you may just be right. Perhaps they were...spacemen from another world!" he finished with a wink.

Just then, the room lights came on and there was the real mummy, towering over me in all his hideous, decayed glory. The loosened wrappings exposed a gaunt, shrunken, distorted face. The eyes were frozen shut, with gray skin stretched tightly over protruding jaws and cheekbones — like Uncle Clark's.

"Look what the X-rays did to that mummy!" I said, breaking loose and racing out of the tomb.

Uncle Clark walked into the Egyptian exhibition room with Bedford at that moment. I ran up to him, grabbing him around the legs. Despite the fact that Uncle Clark looked like a mummy, I was very glad to see him; he seemed less scary than the things I'd just encountered in the museum, both living and dead.

"Don't go in the tomb, Uncle Clark, or the X-rays will get you!" I pleaded.

"Don't worry, I'm immune to it by now," said Uncle Clark, laughing happily to see me.

"Bedford, have you seen all the spacemen from the future?" I asked.

"Oh, those are mummies who lived thousands of years ago," he answered. "This room's just filled with old stuff. I want to go see the new inventions at the Museum of Science & Industry."

"I think we should call ahead to the guards, Wo, and let them know your brother's coming, so they can lock up their radios, airplanes and cars," said Uncle Clark as we walked back out of the Field Museum.

I wondered as we strolled along: could Uncle Clark be the mummy of a great pharaoh, come back? He seemed to know everything and enjoyed life to the fullest like the pharaohs, and his face looked a bit like the mummies in the museum.

Anyway, Uncle Clark didn't look so awful to me anymore. Compared to the mummies I'd just seen, he was rather nice-looking, indeed.

XVIII

Blue Heaven

My nose made little greasy smudges on the window of the train as I gazed at the passing scenery. Huge tree trunks raced by the glass like an endless procession of running giants. Anxious streams of water rushed down hills and over rocks, looking for quiet lakes in which to rest. Sunbeams poked around through the trees, searching for buried treasure, but they couldn't find any. The deep, dark, mysterious forest kept its secrets to itself.

I imagined countless, tiny eyes watching our train rumble through the wilderness...eyes of small, furry creatures scampering over carpets of pine needles as we shook their backyards; eyes of birds perched high in the tree tops, angry because we were puffing smoke at them.

"How long till we get to Blue Lake station?" asked Bedford, breaking the spell.

"There's no station up here," laughed Uncle Clark, "just a wide spot in the woods. I asked the engineer to stop, but if he forgets, we'll end up in Canada. And when you get ready to go back to Texas, we'll have to wave a flag at that ole engineer to get him to stop."

"I get dibs on waving the flag to stop the train when we leave," I said, thus securing the job for myself.

The porter had already carried our suitcases to the platform between cars: Bedford's big blue one, my middle-sized green and David's little brown one. There they sat, in unsuspecting peril on the slipping, sliding steel plates, ready to be gobbled up in the crack if the cars should pull apart.

As the train screeched slowly to a halt, we could see a wooden station wagon and a big ice truck parked on the side of the road. When the porter placed our bags on the ground, the door of the ice truck swung open and out jumped a handsome, determined-looking iceman wearing a plaid jacket and blue jeans. He snatched our bags and swung them effortlessly up on the truck platform, then turned to greet us. We hopped off the train and each got a great big hug as we discovered...the iceman was a woman!

"Hello Bedford...Wo...David. Welcome to the North Woods of Wisconsin," she said.

"Boys, meet your 'Aunt' Gertrude," said Daddy.

"She work so hard, I call her 'squaw,'" said Uncle Clark in Indian dialect. "Sell ice on the side...make heap big wampum...buy me new face!"

After giving our parents a warm reception, she grabbed Uncle Clark and hugged and kissed him as if nothing were wrong with his face. The caretaker loaded the other bags in the station wagon and drove off for Blue Lake with Uncle Clark, our parents, and David. Bedford and I climbed up onto the ice truck with the Finnerud daughters: pretty, plump, brunette Ann, Bedford's age, and beautiful little Mary, her younger sister.

We shyly met and I discovered that this shining, blue-eyed girl was ten years old, but I had to admit to being only nine. Her hair was cut short in a pageboy, and her two prominent front teeth reminded me of an adorable bunny. She was the prettiest little blue-eyed blonde I'd ever seen.

Aunt Gertrude explained to us about the ice truck as she closed the tailgate. She had borrowed it from Sven, the local Blue Lake iceman, for our arrival. After an exciting ride in the cool, fresh, Wisconsin air the Finnerud log home appeared through the dense forest. It sat on the brow of a high hill overlooking the lake and seemed to have grown out of the hill like the rocks, the pines, and the ferns. We jumped off the ice truck and ran inside to explore the lodge. The big living room had a high, soaring, pine-beamed ceiling, rock floor, large windows, and a huge, inviting fireplace. Kerosene lamps had been placed on the tables — there was no electricity at Blue Lake.

I stopped to look at two old photographs on the mantel. One was of a handsome, blond young man wearing a college football jersey. The other photo was the high school graduation picture of a beautiful, raven-haired girl. Uncle Clark walked in just then with his arm around Aunt Gertrude. I followed them through French doors and onto the screened porch that had a dining table, a hammock, and a panoramic view of woods and water.

Blue Lake was truly blue, as blue as the sky it reflected, and it sparkled like a thousand sapphires in the afternoon sun. I looked up at the couple as they enjoyed a quiet moment together, surveying their own bit of heaven, and wondered if they were really the same people in the photographs. Aunt Gertrude's hair had faded to gray, and lines now crossed that girlish face. Uncle Clark's smooth, boyish features had turned to chipped, weathered stone. Nothing is forever it seemed, once again.

The log guest house, where our family would stay, sat a hundred yards west through the pines. A thin wire ran alongside the path, linking the two houses by a battery-operated telephone.

"This is exactly the telephone system I need to replace my shell-phones," said Bedford. "It's powered by two, six-volt dry cell batteries connected in series, but I think I'll build some backup batteries in case they go dead. Since there's no electricity or telephone to civilization out here in the woods, there needs to be alternate power systems and a backup for everything."

"Like what?" I asked.

"Well," said Bedford, "everything you might run out of; things you couldn't get real easy, like batteries, and kerosene...and chewing gum."

"Chewing gum?" I said, wondering what he could possibly discover in the woods he could substitute for that greatest of life's necessities.

Late that afternoon, with the forest silhouetted against the sunset like a black paper cutout, we dined on the big screened porch. A loon laughed across the lake as Uncle Clark and Daddy traded jokes.

"Well, boys," said Uncle Clark, "I met your father because of his bad German, but I'll bet he hasn't told you the real story, has he? Your daddy decided at The University of Texas that if he was going to become a great doctor, he had to learn German first so he could go to medical school in Vienna. He and a friend worked their way over to Germany on a luxurious German passenger boat, waiting tables during the day, and dancing with the pretty girls all night. Those guys literally tangoed their way to Germany!"

Bedford and I looked at each other and laughed, hardly able to imagine our dad dancing at all, much less doing the tango.

"Landing in Germany," continued Uncle Clark, "they went their separate ways. Your dad caught a train and rode it all the way to a small town at the end of the line in the Black Forest. Then he walked till he reached the very last house on the lane, knocked on the door, and asked the family if he could stay with them that summer and learn German. They had this beautiful daughter, who tried to teach him proper German as they strolled the woods each afternoon. Then one day..."

"The Great War broke out," interrupted our dad, "and I only had a steamship ticket and one thin dime in my pocket. I couldn't wire home for more money, so I flashed the dime at the train conductor. He thought it must be worth something, and he let me on. I had to peel potatoes for the German army all the way to the coast, where I caught a steamship home."

"After the war, your dad came back over to medical school in Vienna, the same year I was there," said Uncle Clark. "The first day of class, before we'd met, the professor asked him a medical question in German. Guess what his answer was — 'Ich liebe dich — I love you!' That was all the German that pretty fraulein had taught him. So, I introduced myself to this helpless fellow American and decided to save him with my fluent German and my talent as a ventriloquist. Have you noticed that you can't tell if my mouth is talking or not talking?"

We nodded and laughed with Uncle Clark laughing at himself.

"I had to sit next to him for the rest of the year and answer all questions the professor asked him in my perfect German."

"Well," countered Daddy, "I may not be famous for my German, but your Uncle Clark is infamous for his tall stories."

After supper we sat in the friendly glow of the kerosene lamps and the flickering fire in the fireplace. When Uncle Clark picked up his ukelele to play and sing a few songs for us, words, shadows, and warmth began to dance around the room:

> *In my castle on the River Nile,*
> *I'm gonna live in elegant style.*
> *Inlaid marble on the floor,*
> *Baboons dancin' 'round the front of my door...*

While the words he sang were the words of a pharaoh who came back to earth, his face looked more like an adorable patchwork bear than a mummy. Encouraged by our applause and another scotch and soda, he continued with his favorite numbers — a medley of George M. Cohan tunes, sung with a charm and style that disguised his lack of a singing voice. After that, Uncle Clark's ukelele serenades became an eagerly-anticipated nightly event.

The next morning, Mary invited me to go out in the woods with her to look for wild blueberries, so Aunt Gertrude could make us hot blueberry muffins.

Just as we were walking out the front door of the main lodge, the telephone from the guest house buzzed and I answered it.

"Watson, it's Bell," said the voice at the other end. "Come here. I want you...again."

"I can't," I replied. "I told Mary I'd go look for wild blueberries with her."

"I need you to help me with a new experiment. I'm going to make a back-up battery system for the telephones, and I need you on the other end of the line," said Bedford impatiently.

"No, I'm going to help Mary," I said, with newly-found independence from his inventive magic.

Mary led me into the lush, green foliage of the deep forest, and we moved along a narrow path until we arrived at a great open space filled with sunlight, and surrounded by tall, swaying pines.

"Where are the blueberries?" I asked.

"They're around the edge of the clearing," she answered. "I got lost here one day and had to live on blueberries till Daddy found me."

"How long were you lost?" I asked.

"'Bout an hour."

We began filling our pails, and our mouths, with the sweet, plump fruit. Finally, with pails full, we headed back along the trail toward home. Uncle Clark had taught Mary to know and love these North Woods of Wisconsin, and she unlocked some of its secrets for me on our way back.

"Chew that dark green leaf and taste the wild spearmint they make gum from," she said, as I picked some to take to Bedford. "Now see these mushrooms? Don't eat them or you might die. Then, those red berries over there — the Indians used them to make war paint."

When Mary and I climbed, tired and proud, up the porch steps, our parents were enjoying coffee, conversation, and the magnificent morning view.

"Someday when I'm gone, you're all going to miss Blue Lake," said Uncle Clark, "'cause I'm taking it with me; I've made a deal with the devil."

"Again?" asked Aunt Gertrude.

"Well, here come the gatherers," said Uncle Clark. "In primitive tribes, we have the hunters, and we have the gatherers. Behold the gatherers, returning with the bounty of the forest."

"But I want to be a hunter now," I said, hoping to return to the forest for more adventure.

"Fine, Wo," said Uncle Clark. "After we have some of your Aunt Gertrude's hot blueberry muffins, we'll go out on Blue Lake to hunt for some fish."

When we'd filled ourselves to bursting with blueberry muffins, Mary, Uncle Clark and I walked down to the water carrying fishing tackle and climbed into a wooden rowboat that had "Jack Tar" painted across its bow.

"Let's row down the shoreline, kids," said Uncle Clark, "and I'll show you some fish."

I sat next to Mary on the seat of the "Jack Tar" as we each pulled on an oar. We glided through the crystal-clear water, drifting high over the sunny, rocky bottom as if we were floating on air. When Uncle Clark burst into song, a large school of fish suddenly began following the boat.

"Look at all those big fish down there!" I exclaimed.

"They always come when Daddy sings 'Three Little Fishies,'" said Mary, matter-of-factly.

"Now, Wo, grab one of those minnows out of the bucket," instructed Uncle Clark. "O.K., stick the hook through its back <u>above</u> the spine so you don't kill it."

"But Uncle Clark, this one wiggles just like the little goldfish I got when I was sick with pneumonia," I said, suffering the paralysis of a tender heart.

"Go ahead, Wo, stick it through; we've got to catch some fish for lunch!" said Uncle Clark. I didn't budge. "Okay if you can't do it, I will."

A moment later I cast the shimmering minnow a short distance and watched the weight pull it down to the rocky bottom. Suddenly, the school of fish came darting toward the minnow and one grabbed it. I pulled out a fat, sparkling, flapping silver sun perch with lemon-yellow sides.

"Why, just look what Wo caught," said Uncle Clark proudly. "Pull the hook out of his mouth and run the stringer through his gill, son."

"It might hurt him," I said. "He's bleeding already."

"Just jerk it out quick, Wo."

"I can't," I said. "He's looking at me funny."

"All right, I'll do it," said Uncle Clark.

"Here Daddy, take the fish off my hook too," said Mary at the front of the canoe.

Back and forth Uncle Clark worked between Mary at the front and me at the back, hooking minnows and unhooking fish. Every time he picked up his rod and reel to fish himself, one of us would hook a fish, or need our hook baited. Before long, Mary and I had each a dozen, but then she whispered something in Uncle Clark's ear.

"No! I will not row you kids to shore to go to the bathroom. You should have thought of that before you got in the boat," said Uncle Clark, looking first at me, then at Mary with an anguished look on his tattered face. "All I've done is hook and unhook for you two and I haven't even had time to fish myself. So, Mary, take this coffee can to the front of the boat, and Wo, take this bucket to the back and turn around."

"I've never been to the bathroom with a girl," I whispered.

"Well, I hope it doesn't ruin your reputation or hers, but we're not going to shore," he said with finality.

Soon, we were catching fish at a frantic pace again. Before Uncle

Clark could use his own rod and reel, Mary and I had caught 75 beautiful sun perch and bass. Finally, we made it back to shore and Uncle Clark got out with the "keepers" to go clean them.

"Didn't you ever go fishing, before," asked Mary?

"Sure, but the fish don't come when I sing, like they do for your daddy's silly songs," I answered. "He's funny, and he's not so ugly when you get used to him."

Mary's sweet, smiling countenance turned into a fierce scowl. I knew I'd said the wrong thing and wished I could take back my words.

"He is not ugly. You take that back right now," she said as her temper flared and her eyes welled with tears. "Lots of people have scars on their faces, but that doesn't make them ugly. Daddy just looks different. My mommy says the only really ugly people are the ones who do terrible things to others, or hurt animals."

"Well, uh...," I said, frantically trying to think of something to change the subject, "I did catch a fish one time — a big alligator gar. I sneaked it home in Daddy's car trunk and nailed it up on my bedroom wall, like our uncle's big sailfish hanging in his office. In a couple of days it started to stink really bad. I even had to wear a clothespin on my nose just to go in my own room. Baba smelled it and when she came in, she couldn't believe her eyes. I didn't know the fish was supposed to be stuffed. She made me take it to the alley and throw it in the trash."

"That's a silly story," said Mary, laughing through her tears — much to my relief.

By now, the morning chill had turned to noontime heat, and Mary and I stripped down to our shorts to go swimming in the cool water. She was strong and wiry, and outswam me to the Finnerud's raft, which floated on steel drums.

"It looks like rain," she said, as clouds suddenly appeared with a clap of thunder. "If you're swimming and see lightning, you count one thousand one...one thousand two...one thousand three...and so on until you hear the thunder. The lightning's a mile away for each time you count to one thousand five, and you don't want the lightning to get any closer than that before you get out. Otherwise, you're in danger of being electrocuted when it hits the water. Do you know what electrocution is?"

I had come to peaceful Blue Lake in the North Woods of Wisconsin where there was no electricity. Yet, I had to worry about still another way to get electrocuted. Isn't any place safe, I wondered?

XIX

Waving the Flag

The days flew by all too swiftly — cool mornings occupied with strolls in the forest, unlocking more of nature's secrets, and eating hot blueberry muffins...warm afternoons spent swimming, sailing, and fishing in the "Jack Tar" with Mary...crisp evenings filled with crackling fires, ukelele serenades, and smiles glowing in the light of kerosene lanterns.

We began to wonder what we could do to thank the Finneruds for their wonderful hospitality, but there didn't seem to be one thing they needed, or lacked at their verdant paradise-on-earth called Blue Lake. Uncle Clark had wanted a new face, and our dad had given him that.

Then one day, while I was chopping down a small pine that blocked a new path Uncle Clark had been clearing, Bedford and Ann walked by.

"Want some more chewing gum, Wo?" asked Bedford.

"No thank you. My jaw's still tired from chewing on that stuff you made from beeswax and the wild spearmint I brought you."

"Ann, I'm trying to show him how to replace things he runs out of so he can survive in the woods," said Bedford.

"I never knew you could die from not having any chewing gum," laughed Ann.

Just then the tree crashed to the ground, narrowly missing Bedford. He stepped back, lost his balance, and slid a short distance down the steep hill toward the lake.

"If this were winter," said Ann, "you'd have slid all the way down to the water on the snow, like we do on our sled."

Bedford climbed back up with a look I recognized as a germination of the seed of an invention, then raced to the guest house to find our parents.

"Baba, Daddy!" he shouted. "I thought of a present for the Finneruds. We could build a long, wooden slide...that runs from the top of that hill...all the way down through the woods and out over the lake...covered with sheet metal...and water running down it to make it slide better, and..."

"Wait!" said Daddy. "That's a crazy idea...but your water slide sounds like a lot of fun. I hear Sven, the iceman is quite a carpenter. Think I'll go talk to him to see if he can build one in the week we have left."

A few days later, the Fourth of July arrived. Back home popping firecrackers and screaming rockets would have awakened us, but here the morning was quiet, and placid Blue Lake echoed only the sound of Sven hammering on the water slide off in the distance. I caught a faint hum, that got louder and louder. Soon I saw a powerful speedboat racing toward us across the lake, cutting through the blue mirror of water and leaving a foaming trail of waves. I ran down to the pier in time to watch the huge Chris Craft pull up to the dock, driven by a fat, jolly-looking man. The boat was made of varnished boards and trimmed with bright chrome. It had white leather seats, a big horn, searchlight, and a magnificent American flag flying from the stern. Steam bubbled up from the rear of the boat and the motor murmured with a sound that seemed to come from the depths of the lake.

"Bedford and Wo, meet our neighbor from Chicago who owns the house across the lake, Mr. Wheeler Sammons," said Uncle Clark. "He's come to take you boys, Mary and Ann on a speedboat ride to celebrate the Fourth. Mr. Sammons is editor of *Who's Who in America*."

"What's your book about — some owls?" I asked.

"Oh no," he said. "It's about notable Americans, like your fathers, Drs. Shelmire and Finnerud. They're in my book."

"Well," said Uncle Clark, "I don't see how Shelmire made it with his bad German."

"They put me in because of the great job I did on you, Clark," said our dad. "I made you beautiful. That's my notable accomplishment!"

We cruised around the shoreline past the other Blue Lake houses, each one with a pier, each one with an American flag proudly displayed by its occupants, who waved as we sped by. I looked around admiringly at our flag being held straight out by the wind. It was beautifully made of vivid red, white, and blue cloth, with each of the 13 stripes for the original colonies, and 48 stars for the states sewn on separately.

I sat next to Mr. Sammons, awaiting my turn to steer.

"Did you know that Uncle Clark's great-great-great grandfather discovered America?" I asked. "He was a Viking and sailed over in a ship with a dragon on the front."

"No, I had no idea. Thanks for telling me so I can put that in the book," he said.

"Well," said Mary, "Mom says her great-great-great grandmother was here to meet him, and made a fortune selling blueberry muffins to the Vikings as they walked by Blue Lake."

As we pulled back up to the Finnerud boat dock, Old Glory hung limply from its pole on the stern of the speedboat, looking now like the flag in the corner of our classroom at Armstrong School. This being the Fourth of July, I suddenly stood at attention, putting my hand over my heart; saying once again:

I pledge allegiance to the flag of the United States of America, and to the Republic for which it stands: one Nation, indivisible, with liberty and justice for all.

Because it was the Fourth of July, Mr. Sammons unhooked the flag and handed it to me as a gift. Now I had just the flag to wave the train down at Blue Lake crossing.

After supper, Sven drove up to the lodge in his ice truck, loaded with blocks of ice he'd sawn from the lake during the winter and stored in his ice house under a layer of thick sawdust. When he invited Mary and me to make the rounds with him to deliver ice to the Blue Lake houses, we jumped up on the truck and sat down on the shavings-covered ice.

We drove around the road that circled the Lake, stopping at each house to make an ice delivery. Sven would put a long, slick piece of leather over his shoulder, sink the sharp pincers of his ice tongs into a frozen piece of Blue Lake, and swing it onto his back. Then he would carry it in the house and put it in the icebox.

At dusk, Sven finished unloading the last block of ice, and we headed home. As we made our final turn, Mary's cute sailor hat flew off and landed in the road. I knocked on the window to get Sven to stop, then headed to the back so I could jump off and retrieve it. But Sven's ice tongs lay in my way on the bed of the truck, and as I ran across the empty platform in the twilight, I slashed open the side of my foot on one of the sharp prongs.

Sven carried me into the lodge and Uncle Clark examined the bleeding wound, deciding it would require several stitches to close.

"Why is there only candlelight in here?" asked Uncle Clark, impatiently. "Where the hell are the kerosene lanterns? I can't see to sew him up."

"We ran out of kerosene during the night," explained Aunt Gertrude. "The general store was closed today for the Fourth and I couldn't buy any. So, I put the lanterns in the storeroom."

"Well, I may be the first surgeon in history to operate by the light of Fourth of July sparklers!" lamented Uncle Clark, going off to get a shot of novocaine for my foot and a shot of scotch for himself to steady his hand.

When he'd left the room, Bedford raced into the kitchen, grabbed a bottle of vanilla extract, and disappeared through the back door and into the darkness. They had both gone for a drink, I thought, and I was the one who needed it most!

A few minutes later, Bedford returned carrying the kerosene lanterns, now brimming with fuel. When Uncle Clark returned with a syringe to deaden my foot, he was relieved to see the full lanterns. He struck a match and began to light them.

"Wait," he said, pulling the match back. "What's in those lanterns? Smells like gasoline."

"It's my new backup fuel," said Bedford. "First, I put in gasoline. Then I added vanilla extract that has alcohol in it to give off a nice flame, and flavoring in it to reduce the flash point of the mixture."

"Godamighty, kid, if I'd lit that wick those lanterns would have exploded like bombs!" exclaimed Uncle Clark. "Get Aunt Gertrude to pour that volatile liquid out. She'll find you candles or I'll have to operate by Braille."

Bedford had another idea, borrowed from young Tom Edison. He went to the entry hall and returned with a large mirror, placing it behind the dozen or so candles Aunt Gertrude had just placed on the table next to me. Instantly, the candles and their power became two dozen, and a surprisingly strong light bathed my foot.

"Wo, your brother is going to make a great scientist or doctor someday if he doesn't blow himself up," said Uncle Clark.

By the time the others came in from fishing, I was all stitched up and looking forward to tomorrow's activities.

The next morning we all followed the sound of hammering — with me limping along — until we came to the magnificent, just-completed water slide. It started at the crest of the hill, ran down through the trees and out over the water. Sven had just finished securing the last piece of the sheet metal cover, and Bedford turned on the hydrant at the top, transforming the steep trough into a flume. Ann, Mary, and Aunt Gertrude gathered behind Uncle Clark, all sharing the excitement.

In a moment, Bedford came shooting down through the trees on a boat cushion, and sped off the end of the slide into Blue Lake. Uncle Clark laughed and danced around as he took off all his clothes, except for his B.V.D.'s. There he stood in his buttoned-up long underwear, which came to his elbows and knees, with rear trap door and all. Then he clenched his cigarette holder between his teeth, and took off down the slide in his underwear, looking like Franklin Delano Roosevelt savoring a political campaign victory. He and everyone else took turn after turn, except for me — and my injured foot. Our appropriate gift had been an instant and overwhelming success.

That night Uncle Clark serenaded us for the last time by the light of a few remaining candles. I looked over at Mary. What a day it had been. What a three weeks it had been. We'd done so many things together, even gone to the bathroom together. I would miss her very much.

The next afternoon, after everyone had had a morning of fun on the water slide, the time finally came for us to leave Blue Lake. As we waited for the train at the railroad crossing, I looked back at the station wagon and ice truck. They were parked exactly where we'd first seen them three weeks before. Bedford, David, and I were dressed, once again, in our pressed navy blue suits with starched white collars.

We all hugged each other, just like the morning we'd arrived, only now we said warm goodbyes instead of cool hellos. It was as if Daddy had put the movie he'd taken of our North Woods vacation on his projector and run it back to the beginning. Life seemed to be an endless series of hellos and goodbyes, with hellos turning into goodbyes, and goodbyes turning into the scrapbook pages of our memory.

I smiled at Uncle Clark. He winked and smiled at me with his eyes, seeming to express pride in us and confidence in our future. As for him, he had already begun his final retreat from the world and society, but not from life.

"It's coming," said Bedford, kneeling and putting this ear to the tracks.

"I don't hear it," I said.

"Of course not. Sound travels fifteen times faster in a steel rail than in the air, but you'll hear it pretty soon."

The tracks glistened in the late afternoon sunshine. Two families, living apart, had been brought together in love and friendship by these shining steel rails that connected Dallas with Blue Lake...and by Daddy's bad German. I unfurled the Stars and Stripes, and started practicing my wave that would stop the train in front of us.

"Wish I could wave the flag at the engineer," grumbled Bedford, putting a penny on the rail.

I reached in my pocket and put a penny on the rail, too. Mary discovered she only had a nickel, but placed it on the rail, anyway. Just then we saw the chugging, puffing steam engine approaching through the woods. Bedford was surprised and delighted when I handed him the flag to wave at the engineer. Then I opened my suitcase, with Mary watching intently, and took out my camera.

"What are you going to do?" she asked.

"I'm going to take a picture of the train derailment," I said.

"What's a derailment?" asked Mary.

XX

Starring on the Radio

The cold blast of frigid air felt good on my cheeks as I trotted along behind the dog sled. Up ahead, the magnificent team of huskies seemed to sense that we raced against time on a mission of international importance. I gripped the sled handle tightly with one hand while waving Old Glory with the other.

My frosty breath mingled with the vapor from the panting dogs, leaving a cloudy trail to mark our path as we sped along toward our secret destination. We were now only moments away, judging by the sun's angle and the needle of my official Jack Armstrong compass, which guided us due south. I had carried the flag 8,468 miles, all the way from Wisconsin according to my genuine Jack Armstrong pedometer — by land, sea, air, and now over the frozen ice masses of the Antarctic.

No American had ever planted the Stars and Stripes on the South Pole. Admiral Byrd had only flown over it in his airplane. I would be the first — me, Overton Shelmire, age nine. Baba and Daddy would be very proud and I sure would like to see the look on Bedford's face when he heard about it.

We finally reached the Pole in triumph. I gave each dog a pat, then prepared to plant the flag. Suddenly, I felt a hand on my shoulder. Mr. Jones in his starched, white grocer's apron and cap, stood over me. What was he doing here at the South Pole?

"I know you miss that cold Wisconsin air, Wo," he said, "but I can't let you kids hang around here daydreaming all morning in my vegetable room just to keep cool. I need the space for my customers."

"I've been passing out these handbills for Bedford and his friends, trying to get them some customers, too," I said. "It got so hot out there I just about died."

"Customers for what?" asked Mr. Jones, taking one of the handbills.

It read:

ANNOUNCING KPIA, THE 'PLAY IT AGAIN' STATION
DIAL 980 ON YOUR RADIO, 58-9943 ON YOUR TELEPHONE

  * *All the broadcasts of your favorite programs*
  * *Call us for the one you missed*
  * *We'll play it again for just 25¢*
  * *Come in and see our broadcasting station*
  * *Free phonograph record each week to some
      lucky listener*

"Well, I'll be," said Mr. Jones. "How'd the boys get their hands on a radio station?"

"They built it in John Trimble's bedroom out of a radio, phonograph, and loudspeaker combination," I said. "They plugged a microphone in, put an antenna on top, and now they rebroadcast programs from all the stations."

"All the stations, they claim? We'll just see if they have 'em all. My wife and I get a kick out of Dr. Brinkley's health pitch, but we had to miss it last night," said Mr. Jones, winking. "Have Bedford play that one tonight. If he does, I'll sure give ya a quarter."

"I'll see if they have it. If they don't, they'll do a re-creation for the same price," I said.

Reluctantly, I trudged out of one of the few refrigerated rooms in the city, passing between the food shelves of the Hunt Grocery Store and out the front door. Finding myself back on the sizzling pavement, I squinted as my eyes adjusted to the hot sun reflecting off the tall, white, plaster walls that surrounded me in every direction. I looked up at the red tile roofs, arched doors and windows, ornate carved stonework, and beautiful wrought iron that adorned all the buildings.

The Spanish-style Highland Park Village shopping center looked like nothing else in Dallas; like nothing else in the entire nation, for that matter. Built in 1931, it had been the first planned shopping center in the United States with a unified architectural style and stores facing inward toward a parking plaza.

I walked close to the walls, trying to stay in the shade as I delivered KPIA handbills from store to store. Finally I entered the huge, sheltering arches of the Village filling station and cooled my feet in the Spanish fountain that splashed next to the gas pumps.

"I missed hearing *Lorenzo Jones* yesterday just as he was about to try out the new invention," said Joe, the mechanic, as he read the handbill. "Get the boys to play it again at noon today so I can listen while I'm eatin' lunch."

"They can't; they're having technical difficulties right now," I said.

"What kind of technical difficulties?" Joe asked.

"It's Jimmy Strauss' little brother, Frank. They used part of his radio to make the station, and he wants it back. They're borrowing the parts somewhere else so the station can be back on the air tonight," I said.

Just then, Baba drove in to have her car filled with gas.

"Here's a dollar, Joe. I just need ten gallons."

"Well, Mrs. Shelmire, I understand Bedford has become a radio announcer," said Joe.

"Yes, I heard that Bedford and his friends built a radio station. I do know he's hardly been home lately except to mess up his bed. I've turned and turned the radio dial but haven't been able to find them."

"KPIA only has a five-block range, so our house is too far away to pick up their signal," I explained. "You and Daddy should drive up close to John's house and tune 'em in on the car radio."

"We just might do that tonight. In the meantime, you're coming home with me for lunch and a nap," she said.

I was required to spend the heat of the afternoon each day resting on the sleeping porch. I would lie there, unable to sleep, sweltering as the ceiling fan droned on and on. The boredom was only made tolerable by reading the endlessly fascinating Johnson Smith mail order catalogue. Each page in the great volume held excitement, full of provocative illustrations and jaunty, ribald text. It was zippier reading than anything found on our library shelves.

The catalogue contained every conceivable type of gimmick and gadget: card tricks, puzzles, magic acts, joke books, badges, serious and silly disguises. It had an enormous assortment of practical jokes: exploding books, cigars, and toilet seats; squirting flowers, mirrors, and rings; the joy buzzer, a hand shaker and tickler that was "the funniest joker's novelty ever invented;" itching powder — "thoroughly enjoyable. The intense discomfiture of your victim is highly amusing." Finally, there was the classic Johnson Smith whoopee cushion — "when the victim unsuspectingly sits upon the cushion, it gives forth noises that can be better imagined than described."

Items in the catalogue appealed to every human vice and fear. The intriguing description of the automatic, break-open target revolver suggested:

> *You may find yourself dependent upon your skill in shooting*
> *for a meal of game, and you never know when war may come.*

There had been much talk of the upcoming dove hunting season. Too bad I couldn't afford to buy a gun so I'd be prepared for the doves...or a war.

I had read lovingly through the thick catalogue at least a dozen times, and on this particular afternoon my attention riveted to one item:

> *Crystal radio detector, complete with crystal — reception positively guaranteed, 25 mile range, completely assembled, wired, and ready for use, including stand, crystal cup, arm with cat whisker and an ultra-sensitive crystal of the finest grade. Price, postpaid, 25¢.*

I picked up the quarter the boys had paid me to distribute the KPIA handbills, put the coin in an envelope, and scurried to the mail box the minute "rest" ended.

After supper, Daddy drove Baba and me to a street located a couple of blocks north of the Village so they could finally hear KPIA for themselves.

"All right, Wo, this is San Carlos Drive. Which house is it?" asked Daddy.

"I don't know. They all look alike. I always come in from the alley, but better turn on the radio; they're supposed to start broadcasting at seven."

Daddy parked and tuned the dial to 980. We heard the voice of the KPIA announcer that I recognized as Bedford's friend, Roland Bond.

> *Good evening ladies and gentlemen. We're pleased to bring you the following re-created program as requested by Mr. Jones at Hunt Grocery:*
>
> *Tonight, Station XERA, Mexico, the 1,000,000 - watt 'Sunshine Station between the Nations,' brings you that great healer and disciple of health, John R. Brinkley, MD, PhD, MC, LLD, DHP, ScD — and member of the National Geographic Society with his message of health and happiness for you millions of sickly listeners in radio land.*

The real Dr. Brinkley had originated a goat gland operation which, he claimed, could restore lost male virility. The American Medical Association took a dim view, and the Federal Radio Commission questioned the advertising claims he made on his Kansas radio station. When Brinkley's medical license to practice was revoked, he moved his clinic to Del Rio, Texas. Just across the border, in Villa Acuna, Mexico, he built the world's most powerful broadcasting station. There, free from U.S. regulations, he took to the airwaves to tout the wonders of goat gland surgery, his station's powerful wattage disrupting other station's programs. Soon he had amassed a fortune treating, among nearly everything else, impotence with goat glands. Tonight Bedford and his friends were disrupting the local Highland Park airwaves.

Bedford knew the doctor's colorful message by heart, having listened, fascinated, to XERX night after night. He found the Brinkley pitch for patients more ludicrous than Ed Wynne, more humorous than Jack Benny, more entertaining than "Gangbusters." The doctor's power to lure people into driving to Del Rio for the terrifying operations impressed Bedford just as much as Orson Welles' power to send people into their automobiles to escape those terrifying Martians. Bedford, disguising his voice to sound much older than his 13 years, began Brinkley's pitch:

> *Hello, my dear friends, my many patients in Texas and everywhere. This is Dr. John R. Brinkley. Your many hundreds of letters lie here before me — touching testimonials to your pain, your grief, your wretchedness. Well, let me tell you right now — all your diseases, all your ailments are curable. I can take care of everything from indigestion to impotence, from high blood pressure to hemorrhoids. How many of you suffer from constipation, gas, indigestion, bloat, or belching? Well, come to my stomach and rectal clinic. We offer guaranteed treatment for your two sewers...your waterworks and your garbage. We'll clean you up and clean you out. If you have high blood pressure, we'll put you on my special salt-free, sex-free diet at my blood clinic. But be careful till you get here. Remember that alarming statistic: most people with high blood pressure die during sexual intercourse.*

"Good heavens," exclaimed Baba. "I think that's Bedford trying to disguise his voice. I've never heard him talk like that!"

> *Now you men with infected, diseased prostates, why are you holding back with that old cockleburr? You know you're sick. Why do you delay any longer? Unless you come in at once to the Brinkley gland clinic, you're going to be in the undertaker's parlor, on the old cold slab being embalmed for a funeral. So take advantage of my low rates before it's everlastingly too late! And men, you poor fellows who are feeling sexually weak, aren't you disgusted with being below par — you know what I mean? Well, a man is only as good as his glands. So come to the border, and for only $1,000 you can get the Brinkley goat gland operation. I can assure you it will restore your lost vigor, and you'll be performing like you were twenty-five years younger.*

"Bed, that really isn't Bedford, is it?" asked Baba, shaking her head in disbelief. Then Bedford continued, interviewing someone I recognized as Jimmy Strauss, trying to sound old and feeble.

> *Now, folks, we have a new patient in the waiting room who just drove 1,000 miles to get here. Sir, why did you come such a long way to the Brinkley gland clinic?*

'Cause, I'm gonna get me some goat glands and be like I
used to wuz — a ram that am with every lamb!

"That's enough of that," said Baba. "Wo, go in and tell Bedford to
come out this minute; we're going home!"

"I told you, I don't know which house it is," I said.

"Please try to remember the house, Wo," Baba pleaded as she turned
the volume down. "This program's getting worse and worse."

"Wait," said Daddy, turning the radio back up. "They're going to do
another program."

After a moment of silence for the crew to catch its breath, station
KPIA had proceeded to satisfy another request. We felt anticipation
when we heard the surface noise of a record, and then:

The Tom Mix Ralston Straight-Shooters are on the air, said
the announcer.

"Now that's more like it!" said Baba, pacified at last as we drove
out of the KPIA range toward home.

The next morning I ducked down the alley behind San Carlos Drive
and turned in at the fourth chain link gate, climbed the back steps and
entered Station KPIA. The boys were just getting ready to go on the air.
Bedford threw a couple of switches, tapped the microphone, and spoke:

Testing, testing...one, two, three...good morning, ladies
and gentlemen. This is Radio Station KPIA, the 'Play it Again
Station,' bringing you the best in missed programming. And
we've got 'em all: 'Vic and Sade,' 'Stella Dallas,' 'Lum 'n
Abner,' 'Backstage Wife,' and 'Mr. District Attorney.' Then
there's 'One Man's Family,' 'I Love a Mystery,' and 'Let's
Pretend.' So call in your requests for a replay of your favorite
missed program and we'll bill you a quarter after we play it.
And now, for your listening enjoyment, we have a request for
last Thursday's exciting episode of 'Ma Perkins.'

After a few dull minutes of the story about the warm-hearted lady
lumberyard owner, I tapped Bedford to tell him about a request I'd had.

"Shhh," he whispered, "we're on the air."

"Peggy at the candy shop wants to know if you can do *War of the*
Worlds," I whispered in his ear. "She missed it last Halloween."

Bedford sat motionless, with a faraway look in his icy-blue eyes. A
sinister smile came over his face, as if he had just received a long-
awaited answer to an unholy prayer. This was the moment he'd schemed
and dreamed of for months. He felt a surge of power, the power to
terrorize through mass communications, through his own deceptive

creativity, just as Welles and Brinkley had terrorized so many before.

Bedford thought back to the only time his own extraordinary self-confidence had been shattered by fear. He and his friend, Mirza, had gone downtown to the Capitol Theater to see *King Kong*. When the monstrous ape appeared on the screen, the boys ran up the aisle in a two-man mass hysteria and got their dimes back.

Kong's fearful power, Bedford now realized, was based on the terror he and Mirza had created in their own imagination. Brinkley's success in terrorizing patients into expensive, often worthless operations was due to the doctor's successful spiel based on fear of real or potential, sometimes fatal, physical ailments.

Orson Welles with his *War of the Worlds*, Bedford thought, terrorized with what can often be the most gripping, deeply felt fear of all — fear of the unknown. Just as radio preachers who followed Brinkley across the border capitalized on the fearful uncertainty of a hell of fire and brimstone, no one really knew for sure whether or not Mars was populated by frightful, warlike, bloodthirsty creatures. Welles had taken extraordinary advantage of this uncertainty. Now, finally, Bedford's turn to terrorize the masses had come. He began:

> *We interrupt 'Ma Perkins' to bring you a special announcement. Following a series of mysterious explosions on the planet Mars, a large flaming object, believed to be a meteorite, has fallen on a farm in the vicinity of Waxahachie, Texas. Now, we bring you an interlude of music while our on-the-scene reporter is en route to the farm.*

While he played a tango, Bedford assigned the various parts to his friends so that they could reenact the epic *War of the Worlds* broadcast which had made such a lasting, indelible impression on each of them. Returning to the air, a reporter interviewed the farmer who'd witnessed the landing of the strange object in this backyard. Then, true to the original script, the huge green cylinder opened up and horrifying monsters from Mars climbed out, using death-ray guns to zap everyone and everything in sight.

With voices and emotions even more frantic than those of the original actors, Bedford and his troupe continued the terrifying drama until the Martian's relentless march in their giant tripod machines had brought them to the very city limits of Dallas. Then Bedford made a desperate, final announcement:

> *All our defenses have proven useless, so you people better run for your lives...now the Martian machines are in sight! Some poisonous black smoke is pouring out of them. It's drifting toward us...100 yards...it's 50 feet...ahggg...gasssp...click.*

A welcomed silence followed and the microphone was turned off.

"Wo, quick. Go in the living room and look out the window. Do you see people running, or packing up their cars?" asked Bedford.

"No," I said, "Just the Italian knife sharpener pushing his cart down the street, blowing his strange little pipe like he always does. Everything looks normal."

"Darn Italians," said Bedford. "They never worry about anything."

The Martian invasion was over. The earth's population had been annihilated and no one had seemed to pay a bit of attention. Bedford's rational side sensed failure, but his pride and ego would not let him concede. Like a defeated politician, he insisted on the gentler letdown of waiting to see how tomorrow morning's headlines read.

"Did you bring any other new requests, Wo?" asked Bedford.

"Yeah. Mrs. Simpson's dog is lost and would you please make an announcement? She named it 'Fala' after President Roosevelt's dog. It got lost in the Village."

Bedford stopped the spinning record and opened the microphone.

We interrupt 'Young Widder Brown' to bring you a special announcement:

Fala is missing, ladies and gentlemen. Yes, President Roosevelt's little dog Fala is nowhere to be found. He's a brown and white beagle and was last seen in front of the Village A&P. If you find Fala please call the station.

A moment later there came a loud knock on the front door and I went to answer.

"Hello. Did you find Fala?" I asked the tall, somber-looking man. He was dressed in a dark suit and hat and carried a large camera.

"No, I'm a neighbor," he said. "I'd like to examine your radio station and take some pictures."

"Oh, good," I said, taking him in John's room. "They're on the air right now looking for the President's dog."

Bedford nodded and smiled as the visitor entered the room; then he continued broadcasting. The man looked perplexed, showing no sign of amusement as he squinted through his bifocals at the radio equipment and took notes. When he raised his camera to take pictures, Bedford sat up erect as the flashbulbs popped, one after another.

"Are these pictures going to be in the newspaper?" I asked the man.

"No, probably in court," he muttered. Then Bedford continued:

This has been a free public service announcement from KPIA. And now before we go back to the conclusion of 'Young Widder Brown,' we want to welcome a visitor to our station and see if he has a request.

"Yes, I have a request," said the man, solemnly. "I want you boys to accompany me downtown to the office of The United States District Attorney in the Federal Building. You are under arrest for operating a broadcasting station without a license!"

"Are you a policeman?" I asked.

"I'm Agent W.I. Abbott of the Federal Communications Commission," he answered. "An airline pilot, landing at Love Field, complained to us that he kept getting something on his radio that sounded like a Mexican station."

The boys looked stunned and the room suddenly became very quiet and still. When Agent Abbott went to the telephone to call FCC headquarters, Bedford spoke softly into the microphone, one last time:

> *Folks, we've just experienced a really big technical difficulty, so it's goodbye from KPIA, the station of missed programming. We may not be the 'Sunshine Station between the Nations,' but we've played your programs from all the stations. Goodbye, and signing off.*

I stood at the door feeling sad as the FCC agent ushered the three lawbreakers to his waiting automobile. I had been spared, being only nine, and because — according to the older boys — I'd had absolutely nothing to do with the great technical accomplishments of Station KPIA.

The next day, *The Dallas Morning News* did indeed have a headline about Bedford, but it mentioned no panic in the street as he had hoped. It read:

THREE HIGHLAND PARK HI BOYS, HALED INTO COURT FOR RUNNING RADIO STATION, DISMANTLE UNIT

> *All is quiet in the ether air waves in the neighborhood of San Carlos Drive these days, but three Highland Park High School boys, who had established a radio broadcasting station, have wound up the first business venture of their young careers.*
>
> *W.I. Abbott of the Federal Communications Commission, answering distress calls of neighbors who could tune in nothing else, attended one of the broadcasts posing as an interested neighbor. Abbott brought the three sheepish youngsters to United States District Attorney Clyde G. Hood Friday morning. Hood lectured them sternly and when they left, they promised:*
>
> > *1) to dismantle KPIA and*
> > *2) to work for the government as junior investigators in locating any other infraction of United States laws.*

The boys obediently dismantled their radio station and returned the various parts to their rightful owners. KPIA was now radio history. Ironically, Mexican "federales" confiscated the real "Sunshine Station Between the Nations" and blasted its antenna down just a few months later. Freedom of Speech in the U.S. and Mexico had been squelched, Bedford maintained, with the radio stations at the ends of the spectrum — the world's largest and smallest — having been stamped out by their respective governments. Suddenly, the position of radio as the mass communications medium of the future was in doubt.

Late one night, Bedford sneaked downstairs to the living room radio to see if Brinkley's demise was really true. When he turned to the spot on the dial where station XERA used to be, he heard a border evangelist singing gospel music in Villa Acuna, Mexico:

> *Turn your radio on,*
> *And listen to the master's words of love.*
> *Turn your radio on,*
> *Hear his message from above...*

"That sure fixed those 'federales,'" said Bedford as he jumped back in bed. "They wouldn't dare arrest Jesus...while he's starring on the radio!"

XXI

Starting a War

With his radio station gone from the airwaves, Bedford was relegated to spend the long, hot, afternoon rest periods with me on the sleeping porch. To help pass the time, he buried himself in the pages of the thick Johnson Smith catalogue, trying to decide on his next "endeavor."

"What are you sending off for this time, Bedford?" I asked.

"I think I'll order a cannon. Just listen to this:

Big Boom! Authentic reproduction of a World War army field cannon shoots carbide with realistic flash and loud bang."

That sounded serious to me. When my older brother ordered from Johnson Smith, he had no use for the capricious, trivial, or facetious item. His acquisitions from that catalog always had to have a practical purpose for his scheme of things, like his electric motor, telegraph set, chemistry experiment kit, and book, *The Secrets of Hypnotism.*

"What are you planning to do with a cannon, Bedford...start a war?" I asked.

"No, but I think the Gillon Street gang's about to start one. Haven't you seen the nasty signs they make, and heard the names they call us when they ride by on their bicycles?"

"No, they never bother me," I answered.

"Oh, that's right," said Bedford. "During hostilities it's traditional to spare the women and children. That's why they ignore you. But this war may be different — that Gillon Street gang is a tough bunch of cookies. They may do terrible things to you little kids. That's why I want the cannon. The only way to stand up to a bully is to be prepared for him with a secret weapon."

"Will it shoot real cannon balls?" I asked.

"No, but it'll scare 'em to death. Wo, the element of fear is the best offensive weapon there is. It's the most immobilizing force an army can have in its arsenal. During the Civil War the Confederate troops always let out their bloodcurdling rebel yell before they charged. It scared the pants off the yankees."

"But I thought the yankees won," I said. "It must not have scared 'em too bad."

"The South lost because they ran out of rifles, cannons and ammunition. We're going to have to stay ahead of the enemy in the arms race," said Bedford. "First, we need an army to arm. Go get a big jar, and we'll have a draft."

When I returned with the glass jar, Bedford blindfolded me and told me to draw out names he'd written on scraps of paper.

"Richard Stetzel, the first man drafted will be our field marshall," announced Bedford, unfolding the names. "Cousin Bedford Wynne can be our military strategist. Then Cousin Bill Troth can help me with armaments and munitions, since he has that neat hobby shop."

"As for Leon Harris, our fourth draftee, he'll have to be a private, I guess. Every army has to have foot soldiers to slug it out with the enemy in the trenches."

"Leon's not gonna like that," I said.

"Can't be helped," said Bedford, impatiently. "The lottery was fair and square. Besides, Leon has the best chance to become our unknown soldier...who knows? Wo, get going and deliver those draft notices."

"What can I be in the army?" I asked.

"Nothing. You're too young. You can be the Red Cross and bring us bandages, cookies, lemonade, and messages from home; there'll probably be a lot of those from our moms," he answered.

"Wait," I said, as I walked out the door. "What if there's no war?"

"There has to be a war, now that we're all prepared for one," said Bedford. "That's what armies are for."

"Bedford, Bedford," I shouted the next afternoon when the postman finally came with an extra bulge in his big, brown leather bag. "My crystal radio's here!"

I opened the box marked "Johnson Smith Co." and gazed proudly at my new possession, admiring its simple electronic wizardry: a platform which held a lever with a cat whisker, several terminals with thumbscrews, and a small, round, crystal — all connected by sparse, neat wiring. The set gleamed with high technology, and the crystal sparkled like a diamond ring, each facet holding the promise of hours of entertainment.

"Years ago, all radio receivers used a crystal and a cat whisker to receive and tune in the station," explained Bedford, "but the crystal set became old-fashioned when the radio tube was invented." You've gone and bought yourself an antique."

I moved the lever around, setting the thin wire end of the cat whisker down on the crystal, but no sound came magically forth as I had expected.

"Looks like you forgot to order earphones," said Bedford, putting his book down. "You can't hear anything without a headset."

I stood there stunned, realizing that my crystal radio was useless. I hadn't read the fine print in the advertisement — earphones were extra. So, my new crystal radio went up on the shelf.

It wasn't long until Bedford's birthday, however, and he received a fancy, big, professional-looking earphone headset to use with his short-wave radio. Baba persuaded him, in the interest of being a sharing family, to give me his old, thin, tinny earphones. After I'd devised an antenna, my radio was finally complete, and those earphones became a part of my anatomy for the rest of the summer.

"Baba, Daddy," shouted Bedford from an upstairs window. "I was listening to Germany on my shortwave radio. Hitler is invading Poland, and if I still had my radio station this could have been a KPIA exclusive, darn it."

It was the first of September, 1939, the opening day of dove hunting season...the opening day of World War II. Bedford and I were going with Daddy to meet some of his friends and hunt doves with them at a ranch south of Dallas. Our parents, who'd been packing the car with hunting equipment and picnic supplies, now dropped everything and raced inside to sit solemnly by the living room radio and listen to the news, but details of the invasion were sketchy. Daddy had been showing me how to load and cock Bedford's hand-me-down 410 gauge shotgun when Bedford had called. He'd left me standing by the car holding the gun, wondering what to do next. The Johnson Smith catalog, I thought, had been right on target with its gun advertisement:

You may find yourself shooting for a meal of game, and you never know when war may come.

Finally, we headed off for the dove hunt, stopping at the drugstore to buy a portable radio.

"They just got these in — a new kind of radio that works on a battery," said Daddy. "We're taking it with us on the hunt so we can hear the war news."

When we got to the ranch, the other men were waiting, angrily discussing Hitler's attack on Poland. We climbed through a barbed wire fence and carried our guns, shells and supplies across a pasture to a large cattle watering pond, called a "tank" in Texas. There, we would hide in waiting and shoot the elusive game birds. After the sun had gone down, we would pick our kill and eat supper around the campfire.

It was too early for the doves to fly in for a drink, so the hunters decided to stalk the birds in a nearby field of tall sunflowers. Bedford joined them, but since it was my first hunt using a gun, Daddy left me under a big, dead tree to try and shoot a few doves off a limb.

Left alone, I felt the adventure of the hunt, the peace and quiet of the great outdoors as I looked out over the fields and pastures and watched the cattle graze. Now and then a lonesome dove flew in the distance, having been flushed from its sunflower patch by the hunters. I kept hoping one would light in my tree, allowing me to bag my first dove.

I put on the earphones and looked down to tune my ever-present crystal set. When I glanced up, I saw a brown bird sitting on a limb high atop the tree. It appeared to be the right size and color for a dove. I hadn't heard the tell-tale whistle of dove wings, probably because I had the headset on, I thought.

I slowly cocked the firing hammer of the shotgun with my thumb, and took the safety off, just as Daddy had instructed. I aimed carefully at the dove until the bead at the end of the barrel sat on top of the gun sight next to my eye. I held my breath and squeezed the trigger. A loud blast issued forth and the gun stock pounded my shoulder. The dove fluttered, then fell into the gully on the other side of the tree.

I ran breathlessly to the flapping bird and picked it up. It quivered with fear and pain, wounded but not dead. Why was its beak bright orange? Finally realizing that I had just shot a female cardinal by mistake, I felt heartbroken. I cradled it in both hands, feeling her warm, heaving breast, not knowing what to do.

As I sat there holding her, I thought back to the time at home when I'd held a string for days, trying to capture a redbird so I could get a close look at its beauty. It all started when I had found a $5 bill. Bedford and Leon, determined to share my new wealth, offered to show me a redbird's nest, and make me a bird trap so I could catch my own, if I'd give them the money. When I agreed, they took me to a sparrow's nest where, first, they'd painted the eggs with red fingernail polish. Then they made my bird trap — an orange crate covered with window screen, propped up on a stick that had a long string running over to the bushes, and their specially mixed redbird seed sprinkled beneath the box. So there I sat, hour after hour, day after day, holding the string. All I got was broke and bored. Now, a couple of years older and supposedly wiser, the only redbird I had to show for myself was a female I'd just shot out of a tree.

She looked at me helplessly until her eyes became glazed and her eyelids closed. Then her head fell over and she was dead. I held her, still warm, in my hands until the shooting stopped in the sunflower patch and the hunters returned.

"Looks like you had a little accident," said Daddy when he got back.

"She was so beautiful," I said, sadly, admiring her soft colors.

"I know," said Daddy. "Lots of beautiful birds and animals are shot each year by hunters who want them just because they're beautiful...or rare...or valuable. A *true* sportsman hunts a bird or animal to eat, and only kills what he can use. Today, you were hunting for meat, like a real sportsman. This was just an unfortunate accident. You'll have to work hard to know all these game birds and animals: what they look like, sound like, and how they behave. Then accidents aren't as likely to happen."

He patted me on the back and went off to join the other hunters as they deployed around the tank to wait for the doves to fly in for a drink. The men crouched in the late afternoon shadows as the gathering birds began to dot the horizon. For an action-packed hour I watched the sights and heard the sounds of dove hunting: singing wings; swinging, blue-steel barrels; shotgun shells exploding; smoking, empty cases flying; feathers floating in the air; doves hitting the ground with a "thud," or going "kerplunk" in the water; hunters fetching the limp birds and stuffing them in their hunting bags.

Everyone had bagged his limit of doves by the time the last slice of sun dipped below the horizon. The shooting finally stopped, and the hunters gathered anxiously at the campfire to pick their doves and hear news of the German invasion of Poland.

Our dad opened the cardboard box and took out his new portable radio. He turned the knob, but no sound came out. He juggled the case; still not a sound.

"The salesman said it came complete with battery, but look — the battery compartment's empty," groaned Daddy.

"Oh no," said one of the hunters. "Now we won't be able to get the news of the invasion."

"There's a man talking about it on my radio right now," I said.

"You mean that's a real radio?" asked the man in disbelief. "Where's the battery?"

Bedford gladly offered the following explanation:

"It doesn't need a battery or other electric power source because the crystal, itself, converts the radio waves into weak electric current and makes the signal audible."

"That's amazing," the man said. "Let's see how it works; we want to hear some war news."

Suddenly, I felt great pressure and a feeling of urgency, of respon-sibility, of importance — those men were depending on me and my crystal radio for news of the outside world. I poked around on the crystal with the cat whisker until I finally located the strong signal of WRR. I began to relay the news coming over the airwaves, trying my best to keep up.

"The announcer said Hitler's attack on Poland started this morning," I said, as the hunters gathered around me and my crystal set, trying to catch some news of the invasion while they picked feathers off their doves. "Thousands of Adolph Hitler's planes flew eastward at dawn...and they bombed lots of old-fashioned Polish planes...before they could get off the ground," I repeated.

The men sat down around me and continued picking feathers, keenly interested in what I was saying.

"Then Hitler's big tanks...smashed through the barricades at the Polish border and rumbled across...with thousands of German soldiers marching in behind them."

"The German army has been cutting Polish troops and horse cavalry to pieces...Poles are dying to the stirring notes of a Chopin polonaise...repeated on the radio every 30 seconds.

"Hitlers' war machine is now slam-banging along the Polish roads...toward Warsaw from two directions...in a 'pincher' movement," I reported as the hunters listened glumly.

"That's pronounced 'pin-sir' movement," said Bedford, eagerly correcting me, jealous because I had the spotlight and because his potential KPIA exclusive had become my crystal set scoop. Being the middle child, I seldom got my share of attention. Bedford was always doing something smarter, David something cuter, but tonight, it was my turn.

When the news broadcast ended, one of the men finally broke the long silence that followed:

"Say, did you hear that Uncle Sam has a new pill to keep the doughboys from getting steamed up about girls? It says on the bottle:

> *If Hedy Lamar gets you excited,*
> *take one pill.*
> *If Zazu Pitts looks good to you,*
> *take two pills.*
> *If Eleanor Roosevelt turns you on,*
> *take the whole bottle — quick!*"

"My mother says Eleanor Roosevelt is beautiful on the inside," I said, as soon as the nervous laughter died down.

No one told more New Deal or Roosevelt jokes that night as the subdued hunters sat there trying to sort out the meaning of what they'd been hearing, pondering all the ramifications of the big story that had just come out of a small, crystalline piece of the earth's crust — earth that men were fighting for halfway around the globe, earth that acknowledged no political boundaries, didn't remember who fought the battles, or cared who won or lost them.

As they finished picking their birds with bloody, feathered fingers, the smell of gunpowder filling their nostrils, the sound of shotgun blasts still ringing in their ears, the men seemed to sense that it would be a long time before the guns of war grew silent again.

XXII

The Gillon Street Gang

I sat under the old stone bridge, fishing for crawdads. Bedford had told me to tie bacon to a string, dangle it in the creek over their holes, and they'd come out. But, as I looked into the placid pool, I saw only my reflection. Was this another of Bedford's tricks, like the useless bird trap he'd sold me?

It didn't really matter. So much had happened yesterday: the dove hunt, killing the redbird, the war. It felt so peaceful just to sit by myself and listen to the tranquil sound of the water as it flowed through the shady parkway. Beyond the creek bank stood the tall brick walls of Armstrong School. Behind me, I could see the red tile roof of my grandmother's house, and overhead arched the strong, sheltering ceiling of stone — spanning from bank to bank.

The bridge was my friend, the link between home and family, and my education. It had watched over me as I launched tiny ships that disappeared downstream; as I hid from playmates, and made things from the clay I'd dug beneath it.

The bridge had shown me secrets of nature: of bugs and butterflies; of turtles and tadpoles; of frogs, flowers, and ferns. It hadn't yet shared the secrets of life that would someday be revealed to me beneath it — I wasn't ready. My body had yet to feel "the rustle of spring," and those secrets were still far upstream in the flow of time.

As I daydreamed, I heard bicycles pull up, kickstands being deployed, then footsteps on the bridge above. Just then, I felt a tug on my string and looked down into the clear, shimmering water. There crouched my crawdad, waving his antennas, looking up at me with beady eyes as he claimed the bacon with his lobster-like claws. I dipped one hand slowly into the water and pulled the string gently with the other, lifting the crawdad from this muddy fortress.

My eager fingers came closer...and closer...and closer to the tenacious prize, when KERPLOP — an explosion splattered the water. A rock had landed just in front of me, and I dropped the string and scooted from the water's edge up to the underside of the protective bridge, hoping I hadn't been observed by the intruders above.

"Quit wastin' ammunition, clunkhead," came the voice of an older boy. "We may be at war before long. Did you see that look on Bedford Shelmire's face when I gave him the finger and called him a 'cock-sucker'?"

Then another boy asked, "You still burned up about the itchin' powder he put on our bicycle seats when we were in the show?"

"Yeah, but we're gonna pay him back. If it's war he wants, it's war he'll get. Watch out for his friend, Richard, 'though. He won his weight in the Golden Gloves boxing tournament," said the first boy.

"I'll break him in half," said a deep-voiced boy who sounded not overly bright.

"Listen Frank, don't get into a slugging match with him, or you'll be sorry! We won't use our fists; this will be a war of strategy, and lots of neat weapons," responded the first boy, obviously the leader.

This must be the Gillon Street gang, I thought. They had simply been a group of unfamiliar boys who lived on another street — until they began showing off on their bicycles in front of the houses of the girls that Bedford and his friends liked. Since then, they were referred to as a "gang."

A bicycle skidded up to the other end of the bridge and I heard the excited voice of a younger boy: "I've been scouting 'em out. Shelmire's gone and drafted a big army; they were on maneuvers when you rode by 'em on your bikes."

"Good work, Peter. That means war; come on guys, we've got to go get mobilized," said the leader as they rushed for their bicycles.

The long, late afternoon shadows enveloped the bridge, and the creek bed took on the somber look of a battlefield entrenchment. The stone retaining walls appeared to be fortifications of stacked sandbags, and the drainage pipes sticking out of them looked like huge cannons. I pulled my bike out of the bushes and pedaled home as fast as I could to tell Bedford what I'd just overheard.

When I rushed into our bedroom, he and Richard were filling a huge red balloon with gas from the stove jet. They tied a note to the bottom and let it float, majestically, to the ceiling.

"We've developed a weather/signal/anti-aircraft barrage balloon," explained Bedford. "If war comes, we might get surrounded and starve under siege, so we want to be able to send a message over enemy lines, and we've got lots of balloons ready. We're gonna use this one to check the weather, prevailing wind currents, and flight range. The note offers a reward to whoever finds it, and..."

I interrupted him to say, "I was fishing under the stone bridge, and I heard the Gillon Street gang talking. They didn't know I was there and they said they're going to start a war!"

"I don't know why they got so upset over my little joke," said Bedford.

"'Cause they felt ridiculous, standing there scratchin' their butts from that itching powder when all the girls walked out of the theater," said Richard. "Whew, were they pissed off!"

"Wars always start with people who don't have any sense of humor over some silly little something like that," said Bedford. "Well, if they want to go to war, we're ready for 'em. But watch out for Big Frank, that moron of theirs. He's as strong as a bear and has about as much intelligence as one, so don't get in a rasslin' match with him."

"I could punch him out," said Richard.

"No!" said Bedford, adamantly. "There'll be no hand-to-hand combat in this war. It'll be won with cunning, with the deft maneuver, with sophisticated weaponry like this. We'll launch it tomorrow morning."

The boys decided to release the weather/signal/anti-aircraft barrage balloon from the tower of the town hall, two blocks away, hoping that releasing it from there would keep it out of the clutches of the enemy, and the hungry branches of the surrounding trees. We climbed to the observation platform under the big Spanish dome, and looked out through the archways over the town of Highland Park. Lush trees, parks, parkways, and flowing streams now filled the peaceful, verdant suburb of Dallas that had formerly been bare prairie. The town hall, library, fire and police stations straddled the parkway a few blocks down the creek from the old stone bridge. When the stream reached the buildings, it flowed beneath them in a wide, open drainage tunnel. When the creek surfaced, it meandered through a picturesque park that welcomed walkers, wooers, and...warriors.

After testing the breeze, Bedford leaned out an archway as far as he dared, and released the balloon. It flew swiftly away, dangling its note beneath that promised a reward for the finder, and soon appeared to be only a tiny red speck in the sky.

"It's heading into the stratosphere, traveling north-northwest," he exclaimed. "It'll probably end up in Idaho."

The launching did not go unnoticed by members of the Gillon Street gang, who were riding their bicycles a couple of blocks away. They pedaled quickly to the town hall, curious to see who had released the balloon and why, and pulled up in front of the building right below us. Bedford and Richard rushed down to the restroom and filled their spare balloons with water. In a moment, water bombs pounded and drenched the enemy. Big Frank, his face red with anger, started to rush into the building after us, but thought better of it when he saw Richard shaking a clenched fist. Then the gang responded with their own barrage of rocks that they took from their bicycle carriers.

As the rocks flew through the openings and bounced around the platform, Bedford shouted down, "Hold your fire; we haven't even declared war yet!"

"We hereby declare war," said the leader, whose voice I recognized. "Now do you surrender?"

"Never!" replied Bedford. "We challenge you to a battle, since a state of war exists; you pick the time and place."

After a short conference, the leader spoke again. "How about 10 o'clock tomorrow morning along the creek in the tunnel under the town hall?"

That sounded eerie to me. It was dark, drippy and smelly under there, and slimy things crawled all over you, I'd heard.

"Agreed. Now we get to pick the weapons. It'll be...matchguns, like these," said Bedford, pointing to his empty pocket.

The Gillon Street gang looked up with bewildered expressions. Obviously, Bedford had caught them completely by surprise. They had no matchguns — only sacks full of rocks. Finally they agreed, and rode off to get armed.

Bedford had been bluffing — he had no matchguns either. When we got home, Bedford commandeered all the big, wooden clothespins from the laundry line while Sally wasn't looking. He rearranged the sticks and strong steel springs, and taped them together, creating guns that would ignite and shoot flaming kitchen matches some 25 feet.

The next morning, precisely at 10 o'clock, I observed the adversaries entering the dimly-lit tunnel under the town hall, advancing from opposite ends until they confronted each other across the flowing stream. Then on a signal, the firing began. It looked like the Fourth of July as the flaming matches streaked through the air, striking opposite walls of the tunnel, splashing into the water with a smoking sizzle, or scorching an opponent. There came an occasional cry of anguish as one of the tiny torches wedged in a pocket or went down a shirt collar.

The battle became a stalemate until the Gillon Street gang started to run out of ammunition, and pulled their secret weapons — rubber guns — from under their shirts. The guns were carved from wood and had long, square barrels and a pistol grip at one end. Rubber tire inner tubes had been sliced into ammunition and stretched over them.

Big Frank now led the charge of the gang's offensive, squeezing his clothespin trigger and letting fly his rubber strips at high speed to inflict stinging blows. Suddenly he stopped and a fearful expression came over his face as he looked down at his ankles.

"Leeches!" he shouted. "They're stuck all over my legs."

Hostilities ceased as each contestant went to check his own ankles. Several, finding they had the slimy, clingy creatures on them, too, ran yelling out of the tunnel. The battle had ended abruptly, with the creek and its leeches the only victor.

"Where have all my clothespins gone?" Baba demanded when we got home.

Bedford's pockets bulged with matchguns and mine with extra ammunition. The burns on our shirts gave testimony that we'd been in some sort of conflagration. She snatched one of the loaded matchguns from him, triggering the spring and firing a lighted match into one of her bedsheets hanging over the line. Within minutes, our entire arsenal was dismantled and hanging back on the clothesline.

Bedford began working feverishly to meet the rubber gun escalation by developing a new weapon — the six-rubber-band repeating rifle. With the paint on the barrels still wet, he issued guns to the troops the following morning for the next scheduled battle — this time in the park, with rubber guns as the chosen weapon.

Our army marched to the battlefield and lined up opposite the enemy. They raised their repeating rifles and fired six salvos of rubber bands in rapid succession, inflicting multiple, painful, slapping blows while the enemy got off only one shot at a time.

Members of the Gillon Street gang, outmatched in firepower, re-treated through the park with our troops pursuing relentlessly past the merry-go-round, up steps, over walls, and across bridges. Soon com-pleting the rout, Bedford's army marched triumphantly toward home.

I had parked my bicycle on top of the high cliff overlooking the tennis court, where I thought it would be safe. During the height of the fighting, I had walked down to bring extra rubber bands to feed the insatiable appetite of our new, repeating rifles. Climbing the steps after the battle, I panicked as I saw Big Frank on top of the cliff, rolling my bike toward the precipice. He stopped and lifted it high above his head, then he tossed it over the edge in an act of cruel retaliation. Helpless and horror-stricken, I watched it fall — remembering the day Phyllis Murphey's father had run over my new bike in their driveway. A second later, my bicycle crashed down on the tennis court, becoming a mangled mass of metal once again — with broken spokes, crumpled fenders, and bent frame.

"Wo, you've had more major accidents with one bike than anyone I know," said Bedford as I dragged the twisted wreckage into our yard, reliving the past heartbreak all over again. "Why'd you let him get away with it? Don't you know you have to stand up to bullies?"

Bedford quickly assembled his troops and their BB guns — a weapon hitherto unused in neighborhood warfare. Sure, he'd heard all the stories of kids getting hurt by BBs — eyes being shot out and stuff like that. But a dreadful atrocity had been committed and, he said, "so much for danger when pride and honor are at stake."

They raced to the swimming pool in the park to ambush the enemy as they walked by for their daily afternoon swim. The barrage from the spring-loaded BB guns targeted Big Frank, and he suffered numerous welts on his legs and fanny before he and his friends found some trees to hide behind.

"Hold your fire," yelled the gang's leader. "We're unarmed. If you want a BB gun battle you'll get one, but we can't have it today — Big Frank has a piano lesson, and tomorrow school starts. How 'bout meeting us next Saturday morning where the creek runs under Beverly Drive? You guys take the north side of the ditch and we'll take the ditch on the south side."

"Agreed...barbarians!" shouted Bedford.

XXIII

Following the Front

The next morning, we reluctantly laced on our shoes and headed for our first day of school. I was glad to see my friends again, but shocked to discover Peter, the young scout of the Gillon Street gang, sitting on the back row glaring at me. He was a new classmate — an enemy in our midst!

After lunch, as I walked out of the building and started to descend the steep flight of steps leading to the playgrounds, someone stuck a foot out. I stumbled, and tumbled head over heels to the ground. As I looked up in dismay, with my knees and elbows bleeding, there stood Peter — laughing and jeering at me in front of my surprised classmates. How was I supposed to stand up to this bully? Till now, I'd been the tallest boy in the class, but this new student towered over me.

Walking out the next day after lunch, I looked for a menacing foot. Not seeing one, I started down the steps. Suddenly, a shove on the back sent me sprawling again. Wasn't there any kind, peaceful place left in the world, I wondered?

"Wo, it's brave of you to volunteer for combat duty, but you're needed behind the lines with the bandages, ammunition, and soda pop," said Bedford, as Saturday's battle neared zero hour. "So go back to the bridge and stay under there until I give you the signal. It's too dangerous up here at the front for you."

The BB gun escalation had brought a serious, sinister new dimension to creek warfare. Before, we could see the tumbling rocks and water bombs, smoking matches, and flapping rubber bands as they flew through the air toward us, giving us a chance to dodge them. The flying steel BB gun balls sped swiftly silently, invisibly, and they struck without warning.

I walked upstream and sat under the old stone bridge just as the conflict started, with taunts, name-calling, and sniper fire. It felt so peaceful beneath it, that I found it hard to realize an armed conflict was taking place a short distance downstream.

Each army had entrenched themselves in one of the concrete-walled bunkers that formed the entrance to the drainage tunnel running beneath the street. Suddenly, the Gillon Street gang climbed from their fortified position, and with Big Frank leading the charge, raced across no-man's land, giving war whoops and firing their weapons. When they reached the other side, Bedford's forces opened with a withering fusillade that drove the enemy back across the wide street and parkway to their own ramparts.

Soon, Richard Stetzel, on command from his general, leaped on top of the wall and motioned for his comrades to counter-attack. He was tough, wily, and street-wise, with a proud, aggressive nature — just the kind of field commander you'd want to lead your army. Richard directed the advance, with enemy fire ricocheting off him and raising welts on his handsome countenance. Finally, he stood at the very edge of their battlement, firing down at them point blank. The stings of the enemy's zinging, brutal barrage had routed the rest of Richard's regiment, however, so he withdrew to cover their retreat.

The charges and retreats continued back and forth with neither side gaining the advantage, both armies having equal firepower and troop strength. Finally, Bedford came running back to me at the bridge to get a fresh cylinder of BBs and Band-Aids for the bleeding cuts on his neck and ears.

"Ouch, that hurts," he said angrily, as I administered to his wounds. "They're aiming for our heads, and if they're gonna fight dirty, we'll throw everything we've got at 'em. Run home quick and get my pellet gun!"

When I returned with the powerful rifle, Bedford grabbed it and pumped the lever beneath the barrel several times to build up the pressure of compressed air inside the firing chamber that would propel the pellet — a thick, thimble-shaped piece of lead about a quarter of an inch across.

"Men, behold the ultimate weapon that will end this war," he said, as he rejoined his troops at the top of the embankment.

He raised his gun over the concrete wall and took aim at a tree trunk high above the enemy. He pulled the trigger and the pellet shot across the street, making a loud crack as it penetrated deep into the tree.

The opposing camp grew silent, knowing full well the serious message that had just been fired over their heads, for while BB's could hurt and sting, pellets could penetrate a kneecap...or skull. They realized their army was now at Bedford's mercy, unless they could figure out a new strategy, or luck into a miracle. One was just about to pass by.

"We've demonstrated our new weapon, and they got the message. Listen, there's not a peep out of 'em," said Bedford. "One more salvo and they'll be ready to surrender."

He pumped the lever a few more times, put a lead pellet in the chamber, and focused his telescopic sight on a tree even closer to the crouching enemy, certain that this shot would bring forth their white flag. Just as he squeezed off another round, the telescopic sight went black, and we heard the sickening thud of his pellet hitting metal, the screech of tires, the sound of a car door being thrown open. He'd hit a passing car.

"Some son-of-a-bitch shot a hole in my fender, and I'm gonna whip his ass when I catch him," shouted the car's owner.

Bedford spun around and pitched the pellet gun right into the arms of his astonished field commander. Suddenly, a tall, red-faced young man appeared at the top of the wall. Richard turned and fled, carrying the pellet gun, with the irate car owner in hot pursuit.

The elated enemy, having observed the sudden departure of Bedford's field commander with the pellet gun, decided on a daring maneuver. Remembering the leeches under the town hall, both sides had ignored the possibility of attacking through the big, dark drainage tunnel that ran under Beverly Drive and connected the two entrenchments. Besides, charging troops would be sitting ducks for an ambush when they came out the other side. Now, the Gillon Street gang figured they could make a quick dash through the tunnel, landing right in the depleted enemy's midst. They would capture Bedford and his remaining army, then victory would be theirs.

Bedford had planned for this eventuality, placing his big carbide cannon at the mouth of the tunnel, its muzzle packed with rock salt, and aimed into the darkness. Hearing the enemy coming, Bedford watched for them to near the end of the tunnel, and when they appeared out of the dimness, he gave his rebel yell. The enemy pulled up suddenly, with a look of fear on their faces as they squinted into the bright light and saw Bedford kneel down beside his huge artillery piece.

"KABOOM...ROOM...ROOM...ROOM" went the cannon, with a bright, blinding flash, the sound magnifying and echoing, and the rocksalt ricocheting through the tunnel like shrapnel. The enemy — shocked, stunned, and scared — turned and ran back through the tunnel and out the other end in disarray, with Big Frank leading the pack. The war had ended, they decided. With the introduction of the pellet gun, and now the cannon, the conflict had become too dangerous.

Bedford led us up onto Beverly Drive, tired, tattered, but triumphant. We circled the wounded car, examining the pellet hole in the front fender.

"Couldn't catch that sneaky bastard and his pellet gun," said the high school boy as he came puffing back to his car. "Now who's gonna pay for that hole in my fender? It looks like hell."

"I dunno, looks pretty good to me," said Bedford. "It gives your car that aura of mystery, drama, excitement; bet this old black Ford used to look pretty plain?"

The youth didn't say anything, but he seemed to feel a new sense of pride because of all the attention being garnered by his old car.

"Only thing is," said Bedford, "it needs a few more holes — bigger ones. Then it would look like a car that had been in its share of high speed auto chases, a collector's item that people would notice wherever you went. I've got some hunting guns at home that could make neat holes in the other fenders, too."

A short time later, at our house, Bedford aimed our dad's big deer rifle at the car's hood, having already put an assortment of small caliber holes in the doors and other fenders.

"Be careful," cautioned the youth. "Don't hit the motor or the tires. How about putting one through the rumble seat?"

"Bedford, come quick," I shouted from the front porch. "Your balloon's come back in the mail, from Frisco."

"It made it all the way to San Francisco? Bet some old gold miner found it," said Bedford, snatching the envelope. A look of disappointment came over his face when he saw that the postmark said Frisco, Texas, a rural hamlet 25 miles northwest of Dallas.

"Some farmer found it. The note says, 'Weather was bright and sunny, but your balloon ran out of gas and snagged on my outhouse. Send reward.' Oh what a tragic end," lamented Bedford.

It was hard adjusting to a neighborhood at peace, especially since I still had my personal war with Peter to fight. I dreaded going to school on Monday and having to face him at lunchtime. On Monday morning, however, an unpleasant drama took place in my classroom.

I sat behind the smartest girl in class, who delighted in letting everyone else know it — and showing up us boys. Behind me sat a new student, a short, swarthy, unpopular boy from the North named David Terk. While the teacher stepped out of the room, he stood up, leaned over, and without his victim knowing it, stuck a sign on her back reading, "PLEASE KICK ME." But the tape came loose and the sign fell off.

"Stick it back," whispered David, persuasively.

As I was sticking the sign back on, our teacher walked in and saw me doing it. Oh, no...caught in the act! Couldn't she see I was innocent? Didn't she know I wouldn't...I couldn't make a sign like that and put it on a girl's back? Nevertheless, she chastised me in front of the class as I sat there, crushed and humiliated. Then she set a time for me to see Mr. Earle, the principal — after school.

When I walked outside at lunchtime, Peter was nowhere to be seen — much to my relief. Reaching the bottom of the steps I received a swift kick in the seat of the pants that knocked me to the ground, stunned and embarrassed. When I looked up, there stood Peter with his hands on his hips, laughing haughtily.

As I got up and began dusting myself off, I saw Baba drive up to have a chat with Mrs. Phillips about my behavior. Suddenly fortified by my mother's presence, I hauled off and hit Peter square in the stomach with all my might. I left him lying there gasping for breath on the ground in front of our classmates, writhing in agony, unable to utter a word of protest.

I met with Mr. Earle after school, and as punishment for my earlier mischief, was instructed to wear the "PLEASE KICK ME" sign to school all the next day to "see how it made me feel." The next morning as I crossed the footbridge, with the sign pinned on my back, my heart sank. There stood Peter, defiantly, in the school doorway. Today, he could kick me with permission!

When I walked up to Peter, he refused to move aside. Instead, he grabbed me by the shirt collar and pulled my head close to his. We stood eyeball to eyeball, nose to nose, and I could feel his breath on my face.

"Shelmire...I like you!" he said. "You've really got what it takes, and didn't deserve that bum rap."

Then he strode around behind me, but instead of getting the kick I had expected, I got an escort. He walked into school behind me — step for step, protecting my posterior. The older boys had been waiting for me inside, to have their fun at my expense. They thought better of it, however, when they saw the fierce look of dare in Peter's eyes.

When recess came, my good friends Bill, Bobby and Charlie came to my aid and, joining Peter, formed a circle of protection around me. All day long they followed my every step — in the hallways, bathroom, cafeteria, playground, much to the disappointment of the upper classmen. No one laid a foot on my heavily protected posterior the whole day.

When the harrowing experience finally ended, and everyone had gone home, Peter removed the sign and we walked outside, basking in our new friendship that had bloomed out of the ashes of war.

"Want to go across and get some string and bacon at my grandmother's?" I asked. "I'll show you a place where we can catch some crawdads."

"I know," he answered. "Under the old stone bridge. They don't call me scout for nothin'."

XXIV

Shooting up the Town

I'd been waiting and watching all day for a lone stranger to ride into town, wearing a white hat. Instead, three cowboys wearing black hats crept slowly down the street with hands on their pistols. This meant trouble, big trouble and I'd just have to rid the town of this scum before they began to shoot up the place.

I put on my boots, red neckerchief, and big, white, ten gallon hat. Then I strapped my gun belt around my waist, closed the curtains, and clomped down the stairs toward the front door.

"Where are you going, Wo, to a costume party?" asked a fellow slouched in the corner of the saloon, reading *Popular Mechanics.*

He looked a lot like my older brother, Bedford, but there was no time for small talk, and I did what you always do with the town drunk — I ignored him. I marched out and stood right in the middle of the street, daring the outlaws to take just one more step. Suddenly, the varmint on the right went for his gun, followed by the rest. Quick as a flash, my six-shooters came out of their holsters in a blur, firing hot lead. I shot two of them dead in their tracks, and was looking down at them triumphantly when I heard the voice of the last outlaw.

"BAM BAM...BAM BAM...I got you. Why don't you fall down? You're dead."

Even imaginary bullets take their toll, eventually, in play-like gunfights, and a conscientious cowboy is bound by the honor code to take only so many before going down. Slowly, reluctantly, dramatically, I fell to the ground — shot dead. The outlaw turned me over with his boot and looked down at me with pitiless eyes.

"Want to play 'Wyatt Earp, Frontier Marshal' with us?" asked Bill Pearson, the gang's ringleader. "We just saw the movie and need somebody to play Doc Holiday, the mean, gunslinging dentist who gets drunk and plugs everybody in sight."

"Sure! I couldn't go with you to see it 'cause I've been waiting on an old friend of my grandfather who's coming to tell us about his ranch and summer boy's camp," I said, opening one eye and then the other.

It was our custom to come home each Saturday and Sunday afternoon and act out the movie we'd just seen. Bill, our neighborhood C.B. DeMille, would take the story line and assign the dozens of movie parts to the three or four of us available, and divide the plot into "play-as-you-go" segments. When we'd acted out one scene, we would regroup to plan the next one.

"I'll play Wyatt Earp, U.S. Marshal," said Bill, proudly. "Bobby can play my brother Virgil Earp, and John, you can be Curly Bill and his gang."

John Pearson, our director's little brother, relished being a group, especially playing gangs; the bigger and tougher the gangs, the better. Putting our imaginations to work, my front yard became the legendary O.K. Corral and we pretended our way hurriedly through the first part of the movie, anxious to get to the exciting gunfight climax. Finally, the guns began to blaze and everyone dodged imaginary bullets in our re-creation of the most violent and famous shootout in the history of the Old West. We hid behind hedges and tromped through would-be flower beds made as barren as the desert by countless previous charades. Marshal Earp and posse had six pistols between them. Little John, playing Curly Bill's gang, had only one, having left his other lying around somewhere.

Our cap-guns used other ammunition, because we looked upon the red paper rolls of caps as child's play: undependable when damp, time-consuming to load, depletable in a long gun battle and, they cost money. No, we preferred to make BAMS with our lips or emit cannon-like sounds from the throat. Firepower and velocity depended on our ferocity, and we cowboy gunfighters counted on the bangs from the throat for survival.

Suddenly, a vintage Mercury pulled up to the curb, its fenders and sides covered with red dirt and scratches that indicated it had been many places where an automobile was unwelcome. The driver, looking confident and purposeful, hopped quickly out of the car and surveyed the chaotic scene without changing expression. He wore all gray — suit, Stetson hat, tie, and scuffed up boots — and his face and hands looked like rich leather that had been burnished by sun and wind. He had an oval face with high cheekbones, piercing, deeply-set eyes, and a boyish, unruly lock of silver hair hung down over his forehead, belying his age.

The shooting halted as we watched this mysterious stranger, with such an imposing presence, stride briskly toward our shingle-roofed front porch which had become Doc Holiday's office. I'd been standing there by my dentist's chair — a big wooden rocker — trying to decide whether to pull my patient's molars, or just murder him so I could get on to the shootout.

"Hello friend. Seems I lost my way. What town is this?" he asked me in a commanding voice.

"Tombstone, Arizona," I answered.

"Well, looks like I'm pokin' my nose into somebody else's business, but if you and your pals will let me pass, I promise to be outa town by dark," he said. "I'm Tom Ellzey. What's your name?"

"Overton Shelmire, but they call me Wo."

"Oh," he said, his stern expression softening, "you're W.O. Bunch's grandson and namesake, the young fellow I came to meet. Why do you need a nickname, when your grandfather's carried William Overton with honor, to pass on down to you?"

"'Cause the kids at school make fun of it. They call me 'Over-a-ton' and stuff like that. My big brother, Bedford, says our family got all the silly names."

"No use worryin' about nicknames. Worry 'bout livin' up to your real name. Say, what's all the shootin' about," he asked as imaginary bullets began zinging through the O.K. Corral again.

"That's Marshal Wyatt Earp and his brother Virgil crouching behind the hedge. They're after Curly Bill and his gang, over there hiding behind the tree."

"You mean that one little guy is playin' a whole gang?" asked Mr. Ellzey.

"Sure. He changes his voice and hops around a lot," I replied.

"Say, I sure could use some energetic cowboys like those on the LZ Ranch," responded Mr. Ellzey.

Grand Daddy Bunch, who'd been dozing in the living room, awoke and walked out the front screen door and greeted Mr. Ellzey with outstretched arms. A big bear hug and a few pats on the back closed the gap of time and distance as only those fond gestures can, between two old friends re-establishing their friendship. They sat down in the porch rockers for a visit as we resumed the gunfight out in the front yard.

"Who is that?" asked Bill, staring at Tom Ellzey. "Wish we could make him marshal. Heck, with a voice and face like that, he could do all the parts: cowboy, minister, Indian, storekeeper, farmer."

Indeed, at one time or another in his life, this complex, multi-faceted individual had been virtually all those things. My grandfather had told me that Tom Ellzey, born in the gold fields of California a few years after the Gold Rush ended, had moved with his parents by covered wagon to Indian territory in what would become Western Oklahoma. At 14, he went to work on a lonely, remote cattle ranch where he shared prairie and campfire with Kiowas and Comanches. After several years of isolation, he joined a trail ride to the bustling cattle center of Fort Worth, where he stayed and got a job as clerk in a large general store.

Grand Daddy Bunch also headed for Texas from Louisiana and settled in Marlin, a small town prospering with cotton, commerce, and courtesy, where he could breathe antebellum-like atmosphere of the Old South. He opened a dry goods store and, needing inventory, headed for Fort Worth up the old Chisholm Trail, made wide, straight, and smooth by numerous cattle drives. The two liked each other the moment they met. The young clerk's self-confident, convincing salesmanship impressed my grandfather. Tom Ellzey appreciated the buyer's thoughtful, polite Southern manner, so different from the raucous, rambunctious cowboys who came to spend their paychecks. A lifelong friendship had begun and today, the two old friends basked in the warmth of reunion, oblivious to the furious battle going on below them as they rocked back and forth in the porch chairs.

As expected, our big shootout ended in triumph for law and order with Wyatt Earp — in the form of Bill Pearson, having changed history to his liking — standing triumphant in the center of the corral, the only survivor. Doc Holiday, drunk but loyal to the end, lay at his side, dead of a pickled liver.

"Say, boys, if y'all can make a quick recovery, come on inside and see some camp movies," said Mr. Ellzey. Suddenly, the entire cast came to life and headed for the front porch.

Our parents arrived home from their usual Sunday afternoon drive just in time to help Mr. Ellzey locate an electric plug for his movie projector. The screen flickered with light for a moment, then a shapeless panorama of soft pastel colors appeared. When the picture became focused, we saw a vast, endless prairie covered with cattle, prairie grass, and bright wildflowers. Here and there, rugged caprocks and an occasional distant windmill interrupted the long, straight horizon. The breathtaking scenes of the color film changed from treeless plain to rugged cliffs and canyons — scenery straight from a western movie, and I kept expecting cowboys and Indians to come riding from behind the rocks.

"Five hundred miles north, at the tip top o' Texas, lies the LZ Ranch. There, Mrs. Ellzey and I and our four sons have created LZ Camp for Boys. Here we are at LZ Camp headquarters, with our new, modern, concrete bunkhouses and dining hall," said Mr. Ellzey as a group of simple, flat-roofed structures came into view. They were scattered around the bleak, treeless prairie, looking like giant shoeboxes that had been dropped off a truck. Everything was flat, flat, flat, except the flagpole and windmill that seemed to point to the sky just to be different.

"LZ Camp has a well-rounded program of all the activities you see here. Then, to swim in the cool, clear spring water of Wolf Creek after the morning doin's feels mighty good," continued Mr. Ellzey as boys splashed and frolicked on the screen. "After dinner, the campers rest for a couple of hours and are required to write at least one letter home per week."

Grand Daddy Bunch, who relished both writing and receiving long letters, nodded approvingly.

"Then, in the afternoon, comes our most essential activity of all — horseback riding, mostly done in connection with some form of ranch work," said Mr. Ellzey.

Next, the movie camera followed the trail, leading from the big rodeo corral across Wolf Creek and up a hill. Beyond lay, unseen, the vast grasslands of the LZ ranching empire. Suddenly, over the crest rode the same lone stranger who'd ridden into Tombstone this afternoon, only now he rode on a magnificent, dark brown steed, and he had the appearance of a frontier marshal. Following him over the precipice, running toward camp and camera came a herd of stampeding horses, being driven by four handsome cowboys.

"Those are my sons running up the horses," said Mr. Ellzey as the movie ended. "Boys, one of those cowponies will be yours for eight weeks if you come to LZ Camp. You'll saddle 'em up for a Texas cattle roundup, and spend the night out on the range with the chuck wagon. Then you'll ride 'em in the LZ rodeo, and by the end of camp, you'll be real cowboys! At LZ Camp, we have a healthful routine of actual ranch life, with both its diversions and responsibilities. The boys learn how to play...and how to work: milking cows, shocking wheat, gardening, fence building, and other ranch work that has to be done, for we believe that every boy should learn to work with his own hands. And we believe, too, that every normal child has the right to discover the truth about the story of life — the 'facts of life,' at the right time and in the right way."

Bedford looked over at me with raised eyebrows and smiled, knowingly.

"Our aim is to send the boys back home with a greater vision of real life, with greater appreciation for parents, friends, and country, and a more reverent attitude toward God," concluded Mr. Ellzey.

"Your camp looks interesting," said Baba, "but all Wo's talked about is going to Camp La Junta in Kerrville with Bedford. He'll need to think it over and make his own choice."

Bedford left the room with a worried look on his face, wishing he could make the choice for me. The last thing he wanted was to have his little brother tagging along behind him at Camp La Junta.

"Well, it's getting late," said Mr. Ellzey, "and I promised to be out of town by dark."

As I followed the two old friends back to the car, Tom Ellzey turned to me and spoke:

"Overton, I hope you choose to ride with me this summer. We'll work and play, and learn and pray together. But whatever you decide, don't let 'em call you 'Whoa' anymore, 'cause where I come from that means 'stop'...not 'go' and 'do' and 'accomplish.'"

Then the stranger rode down the street and was gone.

While I struggled for the next several days with my choice of a camp, Bedford played records of cowboy songs and tuned in to cactus "shoot-'em-ups" on the radio, trying to influence my decision.

"Hi, ho, Silver, away!" shouted the Lone Ranger as he and his faithful Indian companion, Tonto, rode into a radio-land sunset on the clomping hooves of the sound effects man.

"Wow! What an exciting episode," said Bedford. "Made me think of LZ Camp."

"It made me think about Camp La Junta," I said. "Remember when y'all dressed up like Indians and paddled war canoes down the river. That sure looked like fun!"

"Well, there are lots of fun activities at LZ Camp, too," said Bedford.

"I'd like riding a horse," I said, "but not doing all those chores. I want to go to camp to play, not work all the time."

"Gosh," said Bedford, "I just wish we had gardening, milking, shocking wheat, and all those other neat things to do at Camp La Junta."

"Why, are they fun to do?"

"You bet," said Bedford. "You like zinnias, and here's your chance to grow some pretty ones. And remember how old John Battle Jones used to squirt us while he was milking? You could have big milk fights. Then you go around shocking the wheat with a little electric gadget to make it grow faster before your very eyes."

"I don't know," I said, "maybe I just ought to go to Camp La Junta with you."

Bedford could picture me dogging his every step at Camp La Junta — lonely, homesick, and friendless. As I continued to vacillate, he paced the floor, trying to think of some new, irresistible persuasion to convince me to go to LZ Camp.

"Home, home on the range, where the deer and the antelope play," blared the old wind-up Victrola.

Suddenly, Bedford stopped and his face lit up. "Sex...on...the range. That's it," he exclaimed. "He'll learn about sex on the range! That'll get him there when I tell him how exciting 'it' is."

"What's 'it'?" I asked, rushing into the room.

"I can't tell you; I didn't tell you about Santa Claus, did I? So, I'm not telling you about 'it'. But 'it's' bigger than Santa Claus...lots bigger."

"Who is gonna tell me?" I asked.

"Mr. Ellzey, that's who," said Bedford. "Don't you remember him saying that every boy has the right to know the truth about the 'facts of life' at the right time and in the right way? Well, he's going to tell you about 'it' on the range."

That sounded exciting, having the secret of "it" unlocked while riding the prairie at LZ Camp. Bedford decided that the time might be right, just then, to try to nudge me into making my final choice.

"Wo, just think about it. What would you really rather be, a playlike Indian wearing a feather... or a real cowboy earning your spurs?"

He'd struck a responsive chord that appealed to my strongest desire, my wildest dream: to be a real cowboy out in the Old West.

"A real cowboy earning my spurs!" I answered impulsively.

"Baba...Daddy," Bedford shouted. "Wo's decided to be a cowboy. He's going to LZ Camp!"

XXV

Riding the Range

"Hey, boy...you comin' in from Dallas?" asked the old-timer sitting in a chair, leaning back against the front of the Perryton bus station.

"Yessir, I'm from Dallas. My name is Overton Shelmire."

"I 'spose you have a nickname?" he asked.

"No, I don't," I said, having struck "Wo" from my vocabulary.

"Well, the boys out there at camp'll probably give you one, but you may not like it. Anyway, Lawrence Ellzey came to meet your bus. He got tired of waitin' and went to pick up some supplies, but he'll be back, directly," said the man. "You're the last camper to come in, I guess. I've sat here and watched boys arrive now for about a dozen years since the camp opened — on their way out to the LZ Ranch, looking pale, puny and citified. Don't none of 'em pass back through here at the end of camp, though."

"They don't? Where do they go?" I asked apprehensively.

"I dunno, but some other boys take their places — ones with new nicknames. And they're tanner, stronger, and taller, with a lot more sense and better manners than the ones I saw gettin' off the bus at the first of th' summer."

Just then Lawrence Ellzey drove up, but he wasn't the white knight of a cowboy my imagination had been expecting. Instead of a big ten gallon hat and chaps, he wore a curled-up straw hat and khakis. He didn't ride up on his big strawberry roan; he was driving the dented Mercury I saw in Dallas. Lawrence looked like Gene Autry if the singing cowboy hero had decided to be a farmer, instead.

As we drove out through the hills, the dirt road grew narrow and there was no place to turn around, no place to turn back if I decided I really didn't want to go to camp after all. It seemed the end of the world as we drove under the big, metal "LZ Camp" letters suspended from a long, steel cable. The dusty road finally led us to a little "town" of stark, squatty, flatroofed cement buildings — the camp's office, dining hall, and bunkhouses. They stood alone on the bare, treeless prairie, like a remote cowboy outpost of the Old West. But where were the singing cowboys who were supposed to be sitting around strumming their guitars?

"It's suppertime. You run on in and get something to eat; I'll stow your gear in the bunkhouse," said Lawrence, pulling up in front of the dining hall.

Walking through the door into the room, I saw long tables filled with noisy, hungry campers. Suddenly, I heard someone shouting at me from the kitchen.

"Wo, honey. Watchoo doin' here? I thought you were at camp with Bedford."

It was Belzora, who lived with her sister in the servant's quarters down the alley from us in Dallas, and helped our Sally now and then. She would be the camp cook for the summer. I blushed as she gave me a great big hug, hoping no one had heard my old nickname. If they did, there was the distinct possibility I'd be called "Wo" for the rest of my life.

I plopped on a bench at a big table where a quiet young man read his bible. He was Clarence, a tall, slim, soft-spoken divinity student from Southern Methodist University, who'd be our counselor at the "Anchor T" bunkhouse with six of us younger, eleven-year-old campers.

Just then we heard a car racing up the dusty road, and looking out the window, we saw a big, black limousine pull up in front of the "Anchor T." A uniformed driver opened the door for a short, roly-poly new camper, then carried his bag inside.

"Boy, he sure must be rich," said one of the campers.

"Sure is fat," said another. "He looks like Porky Pig. Belzora's gonna hafta bring him two plates and two forks."

After stuffing myself with Belzora's steak and potatoes, I went to our bunkhouse and fell into my cot, dead tired. I'd successfully avoided telling anyone my name, being worried about what nickname they might give me. As I listened to the coyotes howl in the distance, I wondered how I'd ever let Bedford talk me into coming here in the first place.

"Roll out, roll out," shouted someone beating persistently on a loud, insidious gong, rousting us outside just as the sun peeked over the horizon.

"Good morning, cowboys. I'm Skip Ellzey, your trainer. Let's limber up," said the cheerful young man, lining us sleepy campers up in rows and leading us in arm swings, side bends, straddle hops, knee bends and sit-ups.

"Hey, you back there. Get to work and keep up with the rest," shouted the leader at the pudgy camper lying next to me on his fat tummy, unable to do even a single push-up.

"Come on Porky," I said, without thinking, "you can do it. Try to keep your back straight." The boy glared at me angrily, and I felt sorry I had called him the unkind nickname.

The, other campers joined in. "Come on, Porky, push hard," they urged.

The fat boy gave a grunt, pushed with all his might, and finally lifted himself off the ground, smiling with appreciation for all the helpful attention.

As calisthenics ended, Clarence handed each of us a milk pail.

"Our bunkhouse has the milking duty this week," he said, as he marched us to the cow milking pen. But despite how much fun Bedford had said it would be, I discovered milking cows to be a hot, sticky, smelly activity.

After breakfast, the chores continued as we trudged to the garden. But instead of gathering flowers, we dug potatoes. Oh, how I longed to get my tired, muddy hands and gritty fingernails around my brother's throat.

"Now, the wheat has to be shocked," said Clarence, leading our little group into grain fields to join the other campers.

"Where are the shocking gadgets to make the wheat grow bigger?" I asked.

"The only gadgets you'll need to shock wheat are your own two hands," answered our counselor. "You'll be paid 15¢ an hour for this ranch work. I'm keeping your time right here in this little notebook."

With this new incentive, Porky, and I teamed up to lean the bundles of newly-cut wheat upright against each other until we had conical piles that resembled Indian tepees. After two hours of backbreaking work, tepees dotted the empty field, and I wished that Bedford lay beneath one of them.

"Time for the morning swim," Clarence announced at last.

We put on our bathing suits and walked down to take our first swim in Wolf Creek, but were disappointed to find it filled with reddish-brown water only waist deep.

"Where's the raft and the diving board and the rope swing?" I asked, remembering the movie.

"Had a big storm the other night and the flash floodwaters broke the dam; washed half of Ochiltree County into the creek, from the looks of the water," said Clarence. "But Lawrence'll get some mules and rebuild it in a day or two and float the raft back up."

I imagined Bedford down at Kerrville, swimming in the crystal-clear Guadalupe River and pictured myself there — drowning him.

After lunch, the much-needed rest period finally came for us tired, sore hired hands. While a cool, dry breeze blew through camp, the fierce West Texas sun beat down on our small, concrete bunkhouse that stood there defenseless on the treeless prairie. A buzzing swarm of irritating flies circled our hot, crowded bunkroom as I lay there, feeling like a fly-covered roll being baked in an oven. Finally, I dropped off into a deep sleep. But soon, the screen door flew open.

"Okay cowboys, it's time to go get your horses," shouted riding instructor Jack Ellzey, cutting through the haze of my afternoon nap. "We're gonna saddle up and go riding!"

When we reached the rodeo corral, Mr. Ellzey was waiting for us, perched atop his horse, "Bad Boy," who had the star of a frontier marshal on its forehead. He wore wide, leather chaps, decorated with silver medallions and the letters "LZ" spelled out in brads across the flared bottoms, and a tall, crumpled white hat with a personality all its own. Milling around him were 40 magnificent horses — one for each camper. Which would be mine, I wondered?

"How much riding have you done, Overton?" asked the old cowboy with a stern expression on his face.

"Oh, I've spent a lot of time on horseback," I answered, thinking back to the many times I'd been led around the ring on a Shetland pony.

He stared down with piercing eyes for a moment, then rode on to the next camper. After he'd finished his interviews and made a few mental notes, he came back down the line assigning us our horses.

"Overton, you'll be riding Tango. You take good care of him, and he'll take good care of you," he said as a benevolent, protective look came over his face.

He'd made his assignments carefully, for while he didn't want to overly protect us campers, he recognized the potential dangers. Years ago his brother had been slammed into a tree on his horse and killed in a roping accident.

"You've got one of the top cowponies on the ranch," said Jack Ellzey, as he helped me select a leather saddle and bridle at the saddle house. In a moment I came face to face with Tango, a magnificent black horse with rippling muscles, wise eyes, and a nose as soft as a bunny's ears. Jack showed me how to put the saddle blanket on his back, the bit in his mouth, and how to pull the bridle gently over his upraised ears.

I struggled with the big, heavy saddle for a moment, then Jack lifted it onto Tango's back and tightened the cinch. I felt a thrill as I swung my right leg over the saddle and sat squarely on top of my cowpony. I grabbed the saddle horn with all my might as Jack yelled, "Move out, cowboys," and Tango lurched forward. We rode out of the corral, splashed across the creek, and climbed the hill I'd seen in the movie, heading toward open prairie.

When we reached the top, I looked in awe at the splendor of that panoramic view. Most of the 6,000 acres of the LZ Ranch spread before us — mile after mile of gentle, rolling green hills that turned to purple in the distance, covered with bright wildflowers and dotted with grazing red cattle. Here and there canyons dipped, and there were outcroppings of pinkish caprock with boulders tumbling down their sides, looking as if giants had been throwing rocks. A sky full of big, white, fluffy clouds crowned the whole magnificent scene.

Overton in front of "Anchor T" bunkhouse.

My saddle creaked like a great sailing ship being blown by winds of adventure over the sea of grass, along with my heroes from the LZ Camp movie. There rode Mr. Ellzey and his sons — Lawrence, Skip, Jack and Charles — finally dressed like the real Texas cowboys they were. Following them came Porky with his hat flying behind him, holding onto the saddle horn for dear life.

"That's quite a pony you've got," said Charles Ellzey, riding up alongside me with a big smile on his face. "He always wants to be in the lead with that funny gait of his. Most horses do sort of a fox-trot when they go a little faster than a walk, but yours does a tango."

Suddenly, I'd grown to eight feet tall as I strode across the prairie on my wonderful Tango. Together, we were as big and strong, as fast and agile, as old and wise as anyone I thought as we rode on top of the highest caprock. It was glorious riding the range with the Ellzeys, and I still had our first campfire to look forward to that night.

The white-hot skull of the longhorn steer seemed to be looking back through eons of time, as curls of smoke and flying embers danced before its empty eyes and flames flickered below. We took our seats on the rocks around the fire circle, feeling that some mysterious tribal ceremony was about to begin. Then, a voice from the past broke the silence:

"Ten thousand years ago, Indians came to these high plains — wave after wave, spreading out to hunt and live. Here, they found abundant buffalo, antelope and mustang along the watering holes of Wolf Creek."

Tom Ellzey's voice held our imaginations as his face glowed red with firelight, looking like Chief Spotted Bird in the photograph of the two friends that hung in the camp office. Yet the words seemed to come from the huge skull that stared down at us from the pole above the campfire.

"Fifty years after Columbus discovered America," continued the enigmatic voice, "Coronado passed this way on his journey north from Mexico in search of gold. Many people have come here to Wolf Creek for lots of different reasons. We Ellzeys came here 25 years ago to work, make a home, and raise our children. What have you boys come here looking for?" he asked, staring around the campfire at each of us. "Well," he said finally, "you're going to find opportunity. You've been deprived and didn't even know it, 'cause you thought you had everything...but you really didn't. Some of you have never worked with your own hands...or earned anything...or made anything — even your own bed."

Absolute silence followed as the hollow eyes of the longhorn steer stared down at us, seeing into our minds, exposing our guilt. Porky and I glanced at each other, feeling conspicuously singled out.

"When you boys go back home," continued Mr. Ellzey, "you'll have earned more than your 15¢ an hour; you'll have earned pride and self respect. Here, at Wolf Creek, you boys are gonna discover the treasure that Coronado came looking for but couldn't find. You'll be rich in experiences, friendships, and accomplishments, with healthy minds and bodies. *Life*, after all, is the real treasure.

"We'll work together, worship together, play together, and...learn together. You'll get a greater vision of real life. For some of you younger fellows you'll find out, for the first time, things that the older boys already know; things that, often times, are not taught at home."

He asked us to go around the fire circle and introduce ourselves to the other campers. This was the moment I'd been dreading. I had avoided telling my name as long as possible, worried about the nickname the other boys might make of it.

"I'm Jake Hamm," said the fat boy, when the introductions had circled the campfire to our bunkhouse. Then, after hesitating for a moment, he announced his new nickname with a grin and a shrug. "But I'm called...'Porky.'"

When, finally, the rest of our group had had their turn, all eyes turned on me.

"My name is Overton Shelmire," I said, dreading the silence to follow that might be filled with a laugh, a taunt, or a new nickname.

"I understand you're called 'Ovie,'" said Mr. Ellzey, smiling at me. "Is that right?"

"That's right," I replied, smiling back appreciatively, and relieved that the other boys had seemed to find my new nickname satisfactory.

When the fire flickered low, Lawrence and Skip played the guitar and sang cowboy songs. Here, at last, were the singing cowboys I'd been expecting. I thought to myself — what an exciting, action-packed, cowboy day it had been. I had made friends with Porky, and discovered that working hard wasn't so bad after all, especially when I was earning money to buy my spurs. And to heck with Bedford and his old Indian war canoe. I'd gotten a big, beautiful black horse named Tango, who would carry me to exciting western adventures on the prairie where I would become a real cowboy, and, finally, learn the secrets of 'it.'

XXVI

The Big Roundup

"Whoopee ti yi yo, get along little dogies," Porky and I sang as we rode out to the open range, unaware of the ominous danger that lay ahead where the trail came to a high caprock.

Tango and I started up first, and the other horses and riders followed. Halfway up the climb, I heard a sinister rattle and Tango shuddered to a quick stop, the sound having evoked a primitive fear in both of us. I looked down in the middle of the trail and saw a huge rattlesnake coiled in the late afternoon shadows, daring us to come closer.

Suddenly, Tango reared on his hind legs, thrusting me high into the air. I looked down at the steep drop on either side of the trail, with the deadly snake right beneath us, and held onto the saddle horn for dear life. When Tango's front hooves clapped back down on the rock I nearly fell off. But I threw my arms around his neck and somehow held on as he back-tracked down into the other horses.

Just then Mr. Ellzey appeared on top of the caprock above us and shouted down, "Hurry up boys. You're late and we're about to head out with the cattle."

"We can't come up," I yelled back, finally regaining my composure. "There's a rattlesnake sitting right in the middle of the trail."

"Well, either shoo him off, or take this other trail up," instructed Mr. Ellzey, pointing to an alternate route.

"The boys can't come up that way," protested Clarence, who'd ridden up behind us on the chuck wagon. "It's too steep and dangerous for the horses to climb."

"Dammit, I drive up that way in my car all the time, and anything I can drive up, these horses ought to be able to climb up," chided Mr. Ellzey, angry at having his instructions questioned.

He motioned for the chuck wagon to take the long, flat way around, then sat impatiently on Bad Boy, waiting for us at the top of the caprock. Tom Ellzey, a man of impulse and action, refused to let a roadblock or danger stay in his way for long.

"Aren't you going to kill that rattler?" I asked, when we'd finally reached the top.

"Naw," he answered. "There's lots of snakes up here, but we've never had anyone bitten. We've learned to live with them and them with us, without either side disturbin' the other too much. He's just doin' his job, guardin' his territory. Now, you've got a job to do, too, movin' the cattle, so get going," commanded Mr. Ellzey. Then he and Bad Boy turned and galloped off.

We were riding out to the open range to take part in the big LZ roundup and trail drive, toward fulfilment of my wildest dream — becoming a real Texas cowboy. The Ellzeys and some of the older boys had ridden out before noon to round up cattle from the far reaches of the north pasture. We younger campers were bringing up the rear, followed by the creaking chuck wagon full of food and bedrolls. Soon we would help drive the herd six miles south overnight to the ranch workpens, where we would be as surprised as the calves by the fate awaiting them: branding, vaccination, dehorning, and castration.

In the distance we could see the herd, looking like a big ball of red fur swirling in a cloud of dust, circled by running horses and waving riders. We could hear cowboy calls, thundering hooves and calves bellowing for their mothers. As we rode closer we could make out Mr. Ellzey, now back with the wranglers, busy chasing runaways with the same enthusiasm and intensity he brought to everything he did. While each of the sons was an excellent rider, their father was a natural. His motions on horseback were lithe, fluid, and confident, giving him the appearance of a much younger man.

By late afternoon, with the herd finally gathered, Mr. Ellzey gave the order to "move out." As the long-awaited trail drive began, we younger boys felt more comfortable riding at the rear.

"Why are you drifting along back here, Ovie?" asked Mr. Ellzey, dropping back beside me.

"Porky likes to ride beside the chuck wagon, and I thought I oughta stay with him," I explained.

"Well, if you want to be a 'tail-ender' all your life, stay back here," taunted Mr. Ellzey. "If you want to become a leader, get on up there and ride the point with Skip."

A moment later, Tango and I were up at the front, leading the parade of cattle and cowboys. Tango trotted in his funny gait, causing the huge fireball of a sun to bounce on the horizon. I looked behind at the lumbering herd of red cattle flanked by the attentive cowboys, and at the chuck wagon that had now become a prairie schooner with a sail of gold. If only Bedford could see me now!

By the time we reached the halfway point of the drive, the broad valley where we would camp for the night lay in twilight, and the moon came up to spell the sun for awhile. The chuck wagon rolled to a clanging stop, the fire was made, and before long Belzora had the pots boiling.

"Ovie, don't unsaddle Tango yet," shouted Mr. Ellzey. "Your work's not done. I want you to take the first night shift, guardin' the herd with Lawrence and some of the other boys."

Overton on Tango

After supper we took our assigned positions around the big mass of huge animals, then Tango and I were left standing alone. I had an ominous feeling of confrontation and heavy responsibility that I'd never experienced. From the campfire, I could hear singing, story-telling and the rattle of tin plates. Off in the far distance, I could see billowing clouds glowing on and off, as if they hovered over a great battlefield. That's how stampedes always get started in the movies — with thunder and lightning, I thought, growing more apprehensive by the minute.

"Don't worry, Ovie," said Lawrence, making the rounds. "That's just a little heat lightning off about 50 miles away. If the herd starts stampeding and you and Tango can't take care of it, I'll be over to give you a hand."

He rode off, and I felt great assurance that if some cattle should break out, Tango would know just what to do. It wasn't long before a couple of cows started strolling out into the pasture, followed eagerly by their calves. Stampede! I thought. Tango felt me move nervously in the saddle and with a series of agile, graceful moves, ran the errant animals back into the herd.

My heart pounded as we resumed our watch. Feelings of exhilarating maturity, independence, ability, and self-confidence welled up in me — all because of the way Tango and I had worked as a team. What a day it had been. I'd survived a rattlesnake, a bucking bronco, and a cattle stampede. Mr. Ellzey had been right — it was good to be doing ranch work, men's work...to go, and do, and accomplish, at last!

The moon had floated high in the sky now, and its light beat down on the quiet herd and peaceful prairie, capturing a memory that would forever be frozen in time and space. How wondrous, how peaceful — to be eleven, and sitting on the greatest horse in the world, on a perfect night out on the Texas panhandle prairie!

"Oh, Tango, you're my fantastic cowpony, my best friend, and I love you. I wish we could ride away on the range where nobody would ever find us and be together forever, just the two of us," I said, thinking suddenly of having to say goodbye to him at the end of camp. I leaned over, threw my arms around his neck, and lay my cheek on his mane.

By mid-morning the next day we'd reached the workpens with the herd. The older cowboys got busy separating the calves from their mothers, running them into the branding pen, and I wondered, sadly, what would happen to them next. I didn't have to wait long to find out. The larger boys started grabbing the calves, twisting their necks, and throwing them onto the ground. Big Harry Bass put a headlock on a bull calf and twisted with all his might as his own feet skidded through the dirt. The calf's feet finally flipped and it crashed to the ground with a resounding thud. The animal's nostrils flared and eyes bulged, and I thought surely he must be dying from a broken neck. At that moment, Mr. Ellzey rode up beside Porky and me, looking more like a frontier marshal than ever in his flared chaps, great white hat, and leather vest.

"Boys," he said, looking at us angrily, "on the LZ Ranch we don't stand around and watch. We get in and do it!"

With that reprimand, I dove forward and grabbed the legs of the struggling calf, while Porky just stood there, paralyzed.

"I'm warning you kid," said Harry. "If you let go and that critter kicks me, I'm gonna kick the hell outa you!"

Having been duly warned, I held on for dear life as Lawrence walked over with a poker he'd just taken out of a fire. The end — letters "LZ" — glowed red-hot. As the searing metal sank into the fur on the calf's hip, the smell of singed hair and burning flesh filled my nose. The critter bellowed in misery as the branding iron lifted off, leaving raw, red letters on its rump. I looked up at Porky with a sick, horrified expression, feeling weak as Jack walked over with some big, long-handled clippers.

Action at the LZ Ranch workpens.

Just as I began losing my grip on the calf's strong legs, too nauseated to hold any longer, Porky threw his full weight across them, pinning both hooves to the ground. Jack chopped its horns off, and blood flowed into the ground from the stumps left on its skull. Charles followed quickly with another torture as he stuck the poor, unfortunate animal with a vaccinating needle. Then came the cruelest blow of all. Skip knelt and reached between the calf's legs, made a quick incision with his jackknife, pulled a slimly, gray sack of round things out of the hole, and sliced it off of the quivering, flinching animal.

"What's the matter?" taunted Harry, noting the revulsion on our faces. "Haven't you ever seen a bull calf gettin' cut? Well, those things are called 'Rocky Mountain oysters,' and some of the guys will be frying 'em for lunch. Maybe they'll let y'all have a bite."

I looked at Porky, trying to avoid seeing any more horror. His round, funny face was caked with dirt and streaked with beads of perspiration.

Sick as I felt, I managed to smile and give Porky a nod of appreciation, as we finally let the poor calf up, for the way my friend had thrown his weight around to help me.

After tending the next two or three victims, we continued to subdue calf after calf, with dulled senses and robotic motions. By noon, the smell of singed hair no longer permeated the air, and the last bleeding calf had leaped to its feet. Mr. Ellzey, who had surveyed the proceedings on horseback, looked down at me and nodded. I had done my job, and how proud I felt!

After Belzora's tasty chuckwagon lunch of barbecued beef and pinto beans, we began the long drive back to the north pasture, with none of the poor lil' dogies seeming any worse for wear. The trip was hot, dusty, and uneventful. When we'd finally turned the herd loose, we shed our clothes and took a swim in the big tank that stood under a tall, lonesome windmill. I could think of no place else I wanted to be, nothing I'd rather be doing. As we romped and frolicked in the cool water, we were washing away the trauma we'd felt at being part of the torture of those hapless calves. And, as we basked in the glorious, warm sunshine, I couldn't imagine a better swimming hole than this treeless oasis out on the bare prairie.

Our trail drive adventure came to an abrupt end as we splashed triumphantly across Wolf Creek, heading back toward the camp corral. There, waiting ominously for me and my horse stood an old camper who'd come back for a visit. Tango had been his horse the previous summer.

"Let me have Tango," he demanded. "Mr. Ellzey told me I could take him for a ride before supper."

I dismounted and my heart sank when the boy walked over and grabbed the reins out of my hand, rubbed Tango's nose, and talked to him softly:

"Hello, Tango. I've missed you, and I bet you missed me too. Well, all that hard work is over now, so we'll take a joy ride and just have fun."

When the boy climbed on my horse Tango and rode off, I realized I had never seen anyone else ride him. This fellow was messin' with my pony, and I boiled inside with jealousy and anger.

I trudged back to camp, dejected, miserable. As I passed the dining hall, I saw Belzora unloading the chuckwagon.

"Ovie, whatchoo so glum about? Didn't you have a good time on the roundup?"

"Sure, Tango and I had a great time, but some horse thief just rode off on him."

"Oh, Honey, Tango's out there havin' himself a good time; ya gotta turn him loose. He's your friend, but you don't own him...or his friendship. You can earn it and enjoy it, and to be his friend you have to give him his freedom. There's so much trouble in the world 'cause people aren't able to share things. Selfishness is built in all of us. I know it's hard to give up things we love. Someday you may have to share a girlfriend; that's the hardest sharin' of all. But Jesus teaches us to love, to give, and to share. Just follow Him, and He'll show you the way. Now you go on to the bunkhouse and get ready. I gotta make supper."

I walked away feeling better. Belzora had told me a way to overcome my feelings of jealousy and selfishness. I thought back — I'd been jealous over toys, dogs, and now a horse. I couldn't imagine being jealous over a girl, but if that time ever came, I would ask Belzora what to do. While the passing years had grayed her hair and lined her face, they'd done little to diminish her good looks. And, she seemed to know so much about jealousy, I wondered if she hadn't caused a lot of it herself in years gone by?

XXVII

The Last Rodeo

The dazzling silver spurs were blinding in the afternoon sunshine. I stood there holding them proudly, spinning their pointed rowels and admiring the beautiful design etched into their sides. I'd ordered them with the money I made shocking wheat and had just received them in the mail. Now, I'd try them out on our afternoon ride with Mr. Ellzey.

I stuffed the sharp spurs deep into the pockets of my jeans and, feeling no small discomfort, walked, limped and ran to the saddle house. Being the only camper to own a pair of spurs, I didn't want the others to see them until I could display my shining new appendages in all their glory while riding the range.

I lingered in the corral until the last cowboy had ridden out the gate. Then I strapped the spurs on my fancy, brown and white, X-ray-fitted boots, climbed up on Tango, and rode out. By now, the horses and riders were splashing across Wolf Creek, far ahead. Anxious to catch up before Mr. Ellzey reprimanded me for "tail-ending" again, and wanting to show off my proud, new possessions, I decided to use the spurs.

I kicked my heels hard, and drove the sharp points of the rowels deep into Tango's sides, like I'd seen the cowboys do in the westerns when they needed to get someplace in a hurry. Tango shot forward, summoning all his horsepower, and splashed past the startled group of riders. He dashed up the hill, over the precipice, and out onto the open range, running with the fury of a whirlwind. What had I done? How would I ever stop him?

I pulled on the reins as hard as I could, but that didn't change Tango's mind. I held onto the saddle horn for dear life with both hands, feeling terrified, like we were going to run off the edge of the earth any moment. All I could see was the endless, flat plain in the distance, and the bouncing sagebrush and cactus that flew past me. I prayed that Tango would come to his senses and stop, or tire out, or come to a fence, but he didn't. When the view ahead became too frightful, I looked behind us and saw Bad Boy thundering up, with the frontier marshal leaning forward in the saddle, looking more determined than I'd sever seen him.

They drew alongside, and Mr. Ellzey grabbed Tango's reins and pulled him to a stop. Bad Boy, with his white badge of authority in the middle of his forehead, nudged Tango with his nose and looked him straight in the eye like an equine patrolman, seeming to ask — "Do you know how fast you were going, kid?"

Now that I no longer feared for my life, a huge disappointment came over me — Bad Boy was bigger than Tango, and stronger, and faster. I didn't have the greatest cowpony in the world, after all. I sat there waiting sadly for Mr. Ellzey's furious reprimand, but Tango, my adventurous, unpredictable friend received the marshal's mild rebuke, instead.

"There you go, showin' off again Tango," he said. "Well, that's gonna do you in one of these days. There's a 30 foot drop-off ahead."

"I'm sorry I scared Tango when I spurred him" I said, apologetically.

"Scared him nuthin'" scoffed Mr. Ellzey. "Tango thought you were tellin' him you wanted to be somewhere you weren't — fast. He was just tryin' to get you there. Don't you worry; Tango always knows what he's doin', and he woulda turned at the edge, but you might have kept right on goin'."

The rest of the group rode by silently as Mr. Ellzey spoke to us. While the older boys winked, smirked and snickered, the younger campers had expressions ranging from sympathy to wide-eyed envy for all the furor caused by my escapade on Tango.

"Now, Ovie, a cowboy uses spurs to lock into a cinch to help him stay on a buckin' horse, or to punish an ornery horse, or tune-up a stubborn one," explained Mr. Ellzey. "Tango has all the spirit and motivation he needs. Spurring will just make him nervous and he'll want to run with you. So, take those spurs off and don't ever put 'em on again!"

I got down, unstrapped my spurs, and stuffed them deep in my pockets as the rest of the Cowboys looked on. There I stood on the open prairie, de-spurred and disgraced, having brought dishonor to myself and my fine horse. I felt nothing but shame and embarrassment as I climbed on my friend and he began walking ahead, slowly. But when Tango broke into his funny, dancing gait, I felt a sharp pain. I'd put the spurs in my back pockets and now they were spurring me with each bounce in the saddle. Nevertheless, I wasn't about to pull them out again with the marshal nearby.

I jerked the reins sharply, angrily, snapping Tango's head back and hurting his mouth with the steel bar positioned between his teeth. He slowed down to a walk, and while I felt regret, my fanny felt better. I still lagged behind when we passed through the gate into the north pasture, where the LZ Ranch herd grazed. Like the loyal friend he was, Porky dropped back to console me and give moral support.

Riding along a little further, we noticed everyone stopping up ahead to look at some cattle. Mr. Ellzey motioned for the boys to gather their horses in a circle, around two animals having a terrific fight. When Porky and I got closer, we could see a bull on top of a cow, obviously winning but what a strange-looking fight! When we took our places in the circle around the busy animals, we could finally hear the words Mr. Ellzey was saying about the struggle:

"...in a sack located between his legs. Now, those are called testicles — that bull has a pair of 'em just like each of you boys does. They produce the sperm that will eventually fertilize the egg of the cow that is made in her ovaries. And see the bull's penis? It gets big and straight when he's excited, so it can be injected into the vagina of the cow during copulation. Each of you has one, too, only not as large.

When ejaculation occurs, the bull's semen is released inside the cow, and the bull's sperm swims up to meet the egg of the cow in her uterus, where impregnation, fertilization occurs. It's all so simple, so normal, so right, and it's God's miracle of animal procreation."

Mighty big words to explain a cattle fight, I thought. The bull and cow continued their struggle as we campers tried our best to assimilate what Mr. Ellzey had just told us and relate it to what we were now seeing. Mr. Ellzey said no more for a few minutes, sitting there motionless.

Then he raised his arm slowly, and pointed a finger of his outstretched hand, looking as if he were about to issue a decree from God. He spoke:

"Boys...THAT'S HOW YOU WERE MADE!"

The words echoed around in my brain, unable to be turned into meaning. I was shocked, stunned, astonished. As the secrets to the mystery of life gradually unlocked before my eyes and ears, I suddenly realized that he must be talking about 'it.' If this was 'it,' I felt sure that my mother and father had *never* done anything like *that*! Besides, Bedford had said that 'it' was supposed to be fun. The bull and the cow didn't look like they were having any fun. The bull was snorting, his nostrils flared and eyes bulged, and the poor cow looked miserable — like she wished she were somewhere else, doing anything but what she was doing.

Finally, the bull demounted and went nonchalantly off, while the cow just stood there, looking tired and bewildered. Mr. Ellzey motioned us ahead, with lesson over, and I thought to myself as we rode off — surely there's more to 'it' than a big bull atop a helpless cow?

It seemed an eternity since I'd ridden out of the corral with spurs and spirits jingling. Now, I rode back to the corral slumped in the saddle, feeling tired, confused...and older. When we arrived, someone was sitting on the fence. I recognized my good friend from kindergarten days, Dick Bass, Harry's younger brother, who'd come from Dallas for the Parent's Day Rodeo, and was waiting to take a ride on his brother's horse. My heart jumped for joy as I welcomed him to camp.

"Harry," Dick shouted at his brother. "Don't unsaddle Trixie. Mr. Ellzey said I could go riding on her."

"Come ride down Wolf Creek with me, Dick," I said. "I've got lots to tell you."

Dick and I trotted our horses a long way down the peaceful draw, past the huge native cottonwood trees. Finally, we got off and sat down in the cool shadows, talked, and threw rocks in the rushing stream while our horses waded and watered, enjoying an old friendship of their own.

"Are you having fun at camp?" asked Dick.

"I was until today," I answered. "Tango ran away with me, I lost my spurs, and Mr. Ellzey lost his mind. My mother told me it could happen if you stayed out in the sun too long. We saw a bull on top of a cow and, know what he said?...that our parents did that to make us!"

"Ovie, he was telling you the truth; don't you know about the 'birds and the bees?'" asked Dick. "Haven't you heard about S...E...X?"

"What's sex?" I asked.

"It's something new the paperboy told me about. Paperboys know everything. That bull and cow were having sex, and so do people. The man sticks his thing in the woman, then she has a baby," said Dick, showing off his newly-acquired knowledge.

"How does he do that? Sometimes I can't hardly find mine...I have trouble just sticking it out of my pants," I said.

"Oh, it grows real long when you play around and have fun with it," explained Dick.

"Say, did you see the movie 'Pinocchio'?" I asked after a moment of thought. "His nose grew longer every time he told a lie. Is that what happens to a man's thing?"

"Yeah, I think it's something like that," he said.

"What does the woman do with her thing?" I asked.

"Whadda you mean, 'her thing'? Don't you know? A woman doesn't have a thing. They just have a hole."

As that new revelation hit me, I looked up into the tall trees. A whole new world had opened up before my eyes and ears — bewildering, scary, disturbing, but endlessly fascinating! I rode back to camp feeling satisfied and fulfilled, saying little, as Dick talked on and on about 'it.'

I knew now what sex was, and where babies come from, but I still didn't know how to do 'it,' or how to make one myself. I decided to forget about sex, because it was of little concern to me. After all, cowboys don't need babies!

Lawrence Ellzey climbed onto the platform perched high in the huge cottonwood tree that towered above the rodeo ring. He tapped on the microphone of the makeshift public address system and made his announcement:

"Howdy friends, neighbors, and parents. On behalf of all the Ellzeys and our campers, we want to welcome you to the LZ Parent's Day Rodeo, on this final day of camp. Today, the boys will exhibit their skills in roping, bulldogging, tying calves, bull calf riding, and barrel racing. Now, to start things off, my father, Tom Ellzey will lead the parade of campers as they present the colors."

The marshal led us into the ring and galloped around on Bad Boy, waving a big American flag and beaming with pride — in his family, his country, his camp, and his boys. The crowd clapped as we followed him around, each camper carrying a small American flag, and waving it enthusiastically when he spotted his parents in the crowd. I didn't look for mine. I knew they weren't there.

Baba and Daddy had decided to attend Bedford's closing ceremonies at Camp La Junta instead. While I felt disappointed, I didn't blame them. There would be the river pageant, battling war canoes, camp circus, and the beautiful Heart-of-the-Hills Inn. Bedford would have so much more to show for his efforts — crafts he'd made, awards he'd won. All I'd made was my pay for ranch work, and like many a frontier cowboy of yesteryear, my money had quickly slipped through my fingers. Besides, big brothers have first choice of everything, and my big brother had chosen our parents.

We formed a line across the end of the arena, and held our flags high while Lawrence played a scratchy recording of *The Star-Spangled Banner*. As soon as the music ended, the first event began. Campers demonstrated their proficiency in roping, bulldogging, and tying calves, some of them using the ropes they'd made in crafts class. Next came the first of the racing events — the potato and milk stool races. The parents held their collective breath, while the neighbors got a big kick out of watching the city kids riding hard up to the barrels, throwing their potatoes, jumping off their horses and fighting over the one-legged milk stools which, like musical chairs, were always one short.

Now the fateful moment had arrived for Porky — the bull calf riding event which he was determined to enter.

"This bull looks like a killer, Porky," I said, as we boosted him up on the 600-pound calf.

Porky didn't answer. He pulled his hat down, gritted his teeth, and grabbed hold of the rope tied around the animal's waist. The gate flew open and the big calf shot out of the chute into the arena, with Porky on his back, holding onto a rope for dear life. The calf took four or five angry leaps, then veered sharply to one side. Porky kept flying straight ahead and finally came down hard on his seat, stirring up a cloud of dust. He got up smiling and marched proudly off, exuding a new image of self-confidence and ability. He had earned the respect and esteem of his fellow campers, most of whom had not been able to muster the nerve to get on a bull calf themselves.

Tap...tap...tap went Lawrence's fingers on the microphone once more. "Riders in the junior barrel race finals — go to the corral with your horses." My heart sank. While Tango and I were one of the two finalists, Mr. Ellzey had loaned Bad Boy to the other contestant for the race, so I knew from my spurring experience that we couldn't win. As expected, the great brown steed raced ahead to the distant barrel at the other end of the corral and rounded it before Tango and I could reach our barrel. But Tango didn't know the race was over, however, and ran like fury down the home stretch, to finish — first!

"Tango, you really are the greatest horse in the world!" I exclaimed as I gave him a farewell hug around the neck, with the kind of love for an animal that can be, sometimes, stronger than a love for another human. Then Porky and I walked side by side to the center of the ring, where Mr. Ellzey stood busily doling out the winnings.

"Ovie, tell your grandfather that you made a pretty good cowboy after all, and I'll be lookin' for you next summer." he said, as we shook hands and said goodbye.

Then Porky and I started happily back to pack our bags, each of us with a crisp, brand-new $2 bill in our pockets.

"Well folks, that's it for the 1941 LZ Rodeo. Thanks for coming. We're already planning a bigger and better event for next year, so we'll see y'all then," said Lawrence, as he switched off the microphone.

He'd have kept that promise, too, except that other men halfway around the world were planning another event — at Pearl Harbor — and the Ellzey sons would be needed elsewhere next summer. This was, indeed, the last day of LZ Camp...forever, except for those days that we LZ campers would relive in our hearts and minds over the coming years.

When I got home and walked into our room, Bedford proudly displayed his crafts projects, awards, and ribbons on his desk.

"Here are all the things I made and won at Camp La Junta," he said, proudly, sweeping his hand over his braided lanyard with whistle, his Indian bead belt, his three-year award, archery and rifle medals, and a "top camper" arrow with a bright red ribbon tied around it.

"There are mine, now where are yours?' he asked.

"Where are my what?" I said.

"Show me what you made, Wo, at LZ Camp."

"They call me Ovie, now," I said, proudly. "That's short for Overton."

"Oh. I never would have guessed that. What did you make? What did you do? What did you learn?" he asked.

What had I learned, I asked myself? I'd learned to work, to be independent, to cooperate, to share things I loved, like my horse and my parents. I'd gained respect for God, nature, country, and my fellow man. How would I tell Bedford all that? He'd never understand.

"Wo, do you mean you were up there at that camp for eight whole weeks, and you can't remember what you made, or did, or learned? Didn't they teach you anything?"

"Sure, Bedford, come to think of it. I learned how to make babies!"

XXVIII

Getting into Ladies' Underwear

Bedford turned 15 the next day and his birthday sneaked up on me so suddenly that I completely forgot to ignore it.

"Happy Birthday, Bedford," I let slip without thinking.

"Why...thank you, Wo," he said in surprise, heart-warmed by the unexpected nicety on my part. "The folks are giving me a dog for my birthday 'cause I did so good at camp and you can come watch me pick it out."

Bedford's words pierced my heart like he'd just shot his "top camper" arrow right through it for I, too, had been longing for a pup of my own.

While Bedford had now spent the last three summers at Camp La Junta, his first two seasons there were disasters. He had come home to face letters from his counselors complaining about his disruptive behavior and lack of accomplishment. This summer our parents had promised to give him the dog of his own he'd been begging for if he'd come home a model camper. Now, indeed, he'd just returned triumphant with all sorts of crafts and awards. I'd wanted a dog even worse, but had come home awardless and penniless, with nothing to show for my eight weeks but a deep tan, hard muscles, and a scandalous pair of spurs hidden deep in a drawer beneath my underwear.

We'd both been asking for our own dogs for years, it seemed, but Baba had always put her foot down. Daddy already had his eight hunting dogs cooped up out in the pen — more than enough for any family and one backyard, she felt. Besides, we were welcome to play with them anytime we liked, and we did. But I wanted my own dog that would stay by my side, and go places and do things with me. Somewhere out there I knew there was a pup who wanted just me and me alone, and I knew someday we'd find each other.

Our family drove out to the dog kennel so Bedford could select his birthday cocker spaniel. While he made his choice of the largest male, with the longest, shiniest, charcoal-black hair in the litter, a small, frisky pup kept jumping up on me and licking my hand, seeming to have picked me as its master.

"I'll throw that little runt in for nothing," said the owner of the kennel. "I been wonderin' how to get rid of it...wouldn't think of chargin' anything for him."

"Wait until your birthday," said Baba, "and we'll get you a really fine dog — not that one. It's got something wrong with it."

When I pleaded that "Frisky" would be the only pup in the world for me, our parents finally consented to let me take him home with Bedford's "Charcoal."

"When we got back to our house, Frisky and I headed to join my friends at our clubhouse across the alley — an abandoned, clapboard tool shed that once stood behind a large house which had been torn down. Thick fig bushes and cedar trees that had grown up around it now protected the shed from neighbors' prying eyes. Reaching the door, I gave the secret knock.

"Who's there?" asked a voice inside.

"Ovie. Let me in," I answered. A long pause followed.

"Ovie who?" asked the voice.

"Come on, you know who this is."

"Then give the secret password so we'll be sure it's you," said the voice.

Another long pause followed; I'd been away so long at camp I had forgotten.

"Hurry. I want to show you my new puppy!"

"We all got pups this summer," said the disinterested voice.

"But I've got to tell you about sex. I learned how to make babies at camp," I exclaimed.

"So did we...the paperboy taught us."

"Wow, that paperboy sure gets around," I said. "But I just can't remember the password. Let me in."

"Open sesame," said a small voice behind me.

I stood there startled as Bobby Jack's little six-year-old sister walked by me and repeated my knock on the door.

"How does she know all our secrets?" I asked.

"She hid in the bushes one day and heard everything. Now we can't keep her out 'cause she knows the knock and password," said Bill Pearson.

He opened the door, let us in, then closed and locked it. Bill then resumed looking at a girlie magazine with the other club members while their pups dozed by their sides. Bill's little brother John sat there proudly, having been the only one brave enough to march up to the drug store cashier and plunk down a quarter for it.

"This shows girls' parts," said Bill. "Here, take a look."

"I don't see any parts," I said. "They all have bathing suits on."

"You have to use your imagination," said Bill, "but I have an idea. Since we're stuck with Patsy, let's get her to take her clothes off and do the *'Dance of the Seven Veils'* like Maria Montez did in *'Arabian Nights.'*"

"Patsy quickly agreed, hoping to earn her way into the club. Having little else to do, we all took our seats on the rough wooden floor. The room had one small, high window that emitted a greenish, leaf-filtered light — so appropriate for the mysterious, questionable proceedings that went on inside.

We leaned back against the wall boards, which had a multitude of hooks, nails, brackets, and shelves that held clay pots, empty jars, cans of dried-up paint, and an assortment of strange things we'd brought to meetings. It wasn't so much a matter of what those walls included, however, but rather the outside world that they excluded: parents, school, authority, responsibility, big brothers...but not always little sisters, at least not today.

While we eagerly anticipated the dance Maria Montez had done with seven veils, we were only able to hand Patsy six pocket handkerchiefs our mothers made us carry. She took off her shirt, hung it on a nail, and began her dance. She twirled and twirled in her little white, eyelet-ruffled panties, waving the veils around her and seeming to know the dance instinctively, or maybe from overhearing us talk about it. Unlike Maria Montez, though, she had no semblance of a figure or any interesting parts. We'd been hoping for at least a reasonable facsimile, and quickly became bored and uninterested.

"Can I be a member of the club now?" she asked when she'd finished dancing.

"No!" said Bill Pearson, emphatically. "We don't allow girls to be members of our club."

"I'm going home to tell my mommy," she pouted, as she marched angrily out the door.

Fearful of the consequences, we bounded out of the clubhouse and dogged her every step, all the way to her front door, pleading with her to come back.

"We took a vote," I said, "and decided you were just the kind of person we want in our club...if you can keep secrets."

At first she refused, then consented to return to the clubhouse as our newest member, and the not-too-secret society's only girl.

As part of his birthday activities, I was invited to go with Bedford and some of his friends downtown to the ornate Majestic Theater to see a movie and special stage show. Sitting on the middle row, we watched the main feature, then came the live performance — a ballet with scenery simulating an underwater kingdom at the bottom of the sea. In the center of the stage stood a huge seashell, and a muscular man who looked like a mythical God pretending to swim in the sea. Suddenly, the shell opened and out swam a golden-haired goddess — shapely and naked! I sat on the edge of my seat, trying to see her body in the dim, murky light, as the man carried her around on the stage. I'd never beheld so much full, mature, voluptuous bare beauty, I thought, as she danced off the stage and the curtain descended.

When I described what I'd beheld to my fascinated friends, they wanted to go back with me to see my naked goddess. I told my mother I'd enjoyed the movie so much that I simply had to see it again the next day, then asked Margaret to drive us down early so we could get front row seats. But when the naked lady swam out of the shell into the arms of her waiting lover, we all felt tremendous disappointment. From the front row, we could see that she really wasn't naked; my goddess wore skin-colored tights and I hadn't been seeing her bare skin at all.

"You really blew it, Ovie," said Bill as we arrived back at the clubhouse, still not having seen any real women's parts. "I guess we'll never get to see any naked boobs."

"I've seen 'em," said little John Pearson. "Miss Baccus gave me a peep show at school one day when she leaned over to hug me. I looked down her dress and saw her boobs — nipples and everything."

"You did?" we all said in unison, excited and envious. "What did they look like?"

"Well, let me try to remember. One said 'chocolate' and the other said 'vanilla.'"

We all laughed, but I felt insanely jealous. How could fate have dealt me such a blow? I'd wanted to see real bosoms so badly, but Miss Baccus, the pretty substitute teacher, had never leaned over and given me a hug. I could just imagine the naked riches that John's immature, unappreciative, undeserving eyes had beheld.

"My big brother says there are pictures of naked women in art books at the Highland Park library," said Charlie Hall.

We walked down to the library and thumbed through every art book we could get our hands on. Indeed, we found lots of naked women coming out of shells, lying on couches, wading in creeks. The bodies in the pictures weren't real; they were painted on, uninteresting. Besides, the fish-eye we kept getting from the librarian made us nervous.

"Wonder where we could see some *real* naked pictures?" asked Bill

Pearson.

"I guess we could go look at my dad's dermatology books," I said as we left the library. I dreaded looking at those thick volumes entitled *Diseases of the Skin*, because every time I had, they'd made me sick at my stomach.

We got several volumes down and carried them into the bathroom and locked the door. They held a collection of pictures of the most horrible, unsightly diseases of humanity to be seen on earth: people with faces eaten away by leprosy; African men carrying their testicles in wheel barrows, they'd become so swollen with elephantiasis; women with bosoms so riddled with oozing sores that their shapes were indiscernible. These were the only pictures of naked women I knew of that were accessible to an eleven-year-old boy in Dallas, Texas.

We drew matches to see who would be the designated "looker," the person who would pore through the pictures of the undressed, disease-ridden people and find the example having the least amount of sores for the rest of us to look at. John Pearson drew the short match and set out dutifully upon his unpleasant task.

"Here's one that doesn't look too bad," he said, finally.

We all looked at the picture of a naked, pathetic young woman and tried to visualize what she might look like without that red rash peppered all over her parts. Alas, our imaginations weren't strong enough to overcome those afflictions of nature.

"Yuk, John, why'd you show us that one?" said Bill. "Keep looking. You can do better than that!"

"Overton," said my mother through the bathroom door. "What are you boys doing? You've been in there for ages."

"Oh...uh...we're having a secret meeting, electing officers."

Soon, the medical books, with the pictures of the poor, unfortunate souls whose privacy we'd invaded, whose secrets we'd stolen in our quest for enlightenment, returned to the library shelves.

After the boys had gone, I sat down and looked through a copy of my mother's *Vogue* magazine, trying to put all the sickening ugliness we'd seen out of my mind. Amidst the pictures of beautiful ladies in lovely gowns, appeared a seductive brassiere advertisement:

Send a postcard with your name and address to receive a catalogue, with color photographs showing our various styles, sizes, and types of brassieres to fit bosoms of all different shapes.

I felt desperate to get my hands on a copy of that catalogue, sure to be filled with pictures of beautiful, bare bosoms. Feeling certain they wouldn't send one to me since I was a boy, I conceived a devious scheme. I took a postcard and wrote my request, address, and signed it — "yours, truly, Miss O. Shelmire."

Day after day, I rushed home from the swimming pool to beat my mother to the mail, hoping I could intercept my catalogue before she saw it. One day after a swim, I had a strong feeling it had come. When I raced up on my bike, I saw Baba standing on the front porch with her hands on her hips, looking for me.

"Overton, there's a Mrs. Johnson from Bestform Foundations waiting to see you in the living room," she announced.

"Oh, th...there is? Wh...what does she want?" I asked in a state of shock.

"She's here to give Miss O. Shelmire the catalogue she requested and fit her for a bra," said Baba without a hint of sympathy in her voice.

My head began to throb and I felt a terrified panic inside.

"Well...uh...what do I say to her?" I asked.

"Anything you want to," she said, calmly.

I walked inside slowly, reluctantly, and desperately alone, wishing I could face a firing squad instead of Mrs. Johnson. As I entered the living room she sat primly on the couch, holding an order blank and my coveted catalogue.

"Hello, young man. I'm waiting to see your sister," she said, cheerfully.

"That's me...er...I mean...I'm Miss O. Shelmire," I said, as I rolled my eyes toward the heavens, hoping I could survive this latest, greatest crisis.

"Why in the world would you send off for a catalogue about bras that you have no possible use for?" Mrs. Johnson asked, seeming more dismayed than angry.

Each word became a misery for me to utter, each question a torment to answer. How could I tell her I did have a use for it, that we had a new sex library at our clubhouse that was woefully short on spicy books?

"I ordered it for my older brother," I said. "He collects books and magazines on inventions and likes to see how things work."

"Most older brothers do. Well, if I can't be of any assistance here, I'll be on my way," said Mrs. Johnson, walking out on the front porch with my catalogue under her arm.

"I'm so sorry you had to come by for nothing," said Baba, "but if you'll leave the catalogue, I'll see if there's something I'd like to order."

I looked longingly at my brassiere catalogue, but Baba took it back into the house without saying a word. I knew then that the Bestform

Foundation catalogue would never be book-of-the-month at our club, and for years I would wonder what enchantment we might have beheld in those pages, if only I could have gotten my hands on it.

The next afternoon was hot and sultry. The cicadas buzzed outside while the ceiling fan whirred monotonously on the sleeping porch. Baba lay down to take a nap as I rested on the bed next to hers. Her body looked beautifully contoured and shapely beneath a shimmering, white silk slip, and I watched her ample bosoms rising up, then down as she slept soundly. An overwhelming urge of curiosity came over me to see her naked, and a way to do this suddenly occurred to me.

"Oh, I overslept," she said, as she stretched alluringly a little later and got out of bed. "We need to get ready for the Starlight Operetta tonight. It's the '*Desert Song.*' Doesn't that sound romantic? I'm going to take my bath and you take yours, too; your Daddy will be home before long."

As soon as I heard her turn the bath water off, I tip-toed from my bed to her bathroom in breathless anticipation. I got down and opened a heating vent in the wall that enabled me to see into her bathroom. There sat Baba, soaping her arms, neck, and breasts. As she got out and stood there toweling them off, I was overwhelmed by the sight of such loveliness — the very first bare bosoms I had seen since I'd become old enough to care. That ethereal moment of beauty and admiration suddenly turned to shock and embarrassment, however, as she opened the door and caught me peering through the vent.

"Overton! What are you doing down there?" she asked, looking shocked.

"Oh...uh...I...I was just listening to see if you'd finished your bath," I said feebly, looking up at her with eyes that pleaded with her to forgive me, to believe my story. She just gazed down at me with an icy, devastating stare.

"Go get dressed. I'll see you downstairs," she said, in a low, distant voice, sounding like someone I didn't know.

As Baba, Daddy and I took our seats in the open-air theater at Fair Park, I looked up at the stars, wishing I were someone else, somewhere else. The show was a rousing and entertaining spectacle, overflowing with beautiful music. Everyone in the audience and on the stage seemed to be enjoying it, except Baba and me. She sat there still, emotionless, seeming to be preoccupied with her thoughts, sorting out her feelings.

The operetta told the story of the "Red Shadow," a handsome, impetuous French Foreign Legionnaire who disguised himself in Arab garb as he championed the oppressed, and pursued women. While his actions seemed strange and devious, his motives — while hard to understand — were always on the side of good and righteousness. When, finally, he took off his mask, sang his last romantic Sigmund Romberg ballad, embraced the heroine and carried her away, Baba took my hand in hers and held it tightly.

Arriving home, my parents went straight to bed, but I slipped out the back door to find Frisky. Soon, a late-rising moon appeared over the trees as I sat there rubbing his tummy. I felt Frisky licking my hand, and everything was all right again.

XXIX

Naming my Poison

The first day back at school brought the usual culture shock and I barely endured it to the last bell. Speeding around the final corner on my bicycle heading for home, I spotted Mrs. Dill, our next-door neighbor out surveying her front yard.

"Overton!" she called as I streaked into my driveway, hoping to go unnoticed. "There you are, dear boy. Come here, I've been wanting to talk to you."

I got off my bike and reported to her dutifully, knowing I'd be stuck for an excruciatingly long time.

"Just look at my Bermuda grass," she said. "It's gotten out of hand since that no-count yardman walked off and left it growing. Now you've seen all the big trucks with 'Van Valkenburg and Vogel Landscape Company' on the side. When Mr. Van Valkenburg was just your age, he used to mow my yard for a quarter, and just look where he is now! I want to offer you the same opportunity as he had, to become a success. Will you take it?"

"No, ma'am" I said. "Your big yard would take me all day, and I couldn't do it for a quarter. Besides, tomorrow's Saturday and I've got to help Hawkins plant our new garden. Have you asked John Pearson?"

A scowl came over her white, powdered face and the last trace of feigned friendliness left her voice.

"Yes, and he wanted to rob me of a dollar and a half, the impudent little rascal...I was just trying to help him amount to something. So...it seems your mother is finally getting her flower garden your selfish father has deprived her of all these years. I've seen the florist trucks delivering potted plants over there."

"No, those are poison ivy plants for Daddy's new experimental garden," I said, walking off and leaving Mrs. Dill speechless — at last.

When I came to the supper table that evening, I found a single boxing glove, for the left hand, sitting beside my usual glass of appetite tonic.

"Overton, you're going to learn to eat properly with your *right* hand, for a month," said our dad. "Each time you sit down at this table, I will tie the boxing glove on your left hand, and that should break the habit of using it to eat. Now, I have some big news. The Eli Lilly Company is giving me money to pay volunteers for my poison ivy experiments — I intend to develop an immunization. So boys, tell your friends that if they want to volunteer to take part, they should be here tomorrow at noon."

With my left hand rendered useless by the boxing glove, I downed the tonic, gripped the fork awkwardly with my right, and began stabbing at my food like a drunken sailor.

The next morning, Bedford and I went up and down the street, inviting potential volunteers to take part in Daddy's great poison ivy experiment. Lured by curiosity, and the possibility of making some extra money, a group of boys followed us home and into the backyard. The former dog yard now overflowed with lush, green plants, tended by a limping black man with jutting jaw. It was Hawkins, our longtime yardman and the friend of every boy in the neighborhood.

"All my friends that do yards got beautiful flowers and vegetables," he said, "but I'se raisin' poison ivy in my garden. They laughs at me, but I tells 'em it's for medical science. Now I don't know what to say 'bout that meat-eatin' plant over yonder that Bedford brought home. It's supposed to catch flies that buzz around it, but he feeds it hamburger meat. In Africa, they grow so big they eat little kids. I'll take you a picture of one when I goes back to claim my throne."

"What throne?" I asked.

"My family was royalty over there, and I'll be made a king when I goes back and have everything I want."

We believed Hawkins implicitly, such as his exciting tale of how he'd gotten his bad limp when a German shell bounced off his knee in France back in 1917. Then he told us he'd been a big league pitcher, easily convincing us when he stunned a squirrel sitting in a tree with the very first rock he picked up and threw.

Hawkins set his shovel down and showed the boys proudly through the poison ivy garden, cautioning them not to brush accidentally against the leaves. The 48 plants had the tell-tale three leaves per stem, one specimen from each state in the union, including poison oak plants from the western states where poison ivy doesn't grow. The ivy plants had been set in long, wood-curbed bins with gravel paths between, and a cedar post by each plant so that growth and climbing characteristics could be studied as if they were prize orchids. The plants had been sent by patients or doctor acquaintances living in the various states, and when all else had failed, out-of-state specimens had been ordered from a local florist.

Everyone stood there gaping at the treacherous assortment as Daddy drove in from the office, pleased to see so many volunteers.

"Good morning, boys. I appreciate your coming to take part in my poison ivy experiments," he said. "This year, a half million ivy victims will be scratching their rashes 'cause till now, no one has discovered an effective preventative for our native American scourge. That's what we're going to try to develop with the experiments. We'll give some of you small doses of pure ivy extract, hoping that you build up a resistance to the allergy.

"Now human beings are not naturally sensitive to the poison in the plant's sap; newborn infants who have never been exposed to the plant are immune to ivy poisoning. Sensitivity is created by repeated contacts, which is impossible to avoid for anyone who lives where poison ivy grows. How many of you have caught it?"

I raised my hand, along with David, Richard Stetzel, Bobby Jack, and the Pearson brothers.

"And how many have never caught poison ivy?" he asked.

Half the group raised their hands, including Bedford.

"That's about right," said Daddy, "because half the people in the country are allergic to poison ivy, and half are not. You boys are immune. All right, you that are sensitive, let's get down to business. A big pharmaceutical company has asked me to develop a preventative. With the permission of your parents, I plan over the next few weeks to perform two types of poison ivy experiments: external and internal. After you've heard what they are, you can decide which you want to take part in. The external experiments consist of patch tests where I smear spots of poison ivy extract of varying strengths on your back or arms, then cover them with an adhesive patch. From each patch test made, the Eli Lilly Company will pay you $3."

Everyone's mouth dropped open on hearing such a tremendous sum of money. Then he went on to explain the internal experiment.

"I'll make up capsules of ivy juice extracted from the leaves by boiling them in ether. We'll start with a single drop of extract, gradually increasing the dosage to 10 drops as the volunteer attains immunity. For each capsule swallowed, you'll get $3," said Daddy.

"I want to help you make the capsules," said Bedford, who was now busy feeding flies to his meat-eating Venus's-flytrap plant. "Boiling ether to extract the juice will be tricky, since it's so flammable and explosive. You'll need an experienced chemist...like me!"

"Okay, Louis Pasteur," said Daddy, "and you can help me gather the leaves, since you're not sensitive to the plant. Now which of you wants to do the patch tests?"

Richard Stetzel, Bobby Jack, and the Pearson brothers raised their hands.

"How about you, Overton?" asked Daddy.

"Yeah, Wo," said Bedford, "name your poison!"

"I'll take the capsules," I said, adding up how much my "take" would be for a month at $3 per dose a day, "and David wants to do it with me."

"Now Bedford, Overton, David...I'm not paying you anything. It wouldn't look right to the Lilly Company for me to pay my own family to help me with these experiments. You'll get a lot of satisfaction out of thinking of the good you're doing," said Daddy, as our spirits dropped. "Now you other boys run home and tell your folks about the experiments, and if it's all right with them, come back here in an hour to start the tests, when the extract will be ready."

Bedford bravely picked a large handful of leaves off the poison ivy plants and carried them inside the garage to Daddy's makeshift laboratory. Daddy and Bedford began boiling the ivy leaves in ether to extract the juice, then mixed it with corn oil and poured it into capsules. Finally, David and I swallowed our initial doses of the poison, taking our first steps toward immunity.

When we walked out of the garage an hour later, all the eligible volunteers had lined up, waiting for their patches...and rewards. Margaret surprised Daddy by standing with the volunteers.

"Please, Dr. Shelmire, can you use me as a guinea pig? I catch poison ivy when I just look at it, and I sure could use the money."

Like so many other children's nurses in the neighborhood, Margaret was a Seventh Day Adventist, a religious sect that held its services on Saturday. Since virtually every job required working Saturday, and because the Adventists took that day off to worship, being a children's nurse was one of the few jobs open to them. The work paid minimal wages — only a few dollars per week plus room and board. Margaret's husband was a talented but unsuccessful commercial artist, who lived apart from her in a rooming house. They adored each other, but worked so hard to make ends meet they seldom could be together.

Daddy looked Margaret up and down and saw her ample figure in a new light. Instead of a fat body he had to keep fitted in large, crisp white uniforms, he saw a huge experimental territory, and went right to work on it, putting three big poison ivy patch test of varying strengths on her left arm. She took the $9 — equal to a whole week's salary, and walked back to the house with tears of joy and praise for her Lord and his benevolence.

Next came Richard, the oldest of the boys. His muscular arms were thin, so Daddy put two patch tests on his broad back, and paid the elated young man $6. Bobby, John, and Bill stepped up, and each received a single patch on their arm, and $3 — an experiment and payment commensurate with their relative size and needs. David and I walked back into the house glumly having earned only acute indigestion — from the poison ivy juice — for our troubles.

Hawkins, noticing our downcast look, tried to divert our attention and cheer us up. "Lawdy mercy...Ovie, David...did you see Bedford's cannibal plant snap up that fly buzzin' around it! Bedford musta finally taught it to do that after he fed it meat for a few days."

Over the ensuing weeks, Richard proved to be a tough, enthusiastic volunteer with highly sensitive skin, and he took, willingly, all the poison ivy juice Daddy and his assistant chemist could dish out. He, too, needed the money, and knew just what to do with it. His stern, Germanic father lived apart from Richard, his mother, and three mischievous brothers. The Stetzel boys always seemed to be getting in trouble, and often I heard their father whipping them with his belt and denying them their allowances when he came for his weekly visit. Richard, an extremely handsome boy, sought the solace of pretty girls, but he seldom had money to take them out. Now he had plenty of cash to go with his good looks — an unbeatable combination for a guy who wanted to catch girls.

Margaret's vast epidermis turned out to be Daddy's favorite, most fertile testing ground. Over the passing weeks, her arms and back became covered with a multitude of patch tests made using poison ivy extracts of varying strengths, from different plants in his garden. The results proved highly satisfactory, as each patch of the sap formed a rash a day or two after application, with blisters that lasted 10 to 14 days. Margaret never complained or scratched; she remained her sunny, cheerful self, feeling blessed doing the Lord's work and being paid well for it.

One afternoon Daddy summoned our group of volunteers to his garage for the grandest of all his poison ivy experiments — the great smoke test. Promising extra pay, he closed the doors, placed us a few feet from the pile of dead, dry ivy plants, and lit the stack. When we'd inhaled all the poison ivy smoke we could stand, we burst out the doors, coughing and wheezing. The rashes we developed as a result gave testimony that the smoke from the burning leaves carried droplets of sap for a few feet.

During the course of the experiments, Reverend Valentine Lee dropped by one Sunday afternoon for a visit. As he came up the walk, he noticed Bill, John, Bobby and Richard on the front porch, all scratching rashes on their arms and backs. Bedford met him at the front door, and Reverend Lee inquired about their common affliction. "Daddy rubbed poison ivy juice all over 'em." Bedford explained.

In honor of our minister's rare visit, Baba instructed David and me to come downstairs and sit straight, still, and quietly. During the course of the long, boring conversation, we both began to squirm and scoot around on the couch.

"What have you done, Dr. Shelmire, painted their poor little bottoms with poison ivy?" asked Reverend Lee, being close to the truth.

He had not guessed that he'd witnessed the unfortunate side effect of Daddy's new poison ivy preventative. When the Reverend left, Baba insisted that Daddy immediately stop giving us poison ivy juice capsules — before David and I wore the sofa out.

"No," he said, adamantly. "The boys and I have to keep working till we solve the problem."

Six weeks after the experiments began, David and I had been completely desensitized and Daddy had found the answers to all his questions about poison ivy, not without a great deal of discomfort to his "victims." His apprehension about the one, big problem with his capsule-by-mouth preventative came true. The Eli Lilly Company decided not to market a product where the cure was worse, or at least more embarrassing, than the malady itself. Nevertheless, *Life* magazine asked him to write a major article on poison ivy and he became widely known as the "modern master" on the subject.

When, at last, our dad met with his volunteers to give us his thanks, and settle accounts, it was a scene reminiscent of Washington's farewell to his troops.

"Thanks boys...and Margaret, for the sacrifices you made in helping me with those poison ivy experiments. Together, we discovered and proved some enlightening things that are going to help poison ivy sufferers throughout America. For instance, we showed how a sensitive person may avoid the plant, but still have traces of the poison touch his skin indirectly. A microscopic smear of the sap on shoes or clothing or tools retains its potency for months — poison so potent that it can cause a rash when diluted a million times. Then we proved that when someone gets into poison ivy, soaping arms and legs thoroughly within five minutes of exposure will avoid or reduce the rash; after that, the sap won't wash off. And now we know that poison ivy shouldn't be burned. Only when burned does the ivy poison get into the air — the growing plant doesn't exude poisonous vapors.

"The good news, boys, is that despite the way you volunteers have suffered with the allergy as kids, you'll probably become immune as you grow older. Now, as for an effective, practical preventative — immunization by capsule or pill — I'm still working hard on a cure for poison ivy."

"Yeah, Daddy's trying to get to the 'bottom' of the problem," said Bedford.

Back at Armstrong School, we ex-volunteers found it easier to concentrate without the itching and burning backs, arms, and — bottoms. Everything finally seemed back to normal, and then...

As we filed into the classroom after lunch, I noticed Phillip Harmon putting a note on the desk of Rosine Maher, who'd been developing nicely into young womanhood...slightly ahead of schedule. Soon, Rosine came in, looking so pretty with her light blonde hair and well-filled blue sweater. I watched her, like I always did, as she went to her desk and sat down. When she'd read the note she crumpled it up, threw it in the wastebasket, and began to cry. What could Phillip Harmon have written to upset her so, I wondered? At the end of the school day, when the classroom had emptied, I shuffled through the trash and found the note. I read it, and blind with rage, rushed out and caught up with classmate Paul Stephens, another of Rosine's admirers.

"Just look at what Phillip Harmon wrote to Rosine. It hurt her feelings and made her cry," I said handing him the note.

"Paul read the note and his face became flushed with anger. We'll make him pay for that. Hurry — let's hide underneath the bridge and catch him when he walks over it on his way home. He'll wish he'd never learned to write."

When we got to school the next day, Phillip Harmon's seat remained empty. That afternoon Mr. Earle strode into our classroom, looking more somber than we'd ever seen him. He unbuttoned his coat, stuck his thumbs in his vest pockets, and began to stride up and down in front of the blackboard like a courtroom prosecutor.

"Class," he began, "you've seen that Phillip Harmon's seat is empty today, and you probably figured he's sick. Well, he is. Phillip is covered from head to foot with itching, oozing poison ivy blisters. His eyes are swollen shut, and he can hardly open his mouth to talk or eat. His mother has been sitting at his side, hour after hour, putting calamine lotion and wet rags on his blisters, and holding his hands so he won't scratch till he bleeds."

"He had it coming to him" whispered Paul.

"Sh...try to look innocent," I said.

"Phillip will probably be out of school for about two weeks because of his violent allergy to poison ivy," continued Mr. Earle. "Now, he didn't just happen to step into some poison ivy. Oh, no, he was brutally assaulted by two of his classmates, who dragged him through a whole yard filled with poison ivy plants. Those two boys are sitting in this very room, and they know who they are, but what we don't know is why they did it. Their parents don't know. Even Phillip doesn't know. Can any person in this room give me one good reason why Phillip Harmon should have been treated like that?"

The class remained perfectly quiet. I glanced over at Rosine, knowing that she, at least, understood why we'd done it. I kept hoping she would raise her hand, tell all, and exonerate us — but she didn't. Rosine sat there motionless, impassive, never looking our way.

"There, you have it," said Mr. Earle. "Not one person in this room has a single excuse or any explanation at all for this cowardly attack by two bullies on one defenseless, blameless boy who hadn't done a thing to them."

I beamed with pride for a moment, having been referred to as a "bully."

"Now as to their punishment," continued Mr. Earle, "I'm not allowed to inflict one as severe as their misconduct deserves. I will speak with the parents of Overton Shelmire and Paul Stephens and suggest they make the punishment sufficiently strong to fit this dastardly crime!"

Paul and I sank down into our seats as everyone in the class, except Rosine Maher, turned to stare at us.

I put off going home after school until the very last moment before supper. When I walked to the table and sat down, I noticed that Daddy, for the first time in a month, had neglected to put out the boxing glove for me to wear on my left hand.

"Daddy's going to be late for supper," said Baba. "Mrs. Harmon called him and said you'd dragged Phillip all through your father's poison ivy. He's gone over to treat the blisters, and Bedford went with him. I understand the poor little boy's got them from head to foot and is going to miss two whole weeks of school. His mother is furious. Overton, why did you do such a cruel thing?"

I picked up my fork and quickly stuffed my mouth with food so I wouldn't be able to answer.

"You must have had some reason. What did he do?" she asked, but more silence followed. "I just can't tell you how shocked and disappointed I am that you'd do a thing like that. Now you must tell us what he did, or you'll be punished worse than you can imagine."

"He wrote a note to Rosine, and it made her cry all afternoon," I said, between bites.

"What did the note say?" she insisted on knowing.

"I can't tell you," I answered.

"You must tell me!"

"I just can't," I said.

"If you can't tell me, who can you tell?" she said, softly. "I'm your mother."

I thought quietly for a minute, lowered my head, gritted my teeth, and hoped I could get those words out.

"The note said... 'Rosine, your tits are too big.'"

She looked around the room for a moment, then her eyes landed on my fork.

"Overton Shelmire," she said, changing the subject, "do you realize that you're eating with your left hand again?"

XXX

The Big Tooth

When Paul and I arrived at class the next morning our teacher and classmates glared at us like we were hatchet murderers. Mr. Earle's strong indictment had punished us worse than a paddling. At recess we sought the seclusion of the old stone bridge as we discussed all the trouble Phillip Harmon's hypersensitivity to poison ivy had gotten us into.

"Oh my gosh, there goes the bell. We're late to assembly!" said Paul — we'd stayed too long across the street.

We raced to the auditorium and Paul beat me to the only remaining seat on the back row. I spotted another empty seat on the first row and decided to go around to the stage door, duck in and sit down before the program began. When I reached the door and looked in the auditorium, Mr. Earle was standing on the stage starting his announcements. I wasn't about to go in and sit in front of him again after his tirade against us the day before.

As I looked up and down the hall, wondering what to do next, I saw a large, light-colored object floating toward me. As it got closer, I could make out a huge, white, enameled tooth, with roots so long they nearly touched the floor. It walked up to me on thin legs covered in black tights, and it held a giant toothbrush in its spidery arms that stuck out the sides.

"Hello, I'm the Big Tooth," it said, in a strange, far-away voice which sounded neither male nor female, neither old nor young.

Not knowing what to say, I just nodded — I had never met a tooth before.

"Little boy, do you brush your teeth twice a day?" asked the Big Tooth, as Mr. Earle droned on inside the auditorium.

"Sometimes I forget," I admitted.

"Well, when you do brush, do you do it up and down correctly like this?" it asked, demonstrating with the big toothbrush, "or do you scrub sideways like that, which wears your enamel away?"

"Like that," I admitted.

"Do you eat lots of candy and drink sugary drinks?"

"Lots and lots," I said.

"Do you see your dentist for a checkup twice a year?"

"I can't remember," I said.

"Do you drink all your milk and cod-liver oil?"

"Not all of it," I replied.

"Young man, if you don't change your bad dental habits, your teeth are going to get cavities, and decay inside...like this!"

Suddenly, the Big Tooth swung open and I stepped back in revulsion. The inside looked all black, rotten, and puss-filled.

Then, one of the teachers opened the door and motioned for the tooth to come into the auditorium, and we heard Mr. Earle make the introduction.

"And now students, we have a mystery guest who's going to give us some healthy tips during this week's personal hygiene lesson."

The huge molar swung its two parts back together again, and without saying goodbye, pattered inside and climbed the steps to the stage.

"Hello kids. I'm the Big Tooth, and I want to tell you how to keep your teeth bright and healthy, and in your head. We don't want them falling out someday, now do we?"

"No," said the students in unison, giggling with amusement. The audience became more serious as the Big Tooth went over all the hazards of owning teeth. When it opened up and showed its decayed insides, everyone gasped.

The moment the program ended and the Big Tooth had happily gone, the students stood up, and I slipped in and sat down on the front row. A second later, Fairfax Smith, the girl who'd been affected by the Big Tooth more deeply than anyone else, it seemed, threw up on the floor right in front of me. I looked at my teacher who'd seen me sneak in, then down at the horrible mess and realized what a mess I'd been making of my life at school lately.

The welcomed weekend finally came and on Sunday afternoon — with all the furor over Phillip Harmon's demise now forgotten — we decided to go roller skating. We stepped onto our metal skates, took our skate keys and cranked the steel cleats tight over our leather soles. Then Paul, Bobby, Charlie, and I skated down the street to the top of the steep hill overlooking Lakeside Drive along Turtle Creek.

At the signal, we pushed off together, shoving and jostling for position, and raced down the long incline in the middle of the street with sparks flying from the spinning steel wheels that carried us at breakneck speed. Reaching the bottom of the hill, I flew across Lakeside Drive and, unable to make the difficult turn, hit the curb, flipped in the air, and rolled into a clump of bushes at the edge of the lake. I'd skinned my knees and my skates had come off. With blood streaming down my shins, I waved the other contestants on and headed home for first aid.

As I turned into our driveway and rolled past the open windows of the sun parlor, I could hear Baba listening to the Sunday afternoon concert of the New York Philharmonic. Suddenly, the beautiful music stopped, and a man came on the radio with an announcement:

> *We interrupt this program to bring you a special news bulletin. The Japanese have attacked Pearl Harbor, Hawaii by air, President Roosevelt has just announced. The attack also was made on all naval and military activities on the principal island of Oahu. Stay turned for further announcements.*

Trying to fathom the meaning of what I'd just heard, I pulled my skates off and ran inside the house, finding Baba, Daddy, and Bedford staring into the radio as if hypnotized. We sat waiting for more news, waiting for an explanation.

"The Japanese just bombed our fleet at Pearl Harbor, and now we're right in the middle of the big war," said Daddy, with an explanation we could all understand.

"Where is Pearl Harbor?" I asked.

"It's a United States naval base in Hawaii," said Baba.

I left the house feeling angry, frightened, and bewildered. I put on my skates, and set out to find my friends and see if they'd heard the news. As I rolled out the driveway, a big, cardboard box blocked my way. David and his friend, Heinz, who had moved to our neighborhood from Germany, were playing "air raid." Heinz, pretending to be a German bomber, threw rocks while David — an unusually jolly occupant of a London bomb shelter — hid in the box. Being in the mood to throw something myself, I decided to participate in the childish game for a moment. I picked up a rock from the flower bed and bounced it off the box.

"Ha, ha, ya missed me," yelled David, sticking his head out from the rear of the shelter.

I bounced a few more rocks off the side, each provoking a happy response and a taunt from the occupant inside. With no more rocks handy, I picked up a piece of brick, and it made a big, satisfying "explosion" as it bounced off the side.

"You can't hit the side of a barn. Come on, drop another bomb," yelled David.

I didn't want to take my skates off to look for more ammunition. Just then, I caught sight of a hatchet that Hawkins had left sitting on the nearby side steps. That would make a fine bomb, I thought.

I picked it up and flipped it casually toward the box. The blade struck the side with a thud, and it stuck in as neatly as if I'd been throwing at a target.

"Ouch...oh...oo...ah," came sounds of pain and fright from inside. Heinz and I watched in disbelief as David stumbled out of the box with blood streaming from the top of his head, which he'd been holding close to the side of the box. The hatchet blade had split his scalp, but, by some miracle, hadn't penetrated his skull.

Summoned by David's screams and yells, our parents and Bedford rushed out of the house, aghast to see the bloody hatchet lying next to the cardboard box and David's face and clothes covered with blood. Daddy got a bandage and wrapped David's head, then went to get the car as Baba comforted David and dried his tears.

"First the Japanese strike Pearl Harbor, then you hit your little brother with a hatchet. I don't understand what's going on," said Baba as they drove off to Parkland Hospital for stitches, leaving me in a state of shock, fear, and deep remorse.

The next afternoon, Congress declared war on Japan and President Roosevelt spoke to the nation on the radio. While our country entered a world conflict, and grown men planned the deadly game of war, we planned a game of our own after school — football in Tom Dees' backyard, right next to Rosine's house. I always played there with extra determination, hoping that my athletic prowess might not go unnoticed.

"Whew, boy! Did President Roosevelt ever sound mad at those Japs," said Bill Pearson. "I bet he's gonna fix 'em good!"

"Yeah, my dad said he had never voted for Roosevelt, but he's behind the President all the way, now," said Bobby. "How about your dad, Ovie?"

"Oh, he's never agreed with Roosevelt on anything. He's a Wendell Wilkie man," I said.

"Remember that big football game at school we had last year to see who was gonna be elected president, and you Wilkie guys got slaughtered?' asked Charlie Hall.

I thought back to the November just prior to the 1940 presidential election. The boys whose fathers supported Roosevelt had been taunting those of us from Wilkie families, and challenged us to a football game to decide who would be the next President of the United States. When we had lined up that day for the kickoff, the Roosevelt team had

16 players, and only eight of us played for Wendell Wilkie, about the same odds we'd had for the F.D.R. — Alf Landon challenge game back in 1936. On both occasions, our Republican teams had been pounded, bashed, and bruised.

"Yeah, let's divide up and play another presidential game," said Tom. "Okay, all Roosevelt guys at this end, and Wilkie players get down there."

Rosine now sat on her back steps observing the proceedings, so I reluctantly accepted the challenge to do battle to decide the election one more time. The large Roosevelt squad kicked off to our anemic Wilkie team and before long, our side lagged several touchdowns behind. When I got the ball and saw Rosine looking my way, I burst straight through the line and headed for the goal, but before I could get there, someone grabbed an ankle and brought me to a standstill. I closed my eyes and waited for the other players to pounce. A second later, the entire weight of Franklin Delano Roosevelt crushed me to the ground. When the other team got off me, one of my legs was locked painfully at the knee.

"Oh, what's wrong with your poor leg, Overton?" asked Rosine sympathetically as I limped past her house.

"My knee joint's frozen and I can't bend it," I answered. I forgot the pain and felt a sudden surge of excitement. I had worshiped Rosine from afar — her pretty face, hair, figure, but she'd never even spoken to me. Now I discovered a voice, a warmth, a personality to go with those other essentials.

"I'm sorry, but who won the game?" she asked.

"Roosevelt, by a landslide!" I answered as I limped off toward home, having decided to stay out of politics for awhile.

Daddy inspected my knee, but could find nothing wrong. "It's just a bruise, Wo. Your knee will probably be black and blue tomorrow." The next day, however, my knee was still locked in a straight position with no sign of a bruise or injury of any kind. That morning, the war broadened as Germany and Italy declared war on us and we on them.

The coming of the Christmas season found everyone's spirit subdued, especially mine. As the allies continued to suffer defeat after defeat, my leg remained mysteriously locked at the knee. Then, a couple of days after the start of the new year, a blizzard hit the city with ice, snow and paralyzing cold.

The next morning I sat in the window with my stiff leg propped up, wishing I could go out and frolic in the snow. Hawkins worked inside the house that day, taking the Christmas tree down and staying just as near to the floor furnace as he could. We noticed my neighborhood friends coming across the street. They had draped white sheets over their coats, carried barrel staves, and had BB guns strapped to their backs.

"Them boys must be plum crazy, out in weather like this, dressed up like little Ku Klux Klan guys," said Hawkins.

I opened the door, and there my pals stood all garbed in white and breathing frosty breath, obviously enjoying one of Dallas' rare snows.

"Want to come out and play Finnish ski troops with us, Ovie?" asked Bill Pearson.

Since Pearl Harbor, they liked to play war, instead of westerns. There had been no Allied military victories to portray, no living heroes to impersonate, so it took a little extra imagination. The most inspiring battle story to hit the news, some months back, had been about the white-garbed, Finnish ski troops who outfought the Russian invaders in the snowy forests while defending their homeland.

"I can't play with you," I said. "My leg's still too stiff from the Roosevelt-Wilkie football game. Now you've got the snow, but where are y'all gonna find a forest?"

"Well, we might just make one in your backyard so you'll have a forest to look out at while you're shut in," said Bill.

Hawkins and I watched as the boys headed for the alley. In a moment, each returned, dragging a discarded Christmas tree. They spent the entire morning going up and down neighborhood alleys until they'd collected dozens of trees. Our backyard had been transformed into a winter wonderland — a forest of green, and flocked white, pink, and blue Christmas trees, reflecting the tastes of their previous owners this Christmas season. With the scenery complete, the boys strapped the barrel staves on their feet to become skis, took their BB guns from around their shoulders, and disappeared into the "woods" for another afternoon of glorious, heroic, make-believe warfare.

Later, Hawkins put on his coat to go outside, and I limped out with him to see how the war game was going.

"BAM BAM...BAM BAM," went the guns. "Fall down, you're Russian generals, and we just ambushed you!" said Bill as they skied out of the pastel forest and surprised us.

"Let me go carry this box to the alley for Miz Shelmire," said Hawkins, "an' I'll be any kinda general you want. Ya know, I tried to enlist in the army just yesterday to go fight Hitler, but they turned me down, since I still have this piece of artillery shell in my knee from fightin' the Kaiser."

A moment later, Hawkins and I lay in the snow between flocked Christmas trees — a white Russian and a black Russian — each with a frozen knee. Baba was waiting for me when I came back inside.

"Overton, your knee's been stiff for over a month now, and when you won't get out and play in the snow, then I know something's really, really wrong with your leg. I just made a doctor's appointment for you."

The next afternoon, the orthopedic specialist seemed mystified when he'd finished examining my knee and could find no reason for the locked joint. Then, when the X-rays were developed, he looked at the film in amazement.

"Why, it's a Victrola needle. I can't imagine how it got so deep into the middle of the knee joint without being surgically implanted," exclaimed the doctor.

"I'll tell you how it got there," said Baba as she hugged me, showing a mixture of shock and relief. "He fell down playing football, and that needle must have been sticking up in the grass, and it went into his knee without leaving a trace. His leg was bent, and when a friend jerked it straight, the needle must have worked its way into the middle of his joint."

They scheduled me for knee surgery the next day. The nurse placed a rubber mask over my face, instructing me to breathe deeply and count down from 10. The gas smelled sickening sweet, and when I reached six, I felt light and began to fall through a long, checkerboard tube with a loud, buzzing noise in my ears.

I fell and fell and fell, finally landing right in my hospital bed, with Baba sitting next to me. A moment later, the door opened and Daddy walked in, then Bedford carrying a little wind-up phonograph. He set it down, and it started playing a record with the needle that the doctor had just taken out of my knee!

One afternoon when I was home recovering from knee surgery, Bedford walked in our room and found me struggling with a tangled maze of wool yarn and long, metal needles. We'd been told at school that knitting a scarf for a British RAF flyer was one of the projects we could do to help the Allied war effort.

"Wo, you look like you're practicing to become a grandmother," scoffed Bedford. "At the rate you're going, that British flyer's gonna freeze to death before you finish his scarf. I'm gonna make some of those solid, black-painted scale models for the Air Force so they can teach our flyers to identify all the different kinds of friendly and enemy aircraft."

"I thought you were gonna build a big flying model so you could use the little gasoline engine you bought," I said.

"No, the Japanese have cut off the balsa wood and rubber supply.

The model kits come with pine parts now, and a heavy pine plane couldn't make it off the ground. And now with gas rationing, I probably wouldn't be able to keep it running. I can't even make a rubber-powered, wind-up plane anymore or buy new rubber tennis shoes. Then there's sugar rationing, and a good candy bar is hard to find these days. War is hell!"

"Well, if you don't have any use for your airplane motor anymore, can I use it?" I asked. "I want to screw it down to the bench, crank it, watch it run, and tinker with it. Then, when the war's over, I'll build a big balsa wood plane to fly with the engine."

"Okay, I've got other things to work on, and that motor's no use to me without a plane to fly. But how do you think you're going to get gas for it?" asked Bedford.

"I'll just apply to the gas rationing board," I answered, confidently.

A few days later I walked to the town hall and waited my turn in the assembly room to appear before the local rationing board. The war's impact had been felt early in the scarcity of automobiles, sugar, gasoline, tires, and... tennis shoes. Eventually, most basic foods in the U.S. diet were rationed. Today, though, the board met on the subject of gasoline rationing. Most people were only able to obtain "A" cards, which virtually immobilized the family car with about three gallons a week. I stood in a long line of citizens who wanted to request more gas for things like visiting the doctor, and car-pooling.

"All right young man, step up here," said the chairman, having dispensed with all the morning's cases except mine. "For what purpose do you need gasoline and how many gallons per week are you requesting?"

"I have this model airplane engine, sir, that uses about a quart a month," I said.

"I believe we can handle that request without putting too much of a dent in our war supply," the chairman said, finding my request refreshing after all the large quantities that had been asked for.

War was indeed hell. As the Allies continued to suffer setback after setback, the names of many local young men appeared in the growing casualty list of killed, wounded, and missing. I felt like one of the walking wounded, for the Victrola needle operation on my knee had opened a Pandora's box of health problems and anxieties. Baba, having solved the mystery of my stiff knee, decided to check out my other symptoms of ill health she'd noticed, such as sneezing spells, sensitive teeth, earaches, and bad posture. Grand Bunch, who berated me constantly to sit up straight and throw my shoulders back, had convinced my mother that sooner or later I'd slump out of my dining room chair onto the floor and never get up.

Specialists examined my ears, nose, and throat; my bones and muscles; my allergies: I was allergic to cedar and elm, but not poison ivy. Then the orthodontist told me I needed braces, my wisdom teeth out, and several cavities filled. I lamented how my physical condition had gone straight downhill since Pearl Harbor. Bedford said I'd make a perfect 4-F if I were a little older.

My medical marathon finally wound up at the dentist's office, which had the letters DDS after his name on the door. Bedford had said that meant "Don't Dare Stay," and I should have listened to him. I climbed up into the big dentist's chair with great uncertainty, never having had a tooth drilled and filled before.

I looked up at the ominous, long metal arm hanging above my head, with pulleys and drill on the end. Several of my teeth had cavities, the dentist announced after scraping and X-raying them. He turned on the motor of the machine and I saw the rope start moving over the spinning pulleys. Then he asked me to open my mouth wide.

The drill began to grind into one of my teeth, and my hair stood on end as small bits of tooth bounced off the inside of my mouth. Suddenly, the spinning drill hit the nerve, and I felt pain far greater than all the pains I'd ever experienced, rolled into one. It racked my spine, shook my skull, and sent a shock wave down through my body that curled my toes.

Oh, my God, I thought as my fingernails sank into the armrest — first Pearl Harbor, and now this. I should have listened to Bedford...I should have listened to the Big Tooth!

XXXI

Sailing on the SS Miramar

Soon after the Japanese sank the heart of the U.S. battlefleet at Pearl Harbor, a brand-new ship was launched — down the street in the backyard of Dr. Cosette Faust Newton.

Dr. Newton stayed so busy traveling to the out-of-the-way places in the world that she didn't have time to practice medicine. The newspapers, reporting her globetrotting exploits, always pointed out that this eminent scholar and lecturer had earned an MD from Baylor University, a BA and BS from Southern Methodist University, an MS from The University of Texas, a PhD from Radcliffe College, and a law degree from New York University, concluding that she was undoubtedly the most educated woman in the United States.

Her neighbors up and down Miramar, however, saw her as the strange, mysterious eccentric who, a couple of years before, had kidnaped and imprisoned her gardener in the attic. Now she'd gone and built a seventy-foot-long ocean liner right in the middle of her backyard!

Our adventure with the good ship *Miramar* began one day as we walked along the alley past Dr. Newton's tall, ominous back wall and heard the buzz of saws, the clacking of hammers. We just figured she was building a new garage, but as the days passed and the structure rose to three stories in height, with curved walls and portholes where windows should have been, we became mystified.

"One of the carpenters told me she's building a steamship out behind her house so she can take a cruise anytime she likes without going all the way to the ocean," explained Bedford.

"Have you been on board yet?" I asked, as we stood talking to Hawkins while he worked in Daddy's poison ivy garden.

"No, she keeps it locked up, but I'll figure a way to get aboard and see it even if I have to stow away," Bedford answered.

"Now don't you boys be goin' in that crazy lady's backyard," exclaimed Hawkins. "Doncha remember when she locked my friend Mickey up in her attic an' liketa starved him to death? If she catches you on her ship, she's liable to string you up by yall's toes. Naw, you wouldn' catch me within a block o' that place."

It was true. Two years earlier, Cosette Faust Newton had lost what she considered to be a priceless Chinese jade ring and accused the gardener, Mickey Rickets of having stolen it. She had her burly chauffeur kidnap Mickey on a downtown street corner, then haul him up to her attic. Dr. Newton blindfolded and tied the man up for days while she attempted to make him confess the theft of the ring. The police finally got a tip and rescued the unfortunate victim, weak and suffering from malnutrition by the time they found him. Newton eventually paid Rickets $500 to drop the kidnaping charges he had filed against her.

Finally the hammering, sawing, and painting stopped and the *SS Miramar* was finished, but we could only see the tantalizing smokestack and upper deck rising above the wall. Then one day when the Pearson brothers and I walked past Dr. Newton's house and noticed her car gone, we felt an irresistible urge to take a peek at her backyard ocean vessel.

We tiptoed breathlessly down the gloomy, forbidding driveway, shaded by dense shrubbery growing on each side, until we neared the backyard. Before we could get a glimpse of the ship, a long, black limousine pulled swiftly into the driveway behind us. The big chauffeur jumped out, and stalked toward us with menacing steps, followed closely by Dr. Newton — a plump, fiftyish brunette who, while standing not much taller than ourselves, seemed formidable, nevertheless.

"What are you boys doing in my driveway?" she asked in a threatening tone.

"We want to see your boat," answered little John Pearson, the only one of us who hadn't lost his power of speech.

"Well, if you want to see it, you should knock on the door and ask to be invited, like gentlemen."

Sensing that an apology just might work, John removed his knitted green beanie and held it humbly between his hands.

"We didn't mean any harm, Ma'am. We just wanted to see that boat. Now, can we?" he asked in his most angelic voice.

"No! Not the sneaky way you boys have acted, you can't," she answered adamantly.

But as we turned to leave with downcast expressions, a hint of a smile came over Dr. Newton's round face and her attitude suddenly softened. After a moment of thoughtful indecision, she spoke.

"Well, serving as seamen and seeing other countries around the world where children are much better behaved than here might just teach you some manners. Maybe I'll take you and some of your friends on a cruise one of these days."

"When, when?" we all asked in excited unison.

"Oh, maybe next Sunday or so. We'll sail at sunset," she said almost absentmindedly, just to get rid of us.

We raced to our clubhouse with hearts pounding and minds spinning with excitement, and invited John, Charlie, and Bobby to go on the great ocean voyage aboard the *SS Miramar* on Sunday. We vowed not to tell another living soul that we would be foolish enough to venture onto that mysterious phantom ship.

The anxiously awaited, unusually warm February Sunday afternoon arrived. As the sun began to sink in the sky over nearby Turtle Creek, we walked up to Dr. Newton's front door trying our best to look like little gentlemen. John gave three hard knocks, and our knees trembled with anticipation. Hearing no response, John knocked longer and harder. We all jumped when the door finally cracked open. Dr. Newton stood there in her bathrobe, hair frazzled, staring at us sleepy-eyed.

"You're back," she said hoarsely, "and you've learned to knock!"

"Yes ma'am. We're here for the cruise on your boat you promised to take us on today," said John, as we all smiled sweetly.

"No, we won't be sailing today, boys. I forgot all about it, and I have a headache. Go away," she said, slamming the door.

Feeling a tremendous, devastating letdown, we walked slowly toward home, encountering Bedford on our way. When we told him how Dr. Newton had invited us for a cruise on her ship, then slammed the door in our faces when we showed up, I saw his expression of anger turn into a smile as he solved our problem in his mind.

"Wait a minute...I've got an idea. Y'all just come with me and I'll show you how to get aboard the *SS Miramar*," he said.

We followed him up and down all four blocks of Miramar Street as Bedford knocked on the door of every house, and gave the same greeting to whoever answered.

"Good afternoon. Your good neighbor down the street, Dr. Newton, has asked me to invite you to take a cruise with her on the *SS Miramar* tonight. We sail at sunset, about thirty minutes from now and we hope you can join us."

His invitation was greeted with mixed emotions. At first the neighbors seemed hesitant because of the newspaper accounts of the kidnaping episode they'd read, and all the strange stories about Cosette Faust Newton they'd heard. But none of the Miramar residents could resist the opportunity to meet the mysterious doctor and see the unbelievable ship. Before long the sidewalk in front of the Newton home was filled with a crowd of curious onlookers.

The house remained dark and lifeless, and no one felt like being the first to knock on the door. Dr. Newton, hearing voices, raised her upstairs bedroom window and looked out, astonished and dismayed, at the assembled multitude.

"Good afternoon, Dr. Newton," spoke up one brave soul most politely. "One of your young neighbors has just visited our homes and related your kind invitation that we come meet you and tour your ship. He mentioned something about a...uh...cruise. But are we early, or did we get the wrong night?"

Dr. Newton frowned at our little group of backyard intruders, apparently thinking we'd invited all those people, while Bedford blended in with the neighbors. As she continued to survey the crowd, a broad smile came over her face. These neighbors had gossiped about the kidnaping, laughed at her ship, complained about the construction noise, or had shunned and ignored her. Now, she had them assembled in one big bunch, ready to he herded up the gangplank of the *SS Miramar*, where they were sure to be impressed, entertained, captivated, overwhelmed.

"Oh yes, this is the night. Welcome to all of you, but I'm running a little late. Please give me just a moment," she said, shutting the window.

After a few minutes, as the neighbors waited apprehensively, the front door flew open and out bounced the doctor, nattily attired in her navy blue captain's uniform, complete with gold piping, eagle insignia, and white cap.

"Shipmates ahoy! Come join me on the maiden voyage of the *SS Miramar*," she said as she led all the assembled down her driveway.

It felt like we'd been waiting to see the *SS Miramar* for an eternity. Then, there it was! The last rays of sunshine brushed the red, white, and blue bunting that adorned its bow as the colossal craft sailed right through the backyard over a billowy sea of grass.

With the visitors all lined up ready to go aboard, this was the moment Cosette Faust Newton, also, had long looked forward to. Taking the champagne bottle in hand, she smiled broadly and made her announcement:

"This is a ship of dreams, and its cargo is culture, enlightenment, adventure, romance. I built this, the perfect repository for things I've collected in my travels around the world, to take you, my friends, on intellectual and cultural voyages — to stimulate the mind and excite the imagination...to see the world," she said. Then Captain Newton shattered the bottle of champagne over the ships wooden bow. "I christen thee *SS Miramar*."

Bedford stepped out of the crowd, saluted smartly, then headed up the short gangplank with the anxious crowd following close behind. As my friends and I walked past our saluting hostess, her broad smile turned into a menacing frown. And there on the bow stood Bedford, the real culprit, preparing to weigh anchor as if he were her first mate.

Coming aboard we entered a magnificent oval ballroom, encircled by built-in seats cushioned in chartreuse leatherette. At the end, doors led out to a large swimming pool, surrounded by a tropical garden. My friends and I saw a stairway and scampered up it to the second deck, a promenade surrounding the ballroom, so as to avoid an unpleasant confrontation with the captain. Then, from our sanctuary above, we watched as she threw open the bar and offered everyone cocktails.

"Tonight, on this ship of hope," she said, "visualize a world not at war, but a world with all mankind united in peace. Pretend with me that we're preparing to leave New York Harbor for a cruise with stops at many exotic ports-of-call around the world."

Captain Newton rang the ship's bell, then spun a record over the ship's public address system that had the sound of engines and a deep, hoarse-voiced fog horn.

"Look, we're passing the Statue of Liberty on the starboard side!" exclaimed our hostess.

Everyone stared at each other in amusement. But by the time Captain Newton announced our arrival in Rio de Janeiro, and Bedford — her new first mate — had blown the foghorn and put on a record of samba music, all the passengers had caught the spirit and joined in the charade.

A couple of harbor stops later, at Bombay, Captain Newton persuaded several of the younger girls to put on authentic Indian costumes and try native dances. After that, our arrival at each subsequent port-of-call was greeted by an appropriately costumed troupe who would emerge swaying in garb typical of the country "visited."

Somewhere between Singapore and Hong Kong, when the captain decided to climb the stairway with some of her visitors to tour the promenade deck, we boys escaped up to the top deck. Bedford put on Hawaiian music and we could hear the crowd clapping below as the girls, dressed in grass skirts did the hula dance. As soon as the music ended and we'd put out to sea again, we saw the captain coming up the ladder to the top deck with the visitors so we disappeared into the lifeboats that flanked the deck.

"Oh, who'd believe that we are in Dallas, Texas instead of cruising out on the Pacific Ocean?" exclaimed one of the female guests, gazing up at the stars.

"Dr. Newton, is your husband here?" asked another. "We haven't seen him all evening."

"He's off traveling right now," Dr. Newton explained. "When we married, my husband and I agreed that we would do with our lives what we wished, so he and I can be away from home for as long as we like.

There are times when one has to be alone and be just oneself. I have an apartment in New York, a gift from my husband, and I used to keep a trunk in Paris. Before this terrible war, I would be away in Europe and the Orient for maybe a year, writing, lecturing, living my own life, and coming home every once in a while. So, our marriage has been all happiness for me, without ever once having the prison-like feeling I hear so many women complaining about."

Nearing San Francisco, the final destination of our around-the-world cruise, the captain led her group back down to the ballroom to prepare to disembark. Then, as the ship passed beneath the Golden Gate Bridge with Glen Miller's orchestra playing, we jumped out of the lifeboats and circled the top deck looking for a place to sneak off the ship. But our escape to the rear was cut off by Dr. Newton's tall back wall that had sharp pieces of broken glass embedded in cement on the top. We were trapped on a make-believe ship traveling around the world and we couldn't get off!

"We'll have to walk back down the gangplank the way we came in — right past Captain Newton" reported little John Pearson after some scouting down below. "She was standing at the front telling everybody good night and just gave Bedford permission to go ashore."

We crept apprehensively down the stairs and approached the gangway of the ship. Then, when the captain turned her back to close the bar, we dashed through the doorway and down the gangplank. But reaching the bottom, I tripped on a crack in the walk and went sprawling on the ground. As I jumped up and started to race after my pals, I saw Dr. Newton standing in the doorway, glaring at me.

"Stop young man! Come right here to me this very minute," she shouted, then in a calmer tone asked, "What would your mother say?"

The question caught me completely off guard, stopping me in my tracks as I contemplated the answer. What would Baba say? I knew full well what my mother would say. She would say, "If a lady asks you to do something, you should always mind like a gentleman and do it."

I walked dutifully back onto the *SS Miramar* and met its angry captain on the ballroom dance floor. The room seemed so huge, I felt so small.

"You must be the little rascal that invited all those people aboard — am I right?" she asked.

"No, ma'am, it wasn't me."

"Who was it then?" she persisted.

"I don't know."

"I'm sure your mother would want you to tell the truth, now wouldn't she?"

Captain Newton was right. Baba had told me always to be truthful, and since either Bedford or I was sure to be getting the captain's wrath, it didn't take me long to decide who it would be. Besides, Bedford was home safe and sound, out of harm's way, whereas I was talking for my life. Surely she had a dungeon down below.

"It was my brother, Bedford — your first mate!" I blurted out.

"Why, that's mutiny. I'd like to give him a dozen lashes," Dr. Newton said, feeling outwitted by her former crewman. Then she began to chuckle with a twisted smile, seeming amused at Bedford's ingenuity. "That's some way to sneak aboard a ship — bringing his own crew. Well, inform your brother that I don't plan to tell his mother what he's done if he comes over every afternoon after school next week to shine the brass on the *SS Miramar*. And tell Bedford if he does a good job, I'll show him the blow gun and poison darts I picked up in Borneo...a Haitian doll bristling with voodoo pins...and a necklace of human teeth from Brazil. Bet Bedford would like to see those things."

"Bet he would," I answered, backing slowly down the gangplank.

"And I'll let him see my collection of shrunken heads I got when I stayed with a tribe of cannibals in Africa," she said as I turned and disappeared into the night.

My shadow would never, ever darken the bow of the *SS Miramar* again.

As word spread far and wide about our cruise aboard the *SS Miramar*, everyone wanted to see that fantastical backyard ship. A proud Captain Newton proceeded to have one extravagant, late-night party after another to show it off, with bands playing into wee hours. When the neighbors began to complain bitterly over the traffic and noise, she was forced to close her "garden ship of dreams," less than a year after completing it.

Vandals and curiosity seekers began raiding the defunct but tantalizing ship soon after its closing, and ransacking the home. Dr. Newton responded by hiring an armed guard and putting a nine-foot chain link fence, topped by barbed-wire, around the property. For good measure, she had steel bars put on all the windows and jail doors installed throughout the house. Her dream home became a prison.

Finally, after a dozen years of conflict and controversy, the Town of Highland Park took Cosette Faust Newton to court, citing zoning ordinance violations. Months later, following one of the longest, most bitter neighborhood feuds in the history of Dallas, the ship was ordered to be destroyed. The outraged Newtons abandoned their home and lived out their lives amidst Cosette's bizarre collections in a makeshift downtown museum.

When workmen showed up to tear the ship down, they discovered a tall tombstone that read:

SS *Miramar*

Born December, 1941
Died April, 1956.

*Slowly killed by the envy, jealousy
and cruelty of neighbors and
delinquent vandals.*

It had taken 15 years to sink the good ship Miramar. Dr. Newton later recounted that when she showed up to watch the heart-breaking demolition of her beloved ship, a small boy sat down on a bench next to her.

"Did you know that the lady who lived here used to eat little kids," he asked.

XXXII

Nature Boy

As I crossed the old stone bridge one afternoon on my way home from school, I looked down and saw David Terk kneeling beside the creek, peering into the water at two crawdads. I started to walk on by and just ignore him like I always did, never having forgotten the trouble he'd caused me with his "Please Kick Me" sign. I hadn't spoken to him since, and hardly anyone else had either. He was still as unpopular, friendless, and "different" as the day he started school after moving down from the North.

An idea of how to get back at him suddenly occurred to me. KERPLOP went my big rock in the water, drenching David and sending the crawdads back into their holes. As I walked on with a feeling of great satisfaction, I heard the strange little classmate running up the hill after me.

"Why'd you throw that rock at the crawdads?" he asked angrily.

"I didn't...I threw it at you!" I answered. "But don't you know you can't catch crawdads and put them in a jar without a string and piece of bacon?"

"I don't want to catch them. I just want to study how they live in their natural habitat," he said, stirring my interest.

"What's a natural habitat?" I asked.

"Well, it's not a glass jar," said David. "Don't you know the crawdad is a spiny lobster, and its home is in fresh water almost everywhere in the world? They make their houses by burrowing into muddy banks, like this one."

We walked along the creek in uncomfortable silence. Now I really knew why I didn't like him — he talked like a teacher.

"We catch lightning bugs along here in the summer and put 'em in jars to make lanterns," I said, just making conversation.

"I'd rather watch them flying and flickering in the twilight, signaling to each other before they pair off," said David.

"They're signaling to each other?" I asked.

"Yes, they signal for a mate. Don't you know about sex?"

"Of course, I know all about sex but I didn't know that bugs had sex, too."

"Sure, and lightning bugs have the most efficient way known to generate light. They don't have an electric charge in their body — their light is chemical," explained David.

I looked at him in amazement. His dark eyes flashed bright with enthusiasm as he talked about the mysterious secrets of nature. I wondered where he'd learned so much about crawdads and lightning bugs; we hadn't talked about them in school.

"Do you have a big brother?" I asked.

"No, just a little one," he answered. "Do you want to see a vole hole?"

"Oh, I've seen a mole hole," I said.

"No. Not a mole...a vole! There's one at the vacant lot across the alley from your house, under a big log. I take a short-cut through there every day on my way home."

I wondered if he'd seen our clubhouse and learned all our club secrets like Patsy Jack had; we sure didn't want him for a member. I felt relieved when David didn't say a word as we passed the tall bushes that camouflaged our hideout.

"See that hole next to the log, and another one near the other end of the log?" he asked. "Go get a bucket of water and I'll show you something."

I did, and watched as he poured water slowly into the nearest hole. A moment later, a stocky, grayish-brown little animal climbed out of the other hole, wet and angry. It looked like a mouse, but with a shorter tail and ears.

"That's a vole," he said proudly. "It's one of the most numerous mammals on earth. They dig burrows to live in and nibble whatever plants they can find."

"I'll run get a box and we can catch him," I said.

"No!" said David. "How would you like to be standing in front of your house and have someone put you in a box and carry you away?"

"I wouldn't like it," I said, never having thought of that possibility.

"Want to come over and see my zoo collection?" he asked.

"Sure," I answered, fascinated by the small miracle I'd just witnessed.

We watched the little vole go back in his hole, then headed for David's house. Some sort of magic surrounded this little wizard, and I followed him home as if he had hypnotized me.

There, I beheld his collection: cages full of exotic birds, aquariums of slithery reptiles, and little furry creatures. There were skulls and skeletons, and stacks of books on the animal kingdom.

"These hamsters, gerbils, and guinea pigs were born in those cages, and that's their home. Those parrots and parakeets wouldn't be able to exist in the Texas skies. As for the snakes and lizards, I'm just studying them and will let 'em go when I'm finished."

After I'd been shown everything in his one-room zoo, he offered to teach me more, and help me start a nature collection of my own.

When Baba came to my room later to call me to supper, she was startled as she looked in several new boxes that had suddenly appeared. "They're Texas garter snakes. David Terk and I caught them in the alley," I said proudly.

"Who is he and how long do you intend to keep these reptiles in your room?" she asked.

"Oh, David Terk's my new friend. He knows everything about nature," I said. "We'll study the snakes for a little while, then let 'em go. We want to know if you'll drive us out to White Rock Lake Saturday so we can go on a nature hike."

After I promised not to bring home any new "roommates," she consented.

The weekend finally arrived and I met David and his little brother, Roger, at daybreak to pack our naturalist's gear for the safari — including a homing pigeon. Daddy had just begun raising the birds and had built a tall, chicken wire loft on the back of our garage. We had succeeded in catching a pigeon after no small effort, and had attached a message holder to one of its legs. I held the pigeon in a traveling cage as Baba drove us to White Rock Lake.

"No one knows how pigeons and other birds find their way across hundreds of miles of strange territory to reach home," said David. "Some people think they're guided by the position of the sun, but others believe they have a mysterious ability to orient themselves with the earth's magnetic field."

"However they do it, I don't know why you want to lug that pigeon in a cage around with you when you've already got so much to carry," said Baba.

"It's so we can send a message quick in case we're attacked by snakes, or robbers, or kidnappers," I said.

"I hope they wait till your father's home. I've never caught a pigeon before, and if you keep talking like that, I'm turning around," she said.

Baba dropped us off at White Rock Lake with my dog, Frisky, the homing pigeon, and our exploring paraphernalia. We searched, re-searched, and discussed our way along the lake's edge, around pond and marsh, through field and forest. We studied the occupant of each habitat — fish, insects, birds, animals. David taught me their names and how they lived, opening my eyes to the world of nature around us.

As we sat down for lunch and discussed all the exciting things David, Roger, and I had seen, we lamented the fact that we'd had no emergency to write about on a note to send home with the pigeon. Nevertheless, I scribbled a hasty message and sent it aloft with our feathered, homesick friend.

"Ovie...what do you and your friends do in that clubhouse?" he asked.

"Oh, we look at pictures of girls and read *Sexology* magazines, mainly," I answered.

"What's that about?" he asked.

"Well, it doesn't have any pictures, but it has some real neat stories. There's one we just read about this student in Paris, France who invents jack off machines."

David Terk gulped the last bite of his sandwich and looked at me in dismay.

"You know — masturbation," I continued. "He was a medical student and he hollowed out one of his books and lined it with velvet. Then he could jack off in class while his teacher thought he was studying. After graduation, he built a jack off machine out of a bicycle; the faster he pedaled, the better it felt."

"Don't you guys ever talk or read books about animals...or trains...or planes?" he asked.

"No," I said.

"Do you ever talk about geography...or astronomy...or religion?"

"We do at Sunday school," I answered.

"I don't think I want to be in your club," said David.

Baba honked her horn by the water's edge at dusk, and we reluc-tantly walked to the car and climbed in.

"Let me tell you one thing, young man," she said. "That's the last time you're ever going on a trip to the country with a homing pigeon. When it flew back so soon, I was worried and almost killed myself trying to catch it up in the loft...and I nearly ruined a good dress!"

"Ovie, what did you write on that note?" asked David.

"Having a wonderful time — wish you were here," I whispered.

Overton on Safari with David and Roger Terk

Alas, our final day at Armstrong School had arrived. Next fall, we would go to junior high where we would merge classes with two other district elementary schools. There would be strange new students, separation from good friends, and other potential problems that lay ahead such as puberty, pimples, and unpopularity. Today, however, my heart filled with warmth and joy as I traded inscriptions in autograph books with David Terk and other fellow students. We gathered our things and said our goodbyes.

After getting a lecture filled with words of wisdom and a big hug from Miss Young, I went from room to room telling my former teachers goodbye: Mrs. Heisel, Miss Cowser, Mrs. Newton, Mrs. Fulton, Mrs. Manning, Miss Smith, Mrs. Phillips and Miss Beck. Then I walked out the front door and down the steep steps forever — a proud new grade school graduate.

Just then, I spotted Miss Baccus, our pretty young substitute teacher, strolling toward he car. A feeling of excitement, then desperation came over me as I raced after her, hoping I could get there before she drove away.

"Overton, dear!" she greeted me, in that pretty blouse she wore so often. "Yes, I'd be delighted to sign your book."

I stood there trembling with excitement as she wrote — smelling so fragrant, looking so beautifully tall and voluptuous with her long blonde hair falling over her shoulders. She handed me back the book, then responded to my prayers by leaning down and giving me a warm hug. As her loose blouse hung down, my eyes glanced into it, looking for forbidden fruit. I quickly stole away a picture of her lovely, full breasts, and hid it in the scrapbook of my memory.

After we'd said goodbye, I paused as I crossed the old stone bridge for the last time on my way home from Armstrong School. Like my classmates, the bridge had also been a good friend — hiding me away and sharing its secrets. Finally, I turned and headed for my grandmother's house where I'd always found love, encouragement, and links with the past.

"You must have a foreigner in your class that can't write English," said Maw Maw, turning through the freshly-filled pages of my autograph book. "This must be French or German or something 'cause I can't read a word of it."

"No, Chris Semos writes Greek, but it couldn't have been him because he's already left for Greece to see his grandparents," I said, looking over her shoulder to see what the trouble was.

"Well, it's Greek to me," she said with a wink, and we both had a good laugh. "Now you run along, Wo. You need to go out in the sunshine and fresh air. Besides, now you can take your shoes off and go barefooted since school's over. And here's a present to take with you to show how proud I am of you today!"

This inscription had read:

Anne Schilling
(your, friend, anyway

('cause you and David Take put that note on my back)

by writing upside down.
Remember the girl who ruined your book
Remember the girl in the town,
Remember the girl in the city,
Dear Overton,

When I arrived home, Bedford had just returned from his own last day at school and I found him in the kitchen making himself a huge "Dagwood" sandwich.

"Say, Wo — is that a $5 bill I see peeking out of your shirt pocket?" he asked, with an avaricious look in his eye.

"Oh, yeah," I said, almost having forgotten about it. "Maw Maw gave it to me for 'graduating' from Armstrong School."

"So you...finally 'graduated' in...fingerpainting...and <u>Dick</u> and <u>Jane</u> comprehension, eh?" said Bedford between huge gulps. "Well...you better start...getting ready for...the hard stuff...at Junior High next fall."

"What kind of hard stuff?" I asked.

"Stuff like H-I-S-T-O-R-Y...A-L-G-E-B-R-A...S-C-I-E-N-C-E," he said, polishing off the last bite.

"What's science?"

"That's chemistry, and physics. As a matter-of-fact, think I'll give you a little lesson in physics right now. See this plate? I'm filling it with water and putting a penny in it. I'll bet you $5 I can pick up the penny without touching the water or plate, simply by lighting a candle. Wo, here's a chance to double your money."

"Oh, no you don't," I said. "You cheated me out of the $5 I found in the street — with those fake redbird eggs — and you're not gonna gyp me outa <u>this</u> one."

I paused to think. What he said he could do was impossible. Here was the chance to get my lost $5 back!

"Okay, smarty. Let's see you pick up the penny without getting your fingers wet," I said.

Bedford opened the kitchen cabinet and got out a glass tumbler, then a birthday candle which he stuck in a small piece of bread, lit, and floated on the water. He turned the tumbler upside down and placed it over the candle. I watched in shocked amazement when the water rose inside the tumbler as the candle burned the oxygen inside, creating a vacuum. In a matter of seconds the penny, outside the tumbler, lay high and dry, all the water having been sucked up into the glass. Bedford picked up the coin with the fingers of one hand, snatched the $5 bill from my pocket with the other, and walked out the back door.

I sat down at the kitchen table bewildered and penniless, thinking how much I still had to learn...at Junior High...at our clubhouse...everywhere.

XXXIII

Secrets Under the Bridge

So, at last it had arrived — the barefooted, sleep late, do nothing, swim and dive, go fishing, drink iced tea, eat ice cream, stay up late summer vacation — that most blessed time of the year, the prince of all the seasons. And it had taken me all of five minutes to adjust to the pace.

Back at the clubhouse one morning, I gave the secret knock, then the password, and Frisky and I gained admittance.

"I just bought a new *Sexology* magazine and this one finally has some pictures in it," said John Pearson, proudly. "Each of you owes me a nickel."

We leafed eagerly through the pages of the small, thick, wordy magazine until we came across two pages with diagrams entitled, "Cutaway Sections of Male and Female Sex Organs."

"Those aren't pictures," I said, disgusted with John's false perception of what we older boys would find exciting to look at. "They're just more drawings. This one's of a woman's insides — big deal."

The diagrams showed a confusing maze of lines, circles, ovals, and tubes with names of each one.

"Vulva...clitoris...vagina...hymen...uterus...ovary," I read. "Wonder what all those parts are for?"

"Here are the parts of the man," said Bill, going to the next page. "Penis...foreskin...scrotum...testicles...prostate...sperm. Gosh, do we have all those things?"

We gazed at the strange new words — which sounded to me like those I'd heard Tom Ellzey say at camp — trying to fathom their meanings. While the diagrams and words meant little to us at the moment, we sensed that someday they would be important; but for now, their secrets remained locked in words.

"Look what it says here!" said Bill, turning a few pages. "'The Positions of Sexual Intercourse.' Let's read this so we can see how to do it."

"Aren't there any pictures?" asked Charlie Hall.

"Naw, darn it, but let's see," said Bill, with the air of a college professor. "We have the face-to-face position...side position...woman astride position...standing position...and posterior entry position."

"I think Porky and I saw a bull and a cow in the 'posterior entry position' at LZ Camp," I proudly announced.

"Who cares?" said Charlie. "Go ahead, Bill; read us about the face-to-face position."

"All right," said Bill. "Here's what it says:

The face-to-face, or the basic position, is the most conventional and popular coital position. The woman lies flat on her back with legs separated to provide ample access to the vagina. The man approaches by positioning himself between her legs and leaning over her upper body. Then, supporting his weight on his elbows and knees, he guides his penis into the vaginal opening."

"That's face-to-face," said Bill, as the rest of us gazed, bug-eyed, out into space. "Which position do you want to hear about now?"

"It's boring just to read about 'em. Wish there were some real pictures of people doing it," lamented Charlie.

"I saw a book that had pictures of people doing it, last year at our church picnic," I proudly announced.

"You did? Tell us about it," begged Charlie.

"It was a costume party out at Peter Wiggins' country place I went to with some of my Sunday School classmates. One of the church acolytes was dressed up like Daniel Boone in a buckskin outfit and coonskin hat. He saw me starin' at him and told me he wanted to show me a little 'Blondie and Dagwood' cartoon book. He took me to his car, got it out, and started flippin' the pages with his thumb. I could see Blondie and Dagwood take off their clothes, then Dagwood's thing grew big and pointed straight up. Dagwood got on top of Blondie and began to move his hips real fast up and down."

"Then Daniel Boone unlaced his pants, took my hand, and said he'd give me the book if I'd feel his thing. I jerked my hand away, threw the book down, and ran back to the party. Later, we saw Daniel Boone playing bingo next to our Sunday School teacher, Miss Tremble. He sure started to squirm when we walked up and stared at him. Then one of my pals asked...'is that the guy that took his prick out?' Daniel Boone pulled his coonskin hat down and turned beet red!"

"Oh, I just wished you'd at least have grabbed hold of that book and brought it here," said Charlie, wistfully. "Shelmire, you really let us down."

"Gee, it's fun talking about religion!" said little John Pearson.

A warm summer breeze caressed my body, bringing the scent of honeysuckle as it woke me on our sleeping porch. The sweet zephyr promised high adventure, fulfilled expectations, and answers to all our questions about the secrets of carnal knowledge if I'd just get out of bed, and meet my friends who awaited me down the street. The morning had arrived, and we'd planned another walking exploration of the creeks, alleys, and byways of our Highland Park neighborhood.

"Where do we march this morning?" I asked as I joined the small band of explorers.

"Today, we're Lewis and Clark, looking for the elusive Northwest Passage," said Bill Pearson. "Let's go, and keep an eye out for hostile Indians."

We had just seen a movie depicting the famous exploring expedition, the first to cross the continent. Bill was eager to direct the reenactment of that great adventure. We marched, fought, and camped our way down Miramar and along Drexel Drive, with Frisky and the other dogs happily scouting the way. When we reached Hackberry Creek, we launched imaginary canoes and traveling became much easier. After exploring block after block along the water's edge, we approached our expedition's final destination — the mouth of the Columbia River at the Pacific Ocean, which just happened to be at the old stone bridge.

Suddenly, an object lying out in the street gutter caught my eye. Frisky, scouting along in front of me, ran over and gave it a sniff, but found the object to be of no interest to him. Walking closer, I recognized it as a book of some sort. Wondering what might be wrong with this book that someone would throw it away, I picked it up and read the words printed on the cover:

My Trip to the Country
The Story of a Young Frenchman
By Pierre L'Amour
Printed in France

I opened the book randomly to the middle and there, before my startled eyes, was a photograph of a nude man and woman lying in bed, with the man on top of the woman. Staggered by what I was beholding, I stood there frozen, unable to move, trying to make sure my eyes weren't deceiving me. I closed it quickly and hid the book under my shirt, then wheeled around to see if anyone was looking, the thousand eyes of my conscience having seen me pick it up.

"Come on Ovie, let's go," came a shout from ahead, breaking my trance.

"Wait up; I've found something — something big!" I said, waving the book, then putting it back in my shirt.

"Let's look at it," said Bill.

"No, you can't. Someone might see us. Let's go under the bridge where we'll be safe," I said, nervously.

They wondered, as we hurried down the bank, just what I'd found that could be so important, but sensed from my mood that it must be something momentous. A moment later, we stood under the bridge, surrounded by green and the tranquil sound of water rushing over the rocks. I took the book from under my shirt, slowly like a precious treasure. I eagerly showed my friends the cover, then opened the book with an unexplained feeling of trepidation and apprehension. Our age of innocence had been carefree and happy, but this book would soon rob us of that innocence as it revealed its secrets, one page at a time.

I put our dubious, new treasure down on the bank at the water's edge. Then, we all knelt down beside it and began to read together, in this peaceful, familiar, protected spot — far from reality and the prying eyes and ears of parental authority.

Pierre, an innocent young Parisian, told his own story of having received an invitation one summer to visit his aunt at her home in the country. His aunt met his train, and they were driven to her large chateau, where the full staff of servants greeted him warmly — particularly Lisette, the upstairs maid. For the next few days, Pierre and Lisette traded guarded smiles and polite greetings. Then his Aunt told Pierre she'd been called to Paris for a couple of days. In the meantime, the staff would take care of his every need, and indeed Lisette did, beginning on page three.

The next morning Lisette slipped into Pierre's room early to make up his bed, but since he was still in it, she decided to make up Pierre instead. When she awoke him with a gentle kiss, Pierre lifted her prim, black skirt and white apron and put his head beneath them, as we gaped at the full-page photograph on page four.

"What's Pierre looking for?" asked John Pearson.

"I'm not sure," I answered.

As we turned the page, and discovered that photographs had replaced the words to tell Pierre's story, our blood ran hot. Pierre pulled Lisette's dress over her head, then squeezed her bottom as he kissed her front parts madly. In the next photographs, he stood up and she removed his pajamas. Then Pierre lifted Lisette up in the air and drew her close to him.

"That must be the standing position," said Bobby matter-of-factly, as the rest of us remained speechless — knee to knee, elbow to elbow, cheek to cheek, sharing each other's panting breath.

In the next series of pictures, Lisette dropped to her knees, kissing his parts; then they lay down on the bed and felt each other all over.

After that they had sex — position after position after position — all the ones *Sexology* magazine had promised, then more as we looked on in spellbound amazement.

For the next hour, we read and re-read every word, looked at each picture over and over again. Finally, we climbed the hill from under the bridge, having given up our innocence forever. While we felt far wiser, we were bewildered; we had not the slightest idea what to do with our vast new knowledge. I put the book back under my shirt, and we headed toward home.

"What did Pierre do the rest of the time...ride a pony?" asked John Pearson. "Did his aunt come home and catch them naked? Do you think she got mad?"

"Who cares?" said Charlie.

"Listen, I have an idea," said Bill, trying to help us all get over the letdown that had followed such tremendous exhilaration. "Let's go to our house and act out the rest of the story. Then we'll know what happens when his aunt comes home."

Somehow, we saw a strange logic in Bill's suggestion, being in a vulnerable mood for crazy ideas. We went to Bill's and John's house, went up to their room, and locked the door.

"All right guys, everyone get your clothes off. We're gonna do *My Trip to the Country*," said our imaginative and indisputable director.

"Ovie, you're Pierre, and John, you can be Lisette," he said to his little brother. "Bobby, you'll be the butler, and I'll be Pierre's aunt."

Bill directed us to lie down on the bed, with me on top of John, in one of the positions we'd seen in the book.

"Okay," said Bill. "Now you're in the basic face-to-face position. How does it feel?"

"Awful," I answered. "John's skin feels cold and his chest's so flat. He sure doesn't feel like Lisette looked in the book."

"All right, cut," said Bill. "The scene changes to a day later when I come home and catch you two guys...I mean you, Pierre, and you, Lisette, together in bed. I fire Lisette, then I, your aunt, go to bed with you myself, Pierre."

With the script laid out by Bill, we proceeded to act out the next part of the drama. John, now unemployed, sat down in a chair and buried his head in the book. Bill, "my aunt," slapped my face, then pushed me down on the bed and fell on top of me — all was forgiven. We rolled, grappled, and fondled like we'd seen in the pictures, but his pasty-white body didn't feel good, and his touch made my skin crawl.

"This isn't any fun," said Bill. "Look in the book, John, and tell us what we're doing wrong."

"Why don't your wee wees grow long like Pierre's?" asked John, looking first at the book, then at us.

"I don't know," said Bill. "Mine never has."

"Mine neither," I said, "but they're supposed to, like in the pictures, 'cause we're having sex."

"We're doing something wrong," said Bill. "I don't know what, but something's wrong. I have an idea. Let's go see Richard."

We put our clothes back on, with relief, and walked across the street to Richard Stetzel's house. Richard was our hero, our prophet, our guru. He smoked cigarettes, kissed girls and drove cars. Richard would answer all our questions. We found him in his large, attic playroom, lifting barbells. Bedford was there too, busy shooting pool.

Our words stumbled over each other as we told how we'd found the book, studied it under the bridge, then tried out all the positions — but they didn't work. What had we been doing wrong?

"Okay, Wo. Who's the girl?" asked Bedford, frowning apprehensively.

"What girl?" I answered in dismay. "Do you have to have a girl?"

Bedford stared at me in stunned disbelief, then his eyes rolled up in his head as he looked toward the heavens. "Oh, my God...I've heard everything now," he said, shaking his head as he walked out.

We sat at Richard's feet as he flipped through the pages of *My Trip to the Country* with feigned nonchalance. Finally, the prophet spoke, telling us simply that we were too young to understand all that we'd seen, and our bodies were not mature enough to respond to the information it contained. And since the book was no use to us, he would take it off our hands before it got us in trouble.

Somehow we'd heard just what we needed to hear. Relieved to learn that all the confusing things we'd read, seen, and done should be of no concern to us just now, we went next door to our driveway and played basketball with greater than usual exuberance. But the mood of our little group was somehow different for the rest of the day.

We sensed that for some reason, not understood, this signaled the beginning of the end of the bond of our total, innocent friendship. Somehow we each knew, that hot summer afternoon, we had reached the autumn of our childhood when we'd discovered those secrets under the bridge.

At the supper table the next evening, Daddy seemed strangely nervous and uncomfortable. Finally, he cleared his throat and got what he had to say off his chest.

"Overton, I...I put a book on your desk that I think...you should read. It contains lots of good information for someone your age. Please pass the potatoes," he said, turning red and changing the subject.

There it was, I thought, the inevitable sex education book that my friends had told me to expect. They'd said that one day my dad would put a simple "introduction to sex" book on my desk and ask me to read it. That's how everyone's dad taught them the facts of life — usually after they'd already learned them. Now, my friends' predictions had come true for me and I could hardly keep from laughing.

"Go read that book from cover to cover, Wo," said Bedford after supper. "You need it 'bout as bad as anyone could. Your do-it-yourself sex education has really gotten you screwed up."

I went upstairs, intending only to glance at the book in case our dad asked questions. There it was, lying on my desk: *Growing Up*, "How we become alive, are born, and grow." This book explained the whole process of life, beginning with barnyard animals — for the benefit of the child who had no rural background — and continuing through humans. Boy, I thought, if there was one thing I knew about, it was the sex life of the cow!

As I continued to turn the pages, I realized that this book, far from being a children's oversimplified primer, told the story of human reproduction in simple language and meaningful illustrations — a far cry from the bizarre examples cited in *Sexology* magazine. Here it all was, finally — Tom Ellzey's basic prairie sex education lecture, put into words I could understand.

I kept turning the pages with growing interest, as the missing link in my sex education continued to be filled. At last, I knew everything about sex — in theory, anyway. I had learned all about the facts-of-life, not necessarily in the right way and at the right time as Mr. Ellzey had planned, but maybe just in the nick of time!

XXXIV

One's Born Every Minute

I walked in the front door and set my suitcase down, back home after an exciting week on Aunt May and Uncle Bowie's ranch at Egypt, Texas.

"Margaret," I called, but there was no answer. She must be at church, I thought, this being Saturday. Baba and Daddy were in Atlantic City attending a medical meeting. Sally was on vacation and David had gone to visit our grandparents in Marlin.

"Bedford," I finally hollered as a last choice, but still no answer came.

Even Frisky hadn't been there to greet me when I walked up the sidewalk. Nevertheless, I had a feeling of peace and tranquility as I climbed the stairs, welcoming the chance to unpack and be alone with all my "things" that I'd missed. Entering our room, however, I found little evidence that I'd ever lived there.

The floor lay strewn with Bedford's dirty clothes, towels, and wadded up note paper. My prized, battery-operated telephone set had been removed from my desk and gone was my cherished lead soldier collection from the shelves above. Even the half-finished wool scarf I'd been knitting for an RAF pilot had disappeared from over my chair where I'd left it hanging with the yarn and needles, a dropped stitch, and a DO NOT TOUCH! sign.

Suddenly, I remembered the wonderful, big pocket watch Grand Daddy Bunch had recently given me, and I felt panic. The old timepiece fascinated Bedford, and he'd asked if he could borrow it to "study." I had refused, certain that some disaster would surely befall my proud, new possession, and had hidden it away. I pulled my bottom desk drawer out, slid open the secret panel, but there it was — all safe and sound.

As I stormed downstairs to look for the culprit who'd stolen all my things, I heard the back porch screen door slam.

"Bedford. What did you do with all my stuff that's missing?" I shouted.

"It's not missing; it's been 'incorporated' in some things I'm doing out in the tool room. You'll get it all back — eventually."

"I want my stuff back right now or I'll tell Baba and Daddy how you stole it while I was away," I threatened.

Bedford stopped in his tracks, considering his limited options. Seeing no practical choice but to make me a part of his plans, he invited me out to the tool room. The shades were pulled as we stepped inside and a single light bulb hung from a long chord. Frisky greeted me joyously, having been lying with Charkey, Bedford's dog, in the cool shadow of the fertilizer bags, unaware that I had returned home.

I surveyed the room as my eyes adjusted to the glaring, harsh light, and saw a bizarre assortment of unusual shapes and bright colors amongst the mundane, colorless sacks, cans, rakes, shovels and brooms that leaned against the bare wood walls. On a bench I could see the remnant of my once-proud lead soldier army, marching bravely off to a lead melting pot, which sat next to some molds used to make lead nickel slugs.

A bright red and white five-gallon oil can sat on two sawhorses, with shoulder slot cutouts at the bottom, lined with rubber hose, and a view window removed in front and filled with isinglass — Bedford's long-awaited diving helmet! Heavy, rusting weights he'd taken off the tool room windows hung from it. My two green telephones sat nearby, awaiting installation, and a bicycle pump stood at-the-ready to supply air through a long garden hose. He'd thought of everything!

In the middle of the room stood the most majestic motor car my eyes had ever beheld, with a tall, sleek, black and gold racing hood. Behind this colorful cowling nestled a seat, padded with the RAF flyer's half finished wool scarf. On the back was perched a big, silver gasoline motor, with a large flywheel on the side and kick-starter on the rear, taken from Baba's Maytag washing machine. The tires were inflatable white sidewalls with wire spokes. The car had no steering wheel, but rather a foot pedal behind each front tire to steer the wheels.

I stood there pummeled by a confusing gauntlet of emotions: selfish fury over the theft of my possessions; amazement and wonder at all I was seeing; pride in Bedford's awesome accomplishments and in the part my things were playing; fear of the unknown consequences of these mighty inventions. Finally, possessiveness emerged from my plethora of feelings as the emotion of record.

"I want all my stuff back right now!" I growled. "You took my 'Irish Mail' to make your car, and I wanted to ride it today."

"You've outgrown that old velocipede and haven't ridden it in months. And why would you want to keep on pushing and pulling that stupid handlebar to make it go when you can just sit back and let the gasoline motor whisk you along at 10 miles an hour?"

"Whisk me?" I said in astonishment.

Bedford's motor car.

"Sure. Since you're supplying the chassis, it's only fair that you be the first test driver."

"What about my telephones?" I growled.

"I'm planning to fit them in my diving helmet so you can call up to me if you find something, or see a big fish, or need help," said Bedford.

"Me call?" I said.

"Right. You should be the master diver and try the phone first, since it's yours. And about those lead soldiers...Wo, your army was obsolete — World War I stuff: Doughboys, Tommies, and Huns. Your tanks and cannons were harmless relics. What you need is a modern, World War II army. To buy one you need extra income, and that's just what I've been making out of your old soldiers. You'll get half of the counterfeit nickel slugs I take out of the molds, since it's your lead. You can use them for pinball machines, juke boxes, telephones, and maybe even to get in the picture show. Then you can save your allowance for a new, up-to-date army."

I stood there thoroughly confused, not knowing how to react to all the things I'd just seen and heard, when Bedford announced that the car was ready for me to give it a test drive. He put down a board ramp and proudly rolled his speedster out of the tool shed and up the driveway to the street. I sat down on the knitted wool seat and put my feet cautiously on the familiar "Irish Mail" steering pedals. Bedford raised the kick-starter, adjusted the carburetor, then stomped down hard two or three times. Finally, the Maytag motor began purring.

"All right," said Bedford. "You drive it a couple of blocks, then stop and let me have a turn."

Bedford gave the car a running shove, engaged the clutch, and away I went, speeding down Miramar with Frisky alongside, barking, and Bedford running behind like a mother hen, shouting instructions. The car performed flawlessly. and I enjoyed every second of the thrilling ride, especially since my runabout was now propelled by a gasoline engine rather than my own two arms. The test drive went well until I neared the hill where Miramar sloped steeply down to Lakeside Drive.

"Stop so I can take over," shouted Bedford. "Put the brake on."

"What brake? I don't see one," I yelled back, suddenly feeling scared.

"Oh my gosh...I forgot to put it on!" Bedford shouted.

Seconds later the car and driver, unable to stop and running at top speed, careened down the hill and across Lakeside Drive, smashed into the curb, then wobbled, battered and bent into the shallow water of the lake.

"What have you done to my automobile?" shrieked Bedford.

"Me? You're the one that didn't put a brake on it," I said. "Look what you've done to my 'Irish Mail.' I want it fixed or I'm telling!"

"Okay, okay, I'll get the frame straightened after I take the motor off, but it ran like a dream, didn't it?" said Bedford, proudly.

We pushed the wounded vehicle home and after Bedford put the motor back on the Maytag, we hoisted the wreck to the top of Daddy's Buick for the trip to the emergency room of the cycle shop.

"Oh, it's you...again?" said the mechanic, remembering the two times I'd dragged my crumpled bicycle into his shop.

"How much is it gonna cost to straighten this frame out?" asked Bedford.

"I don't know, it's pretty bad off. How much have you got?" asked the man.

"I have a $5 bill," said Bedford, looking pained at the unfortunate turn of events.

"I'll try to do it for that. If not, you can owe me, since y'all have been such good customers," said the man sympathetically.

"What are we going to do now, Bedford?" I asked when we got

home, being caught up in the electricity of all his creative ideas and activities.

"How much allowance do you have left?" he asked.

"None, and since you got my $5 bill, I can't even go to a movie," I lamented.

"Then let's go make some nickels, and we'll spend the afternoon playing the pinball machines, juke box, and calling on the pay phone at the drugstore."

"Make nickels out of my lead soldiers?" I asked.

"Sure. I've already melted the Doughboys and Tommies...there's only the Huns left."

We went out to the tool room and plugged in a little electric kettle that melted the soldiers. As soon as the Germans had been turned into molten lead, Bedford directed me to pour it into his handmade, circular metal molds, so he wouldn't risk burning his own fingers. When the lead discs had cooled, we pushed them out and repeated the process. Soon, our pockets bulged with the coins — exactly the same size as, and remotely resembling newly-minted nickels. Bedford drove us to the Melrose Drugs where we spent the afternoon playing pinball machines, hit records, and telephoning our friends, as the appreciative proprietor — for the moment — looked on.

The air felt cool when I awoke the next morning, with no hint of the scorching midday temperatures to come.

"Today we dive," announced Bedford, confident that his master diver — me — was prepared to meet the unknown challenges of the deep.

Richard and Bedford picked up the diving helmet and weights, and headed down the street for the lake as I followed, carrying the bicycle pump, garden hose, and the other telephone. When we reached the water, I waded out waist deep and Bedford and Richard slowly lowered the diving helmet — laden with the heavy window weights — over my head. The rubber-lined cutouts at the bottom of it crushed down on my thin shoulders, driving my feet into the muck and buckling my knees.

"Wo, testing...one...two...three. Can you hear me all right; are you getting plenty of air from this bicycle pump?"

"I can hear fine and breathe good, but the helmet's so heavy my feet are stuck," I answered, feeling a mixture of fear and excitement.

"Then get down in the water. The helmet will feel light, and you can walk down to the bottom," instructed Bedford.

I followed his directions and finally extricated my feet. Then I cautiously walked deeper and deeper until all the hose had been let out.

Bedford wears his homemade diving helmet as
David pumps air into it with a bicycle pump.

"Wo, you're at the bottom now. Great! Everything's working like I planned. Can you see anything...like fish...or golf balls...how 'bout sunk boats?" asked Bedford over the telephone.

"No. It's murky out the window and I can't see a dumb thing," I said.

"Then come on back up so Richard can take his turn, and I can have mine," instructed Bedford.

"I don't want to yet. I just got down here," I answered over the phone, finally feeling a calm, comfortable sense of well-being.

"Get on up here!" shouted Bedford. "I'm tired of pumping...my arms are about to fall off."

I refused again, telling him I'd take my own good time getting back up, since it had taken so much nerve and energy to get down. I could hear Bedford and Richard conferring, then they started laughing.

"This'll get him back up, quick," snickered Bedford.

A second later I felt water falling on top of my head. I looked up in shock to see it gushing down through the hole where air had been coming in. Bedford had put the bicycle pump in the lake and now pumped water down through the garden hose, instead of air.

I became paralyzed with fear as the water rose higher and higher in the diving helmet until it reached my mouth, all the time Bedford shouting over the telephone for me to come up. Finally, I inhaled the last breath of air, threw the helmet off, and swam to the surface.

"What have you done with my diving helmet?" yelled Bedford, as

I reached the bank. "We might not ever find it again."

"What about my telephone?" I countered. "It's ruined 'cause you pumped water all over it."

I felt like punching both of them in the stomach as I climbed out on the bank, but being outnumbered, I thought better of it. I'd gotten into a fight with Richard once before and he'd raised painful "frogs" all over my arms because he hit them so hard with his knuckles.

When I got home, I found that Baba and Daddy had returned from the medical meeting in Atlantic City and had brought us each a big sack of saltwater taffy from the boardwalk there. I told them all about my trip to Egypt but nothing of our dubious endeavors with Bedford's inventions. Instead, I got my allowance and joined Bill and John for our usual, Saturday afternoon movie at the Village Theater where I could forget about the terrors-of-the-deep I'd encountered that morning.

The matinee feature began, and we sat through the usual western thriller while ushers cruised the aisles, rebuking troublemakers for putting their feet on seats, throwing things, or making noise. There followed an exciting serial episode of Flash Gordon meeting the terrifying "mud men." After that came a special advertisement — for Bosco canned spinach.

On the screen appeared a quiet neighborhood street with a paperboy delivering his papers. Then a big bully walked up, grabbed the boy's bag, and threw all his papers up on the roof of a nearby house — one at a time as the weak, puny paperboy watched helplessly. When he got home, the paperboy saw a can of Bosco spinach on the pantry shelf beckoning to him. He ate the whole can, then he felt a sudden surge of power rippling through his muscles. A sinister, confident smile came over the paperboy's face, up on the screen, as he began lifting heavy household objects with ease, such as the refrigerator and living room sofa.

The next day, as the movie advertisement continued, the bully once again tried to snatch the paperboy's papers. But the paper boy knocked the bully down and gave him a thorough beating as our matinee crowd cheered wildly.

"Gosh, I sure would like to get my hands on a can of Bosco spinach," I whispered to Bill, having just the bully in mind to thrash.

A moment later, my prayer was answered as the houselights went up and the manager came onto the stage. He announced that every youngster attending the matinee the next Saturday would receive a free can of that miracle muscle-maker, Bosco spinach.

That evening, since Sally was on vacation, Bedford and I went out with our parents to a restaurant for supper. After we'd all caught up on family happenings, Baba decided to play the big juke box using the coin-operated, remote control located at our table, but found she had no nickel. I reached in my pocket and gave her a handful of coins. Then, when she didn't hear her selections being played after putting in several nickels, she called for the manager to give us our money back. He came with a screwdriver and took the front off the jammed selector, making a startling discovery.

"No wonder it wouldn't work," he said, giving Baba a reproachful look. "You were putting in slugs!"

Our mother, feeling mortified and blushing from embarrassment, could only offer the explanation that she hadn't noticed, in the dim light, that these nickels were "different." After the manager left, she demanded a full explanation from me, since the nickels had come out of my pocket. But Bedford, feeling the circling vulture of guilt about to land on his shoulder, made a full confession concerning his lead-melting and counterfeiting operation in the tool room.

"Bedford, making and passing off counterfeit money is illegal, immoral, and just plain stupid," said Daddy. "You made a real sucker out of Overton, getting him to help you, but I'm holding you responsible for the idea and making it work. I want you to dismantle everything and then, young man, you're grounded! You'll stay in your room for one, full week till you learn that crime doesn't pay."

"Why'd you have to go and hand Baba those nickels, Wo?" asked Bedford as we were marched out of the restaurant. "Just how stupid can you get?"

"Too stupid to realize I was living with a crook," I answered, feeling mad that he'd ever gotten me involved.

"I'll bet Bedford's counterfeit nickels were only the tip of the iceberg," I overheard Baba say to Daddy when we got home. "There's just no telling what other devilment Bedford was up to while we were away. Maybe he needs to be off in a prep school after all? Aunt Pauline Brazelton sent cousins Berry and Chuck off to Episcopal High School in Virginia, and look at what perfect young gentlemen they've turned out to be!"

As the days of punishment crept by, Bedford paced the floor like a caged animal, or he'd bury his head in books for hours at a time, ignoring food and drink. Finally, his week of confinement neared its end as Friday night arrived.

"Bedford, tomorrow your punishment's done," said Baba softly as she came out on the sleeping porch to tell us good night. "Your Daddy says for you to stay in your room until noon, then you can go out. And Overton, don't forget about your piano recital."

I had begun piano lessons during my confinement after the knee operation, but had yet to make my playing debut. The next morning I reluctantly surrendered myself to Baba and she drove me to the recital at my teacher's home. With the music under my arm, and butterflies in my tummy, I walked dutifully inside to "face the music."

"And for our final number, Overton Shelmire, who just now arrived, will be playing '*Country Gardens*' by Percy Grainger," said the teacher as she motioned impatiently for me to come forward.

I sat down on the stool and placed my music on the piano, petrified and embarrassed as every eye in the room focused on me. When I began to pick at the keys self-consciously, starting the piece, a breeze blew through the room and closed my music. I opened the music and began again, but the breeze blew it shut once more. The other students giggled as I reopened the music and started over. I'd struggled through a few bars of the piece when a sudden, strong gust caught the fluttering sheets and tossed them off the piano and right out the window! Feeling mortified, I walked outside the house to the accompaniment of uproarious laughter. Then I picked up my music and marched straight home, my concert career having ended "on wings of song."

Arriving home, I found our room deserted, Bedford having left at the stroke of noon, the time when his confinement officially ended. Glancing around, my eyes suddenly riveted on a bizarre-looking object sitting on my desk. I realized I was looking at a humorous miniature sculpture of a cowboy riding a horse, made of modeling clay and metal parts. The eyes of the horse and rider peered out of metal wheels imbedded in the clay; more wheels represented the spurs. Some sort of small spring that had been bent into the shape of a flying rope had become the cowboy's lariat, and the shiny buttons on his little clay shirt appeared to be metal screws. The brim of the cowboy's hat was made of a metal case, and the horse's golden reins, he held, looked just like a watch chain.

All of a sudden I reached down, jerked out the bottom desk drawer and slid open the top of the secret compartment. EMPTY! Bedford had discovered my wonderful pocket watch Grand Daddy Bunch had given me, and had dissected the incredible timepiece completely in order to study its works. Then, when he couldn't get it together again, he used the parts in his fiendish sculpture.

Blind with rage, I vowed to pound him with my bare fists until he pleaded for mercy. But how would I do it when he was bigger and stronger than I? Then, I remembered the promised can of Bosco spinach.

I hurried to the Village Theater to claim my prize and sat impatiently through Hopalong Cassidy and the Three Stooges. Finally, the cartoon ended, and as we filed out of the theater, I received a free can of the new muscle building miracle — Bosco spinach.

"What?" said Sally when I got home with my prize. "You want me to fix that whole can of spinach for you? You hardly just pick at it when I put some on your plate?"

She heated the spinach and watched in amazement as I ate it all. Then, as my muscles felt a great surge of power, I went to a mirror so I could see them grow. Soon, I felt strong and self-confident, due to the miraculous transformation the Bosco spinach had suddenly made on my body.

I dashed out the back door and crouched down between Baba's compost pile and the garage, where Bedford would park his bike when he got home. Sure enough, he soon wheeled down the driveway to the garage and got off his bike. As he passed my hiding place, I suddenly flew through the air, landed on my unsuspecting brother's back and dragged him to the ground. I knelt on top of him, pounding his stomach furiously with my newly-powerful two fists.

I was startled, however, when he threw me off with ease, got up, and shoved me down in the compost pile. Then he jumped on top of me and gave me a thorough thrashing, leaving me buried from head to foot in the warm, wet, decaying vegetation that Hawkins had been letting rot into fertilizer for the yard.

Soon, my best friend Frisky began licking the leaves off my face and making me feel better.

"Frisky," I said, stroking his long silky ears with my grimy hand, "I don't know what I'd do around this crazy place without you."

As I lay there, aching and miserable, I wondered what had gone wrong with the promised magical powers of Bosco spinach. Was there simply no truth in advertising, after all?

XXXV

Walking my Dog

That fateful day began just like any other Saturday morning. Bedford, David, and I sat sleepily at the breakfast table, completely oblivious of each other's presence. We three seemed to have only two things in common — the same parents and voracious appetites for Sally's pancakes.

"They'll be ready in a minute," Sally said sweetly, standing there in her starched, blue uniform and white apron, whipping the batter. "You boys are up earlier than usual."

"Wo woke me up bangin' around our room," said Bedford disgustedly.

"I got up early 'cause Frisky and I are walking up to Knox Street to see the Filipino yo-yo man at Woolworth's," I explained. "I've saved up so I can buy a brand-new Duncan yo-yo and get him to carve my name on it."

"I hope you buy one this time that knows how to do some tricks," said Bedford. "Your yo-yo always looks like it's broken."

"It is not...I can 'walk my dog,' 'shoot the moon,' and 'rock the cradle,' and the yo-yo man's gonna teach us how to do the 'breakaway,' 'skin-the-cat,' and 'the man-on-the-flying-trapeze.'"

"I woke up early 'cause Margaret's husband phoned her," said David, who shared his room with our portly nurse. "He said he had a big surprise for her, and Margaret's still upstairs talkin' to him about it."

"Here's the first round," said Sally, putting a tall, steaming stack of her light, fluffy pancakes on each of our plates. Then she walked into the pantry, brought out a metal can shaped like a little log house, and set it down in the middle of the breakfast table.

"Oh, no, Sally," said Bedford. "Don't you have any kinda syrup besides Log Cabin?"

"Now Bedford, we had your Aunt Jemima's syrup last time and Overton's Mary Jane molasses the time before. Your mother said you could take turns and not for me to buy three different syrups and set 'em all out every time I cook pancakes. Besides, I save the empty log houses so David can make his fort bigger," said Sally.

"He better watch out," I said. "Bedford'll melt 'em down or cut 'em up or somethin'."

"I'm not worried," said David boastfully. "Bedford wouldn't dare come in my room and mess with my toys anymore since I cracked him on the head."

David had always been ferociously possessive of his things and once, when he caught his oldest brother pillaging his closet, he'd flung a barrage of dead flashlight batteries, hitting Bedford in the head and stunning him. After that "David and Goliath" episode, Bedford had been more inclined to concentrate on my belongings. Since our fight in the compost bed, however, he'd been surprisingly respectful, even of my things.

We finished our third stacks of pancakes and as I followed Bedford out the back door and down the steps, Sally handed me a can of Red Heart dog food, it being my turn to feed Charcoal and Frisky.

"Don't give Charkey much...he's gotten so fat and lazy," said Bedford, looking down scornfully at his black cocker spaniel whose rotund body had not lived up to the expectation of his fine lineage.

As soon as my sleek, trim Frisky had licked his bowl clean, we began our brisk walk to Knox Street, both of us with full tummies and high spirits. Before long, the town hall came into view and we enjoyed a cool, adventurous shortcut, wading through the creek beneath the building. We walked up Euclid Avenue for several blocks, greeting people who stood at bus stops along the way. Then, when we passed the Highland Park train depot at Knox Street, Frisky went wagging up to the cheerful redcap who waited out front to help passengers with their bags.

"Well, lil' fella, aren't you fulla sass. Bet you'd make me a good bird huntin' dog if your owner would like to sell ya," he said.

"I wouldn't take anything in the world for Frisky," I said, proudly, sincerely.

Beyond the train tracks, Knox Street became a four-block-long shopping strip, situated at the opposite end of the Town of Highland Park from the Village shopping center, and it had held a special allure for me since I'd first been allowed to walk and ride my bicycle up there by myself. This time, I'd chosen a slow, leisurely walk with my dog. Frisky and I passed the radio shop, bakery, and poultry store. Then we stopped at the pharmacy to buy a package of chewing gum. Crossing the street, we walked by the Knox Theater, home of the "B" movie where just a week ago my friends and I had watched a giant tidal wave topple all the skyscrapers of New York City.

Next door stood the Woolworth's variety store, our final destination, where the Filipino yo-yo man was holding court. Frisky sat obediently at the door of the store as I walked inside and spotted a tan, beaming, dark-haired young man wearing a loud floral shirt. He performed extraordinary tricks with his yo-yo, to the delight of an audience of wide-eyed boys.

As he demonstrated "the-man-on-the-flying-trapeze," I thought back to the first time I'd walked to Knox Street by myself. While perusing the toys on this very same aisle, I'd picked up a wooden man-on-the-flying-trapeze. I squeezed the two long sticks together to make him spin, but was overzealous, and they'd snapped in two. Not having a cent on me to pay for my destruction, I'd fled the store, feeling enormous fear and guilt.

Today, however, I had 50¢ burning a hole in my pocket to buy a brand-new, rainbow-colored Duncan yo-yo with my name carved on the side.

"How yoah spell Obie?" asked the Filipino yo-yo man with knife in hand.

"It's Ovie," I answered, "O...V...I...E."

"Okay, Obie," he said as he began to furiously carve the side of my new yo-yo, handing it to me proudly a few seconds later.

"But my name's Ovie, not Obie," I protested, feeling sick as I looked at my name that had been carved so beautifully, so unchangeably.

"Yeah, it say Obie, right," said the yo-yo man, not seeming to comprehend. "Who buy yo-yo now?...who next, boys?"

Not wanting to call attention to myself, remembering the time I'd broken the toy man-on-the-flying trapeze, I left the store having learned no new tricks, with the wrong name on my brand-new yo-yo, and with a dread of having to listen to Bedford ask: "Who's Obie?"

Frisky awaited me outside the store, as did thunder and lightning. We'd walked only a few blocks when a downpour started. Just as I picked up Frisky and tucked him under my shirt to keep him dry, a bus pulled up to the corner where I stood getting drenched. The door opened and I climbed the steps, thanked the driver for stopping, and plunked a nickel in the coin box. Then I took a seat, but when I looked up, I saw the driver staring at me in the mirror and motioning for me to come back up.

"I thought I saw somethin' movin' 'round in there," said the driver as Frisky stuck his bright, smiling face out of my shirt. "Dogs aren't allowed on the bus...you'll have to get off here."

He pulled up in the middle of the block, opened the door, and put Frisky and me off in a torrential rain, without even giving my nickel back. Wiping my eyes, I squinted through the downpour at the big house where we'd stopped. A woman sitting in a swing on her broad, old-fashioned porch motioned for us to come up and get out of the chilling rain. Seeing that we were both drenched from head to foot, she went inside for a towel.

"My, what a beautiful dog," she said as I wiped Frisky off and enjoyed the storm, sharing the swing with her.

"The man who gave me Frisky called him the runt of the litter," I told her.

"Oh, no," she said. "When my husband was alive we used to raise cocker spaniels, so I know how they're supposed to look. Frisky may be small, but he has beautiful conformation. Just look at that head, those ears, his nice body. He could be a show dog!"

When the rain stopped, finally, I thanked her and led Frisky proudly off for home, promising to stop by for a glass of lemonade the next time we passed by on our way back from Knox Street. As we arrived home and walked up the sidewalk, glad to be back from our adventure together, Margaret rushed out of the house carrying a suitcase. I asked her where she was going, but she had to rush to catch a bus for downtown and didn't have time to explain. Frisky and I turned around and started following her toward the bus stop, hoping for an explanation.

"My husband has had a wonderful thing happen," said Margaret as we hurried along. "It's like a miracle. A man who's starting a chain of hamburger stands called 'Topper' needed a sign for each of them, that customers would recognize and remember. My husband drew a top hat and cane as a logo and the man liked it so much he paid $25 for it — just one drawing! We're going to celebrate tonight after church by having dinner and staying at a little hotel downtown."

Then I told her all about our eventful trip up to Knox Street and showed her my new yo-yo as the bus rounded the bend of Drexel Drive.

"Somebody sure needs to learn to spell," she said, looking at the yo-yo.

She hugged me and stepped onto the bus with her suitcase. Then, she continued to wave through the window until the bus had pulled away from the curb, turned the corner, and driven out of sight.

Margaret had never seemed so happy and excited about anything, and I felt glad for her. I started home, then turned to see why Frisky wasn't leading the way like he always did. I saw a squirrel, with a feathery tail, scampering across the intersection of Drexel and Euclid toward its sanctuary of big trees in the park — with Frisky in hot pursuit.

Out of the corner of my eye I noticed a department store delivery truck coming fast down the hill from the right, approaching the stop sign. Though the sun now shone brightly, the streets were still wet...and slick. The driver slammed on his brakes when he saw the sign — and the dog chasing the squirrel just beyond it — but the truck skidded out into the intersection. I watched, horror-stricken, unable to believe my eyes as one of the tires ran over my beloved Frisky.

I ran to him as he lay there, quiet and still in the middle of the intersection. The delivery truck had stopped a few feet beyond and the young driver had jumped out quickly. He just stood there saying he was sorry. I knelt down on the pavement, threw my arms around Frisky's crumpled body, and put my face close to his. He was still breathing, hard and fast, with his pink tongue hanging far out. His eyes bulged as I spoke to him...pleading to him not to hurt...praying for him not to die, but he didn't seem to recognize me. Feeling helpless, bewildered and heart-sick, all I could do was hug and kiss him and tell him I loved him — over and over and over as Frisky lay there, trembling in my arms. Then, after what seemed an eternity in hell, I heard an angelic voice above and behind me.

"Oh, my dear...oh it's Frisky, poor little fellow. Is he still alive?" asked the lady whose porch we'd shared during the rainstorm.

"Y...yes, ma'am," I said, hardly able to speak, "but he was run over awful bad. He can't move."

"I heard the truck skid," she said, "and I looked down the street. I saw it stopped in the middle of the intersection with the driver out, so I came to see what happened. I'm so sorry...I know a good veterinarian near here. You wait with your dog, and I'll run home to get the car and be back in a minute."

When she returned, I picked up Frisky and laid him on her back seat. I sat with my dog as she drove, rubbing him gently, communing and comforting with my trembling hand as best I could until we reached the animal hospital. While distraught and sick with fear, I felt better since this kind lady had come to help my injured friend.

When we arrived, and I had carried Frisky into the waiting room, the lady made me give him to the nurse. I hated so terribly to leave my little dog in this strange place — hurting and afraid — and having to say goodbye to him. Finally, Frisky was taken from my protecting arms, and the nice lady persuaded me to let her drive me home, having convinced me there was nothing else I could do for him there.

Later that afternoon, Baba called the doctor to check on Frisky since we'd received no word. He was still alive and holding his own, she told me. With my spirits buoyed by a faint feeling of hope, I thought of the nice lady who'd come to Frisky's and my rescue, and realized that I hadn't thanked her. I rode my bike to her house and found her sitting on her front porch in the swing as before.

"I was so terribly sorry to hear about poor little Frisky," she said as I climbed the steps. Suddenly, I felt a cold chill of apprehension come over me.

"Oh, he's still alive and might pull through," I said feebly, not quite certain I believed my own words.

She gave me a glass of lemonade and asked me to sit down beside her.

"I didn't realize you hadn't heard," she said, speaking softly. "Overton, life is a wonderful, mysterious combination of happiness and sorrow. I should know, because I've had plenty of each and you will too, as you live yours. We all must learn to accept terrible disappointments, to be courageous, and to keep on going. The veterinarian called a moment ago and said that Frisky died. He'd been unconscious ever since you brought him in and he didn't feel a bit of pain. While he didn't live long enough — people, and animals we love never do — try to think back as you're hurting and remember all of the fun times you and he had together. That's what I do to ease my own pain."

I felt my insides being twisted into a knot, my heart being pierced by a knife. A feeling of utter devastation and sorrow, the likes of which I'd never experienced before, came over me as I finally grasped the reality. Frisky, whose sole purpose was to be at my side every minute, had gone from my life — forever. I thanked the lady as best I could, with my voice cracking while I tried not to cry. Then I raced to my bike and pedaled home, my vision blurred with tears, my insides aching with grief. I needed my mother worse than I ever had in my entire life.

Baba held me in her lap and rocked me for the first time in so very, very long, neither of us saying a word; there were no words that could help. She patted me and rubbed my back like always, for an hour it seemed. But somehow the magic of sitting in Baba's lap, that had always been the answer to any hurt or insecurity, didn't work now; the pain remained inside me. Indeed, I'd grown up, and at that very moment in time, I hated having done so. Oh, if I could only turn the clock back several years, I wished, or for just a few hours anyway. Then I would have slept late, skipped Sally's pancakes, and never, ever have gone up to Knox Street and bought a yo-yo that had "Obie" carved in the side.

XXXVI

The Ultimate Power

As I awakened to the sound of firecrackers popping and torpedoes screaming around the neighborhood, I felt great anticipation for all the Fourth of July fun — until I suddenly awoke again to the nightmare of Frisky's death. It happened every morning, just the same, sad way.

Daddy had unfurled our big American flag and hung it in the holder on the front porch column, joining numerous other flags on almost every house up and down Miramar. After breakfast, Bedford drove David and me up to the vegetable stand on Knox Street so we could each buy our dollar's worth of fireworks. For me, it became a sad, sentimental journey as we passed all the places Frisky and I had visited, stopping and sniffing, the week before.

Reaching the vegetable stand, we filled our sacks with firecrackers, torpedoes, roman candles, bottle rockets, red devils, sparklers, vesuviuses, pinwheels, skyrockets, and punk to light the fuses — enough fireworks for a whole day of fun in the backyard and up and down the street. With Miramar being such a busy street of boys, it sounded like a small war going on. I missed Frisky terribly during the day's hectic activity, for the dogs of the neighborhood always seemed to enjoy racing around between the bangs as much as we boys did. The neighbors never complained about the loudness of our firecrackers, for it was the birthday of our nation and shooting fireworks was patriotism at its best.

Late that afternoon, our whole family went to the country club, as we always did on the Fourth, to sit in chairs on the 18th green, eat watermelon, and watch the ever-spectacular aerial fireworks display. At twilight, we gazed through a constellation of fireflies as a team of young men, across the lagoon, prepared to light the fuses.

When darkness came, the skyrockets began to streak toward the sky. They burst overhead, sending their dazzling, colorful tracery across the heavens, reflecting in the placid water and turning our faces aglow. I began to feel light-of-heart for the first time in a week, since Frisky had died. Perhaps life could go on without him, even richly at times. But, soon, life would have to go on without Sally, too.

Sally's husband, Clinton had a fatal heart attack a few days later. She told Baba at the funeral that, with much thought and soul-searching, she had decided to live in California — after being with us all my life.

The morning Sally returned to work, I got up early before anyone else awoke.

"Good morning, Sally. I'm sorry about Clinton," I said quietly as I tiptoed into the kitchen.

"Thank you, honey," she said, standing at the sink, not turning around. "It was a terrible shock for me, but I'm better now."

"Baba says you're gonna move to California. Why Sally? Why do you have to leave us?" I asked, pleadingly.

"I don't want to leave, especially you, but I have to," she said, staring out the window. "I need to be with my sister who just moved to Los Angeles. We've never been this far apart. Besides, things are...better for us...out there."

"But I'm gonna miss you so much I don't know what I'll do?" I said, tears welling up in my eyes.

"And you think I'm not gonna miss you, too?" she said. "Why lawdy mercy, when you went off to that Camp LZ, I could hardly stand it I missed you so much. When it got real bad, I'd just hafta go up to your closet and look at your shoes and suit hangin' there, so I'd feel you were close by. Why, I bet you never gave your Sally a thought while you were up there havin' fun."

"I did, too," I said, hugging her around the waist from behind. "Will you write me lots and send me molasses pies and come see me sometime?"

"You know I will, honey," she said.

I sat down at the kitchen table. My world had suddenly come tumbling down around me. Frisky had died, and now my second mother was leaving. I watched her make breakfast, each of us solitary in the sadness of our own thoughts. Her world had crashed down too, I realized.

Bedford's 16th birthday arrived the fifth of August, and he began the day acting so pompous about it that I left the house early to go see Bill and John. They'd planned to go to the Esquire theater after lunch to see a movie called *The Biscuit Eater* and asked me to join them. Their mother dropped us off at the theater, and as soon as we'd found out how long the feature ran so she'd know when to pick us up, we raced inside and grabbed our seats.

The Biscuit Eater began as a heart-warming boy and dog story that took place in the Georgia hunting country. It ended as the most devastatingly sad, monumentally tragic motion picture that any of us had ever seen — especially me.

The poignant story paralleled my life with Frisky. A boy had been given a runt from the litter of thoroughbred Georgia pointers. He and a young playmate set about the secret, difficult task of training the runty pointer for the annual field trials, where the dog would have to compete against the boy's father and the father's dog, two-time winner of the Grand National Championship.

At the field trials, the boy's well-trained runt easily outpointed the other dogs with whom he was matched. Finally, he and the champion owned by the boy's father were the only two dogs left in the finals. Just as the runty pointer froze into a beautiful point that most certainly would have clinched the finals for him, the boy's friend ran up to tell him some disturbing news. He had just heard that if the boy's dog won the championship, the wealthy owner of the kennel and farm planned to fire his father.

In desperation, the boy went up to his runt and berated him softly, under his breath as a "no-count biscuit eater" — a bird dog too sorry to hunt for anything except his own food. I ached inside for the little pointer when this caused the puzzled animal to break point and run off into the woods.

That night, the boy's dog sneaked back into the father's kennel to visit a champion bitch, and nuzzle her litter of puppies he had fathered. Finally, the little runt and I had both found contentment, and I waited expectantly for the movie's standard, inevitable happy ending.

At that moment, however, the old trainer, assistant to the boy's father, was awakened by the noise of the happy reunion. I watched in unbelieving horror as the trainer took slow, careful aim in the moonlight, and shot and killed the little runt, thinking him a stray dog. I became the boy in the movie as it ended with the boy cradling the dying dog in his arms, crying his heart out.

While my eyes had been moist throughout the movie, having felt the desperate pain of association, the ending was so withering that I sat sobbing in my chair as the houselights came on. I looked around in embarrassment, and to my surprise, there was not a single boy or girl in the theater who wasn't sobbing with me.

Mrs. Pearson picked us up, and when we three plunked down on the back seat, we all burst into tears.

"What's the matter?' she asked.

"Th...that was...the saddest movie...ever made," we all said in tearful unison.

I walked in our dining room just in time for dinner and Bedford's birthday cake, my eyes bright red from crying.

"Well what's the matter with you, Wo?" asked Bedford.

"We saw the saddest movie in the world," I said, as tears began to stream down my cheeks once again.

"Well, I never saw a movie sad enough to cry about," announced Bedford proudly. "I'd never let a movie make me cry — like that."

"You would in this one," I said, sniffing.

"What in the world was the movie about?" asked Baba.

"It was about a boy who trains a little bird dog to enter the field trials and...oh, I don't want to talk about it," I said.

"Wo's still just moping about Frisky," said Bedford unsympathetically. "He'll never get over that. If something happened to Charcoal, I wouldn't go around crying all the time about it."

"That's 'cause he's not as cute as Frisky. He's a fat slob that lays there all day and just eats," I said.

"You say the movie's about bird dogs and a field trial?" asked Daddy, thinking back to the glory days of the pointers in his own kennel.

"Let's go tonight for Bedford's birthday," suggested Baba.

"Sure," said Bedford. "I'd like to see what broke up my little brother."

Suddenly, my heart grew light again at the prospect, the possibilities. Bedford said he'd never cried in a movie. Indeed, I never remembered having seen him shed a tear about anything at all, but tonight he would, giving me great pleasure.

"Hurry up! We'll be late for the feature," said Baba, as I stuffed my pockets full of Kleenex for them — I knew how much they were going to need it.

My eyes welled up once again when the movie began, but by the time the dog was trained, there were no more tears to shed. When the runty pointer took his stance, about to beat his father's dog, I began to get out the Kleenex. When the boy called his little dog a "biscuit eater" and ran him off, I looked at Baba, Daddy, David and Bedford. Tears were streaming down each of their faces, and they accepted my pieces of Kleenex with appreciation.

The movie ended tragically, once again, with the boy cradling the dead dog in his arms. When the houselights came on, there wasn't a dry eye in the theater, old or young. Bedford-the-brave sat there sobbing uncontrollably. He continued to cry all the way home and went to bed, humiliated, without saying a word.

Bedford seemed subdued and different after that, as he got ready to go off the prep school. Gone was his sarcasm, his meddling, his cynicism. It may have been the unknown challenges that lay ahead that had brought on the big change in him. It seemed to me, however, that I'd discovered the ultimate power that had brought Bedford to his knees. The ultimate power is love, and through the saddest movie ever made, he'd learned — and felt — what love and affection are all about...and how with love, invariably, comes sadness.

The three Shelmire brothers — David, Overton, and Bedford

September first finally arrived, the day Bedford would board the train for prep school in Virginia. As I looked around the room, seeing little evidence that my big brother had ever lived there, I felt a twinge of sadness. Hawkins and Daddy had already carried the big trunk containing most of Bedford's things downstairs. At strict, thorough Episcopal High, Baba and Daddy hoped Bedford would learn to channel his brilliant mind, his facile ability to learn, and create an outstanding record that would enable him to enter Princeton University the following summer, and medical school after that.

We pulled up in front of the Highland Park train depot and when the smiling redcap saw Bedford getting out with Charcoal, he asked me where my dog was, but I couldn't answer. I'd missed Frisky so much, and my beloved Sally, that the possibility hadn't occurred to me that I might miss Bedford, too. Now, I realized I would, and that feeling surprised me.

Finally, we stood on the station platform, waiting to see Bedford off to his learning adventures in the East. He had remained unusually quiet, seeming to anticipate the difficult tasks that lay ahead of him for the next several years, and feeling that this might have been his last summer at home for a long, long time.

Bedford gave Charcoal a pat on the head, then turned and hugged first Baba, then David, then Daddy and, finally — to my great surprise — me! While we'd fought on occasion, he'd never really hurt me. On the other hand, he never had given me a hug, so his affectionate, sincere embrace came as a complete surprise.

"Charcoal is your dog now, Wo. Take good care of him," he said with uncharacteristic emotion.

His eyes grew misty, for giving up his dog was symbolic of giving up his family, his home, his security and...his childhood. Or, perhaps he was lamenting a childhood he'd never had, for Bedford always seemed to have been an adult. The hug I received established a sacred trust he was putting in me to look after Charcoal, cementing a bond among the three of us.

A moment later, as the huge steam locomotive chugged down the track and clanged to a stop, Bedford leaned down and put his arms around his rotund dog.

"Be good, Charkey, and you mind Wo — he's your master now. He'll take good care of you, and you're gonna become great friends."

"Good luck, Bedford," I said, as he turned and headed for the train. "Watch out for the derailment!"

"Okay, Wo...see ya, and don't take any lead nickels," he said as he hopped on the train — always Bedford, evermore Bedford.

Baba, Daddy and David got back in the car, but I said I wanted to be alone and walk Charcoal home. They drove off, and as my new dog and I began to walk along, I felt the pain inside again.

"Oh, why can't you be Frisky?" I asked, but the chubby cocker spaniel just tilted his head quizzically, not seeming to understand.

After we'd walked a couple of blocks, I looked around, almost having forgotten Charcoal was following me. He was sitting down, being very still, with his nose pointed straight up in the air. An aggravating fly buzzed around his fat face and long black ears.

Suddenly, he opened his mouth and snapped it shut, swallowing the fly. Then he looked up at me with what appeared to be a comical, satisfied smile as he seemed to wait for my approval. I began to laugh at Charcoal through my tears...and laugh...and laugh. I dropped to my knees on the sidewalk and hugged him with all my might.

"I'll bet Bedford taught you to do that!" I said, finally laughing without tears. "I love you, Charkey. You're my dog now and we're gonna have lots of fun together."

I got up and began to walk along, feeling light-hearted and gay for the first time in weeks.

"Come on, Charkey, come on," I said. "There's a lady in the next block I want you to meet. D'ya like lemonade?"

THE END

EPILOGUE

December, 1980

A shroud of murky darkness covered the sleeping town and wrapped my heart in grief. Having just heard the tragic news, I called my Labrador retrievers and headed for Hackberry Creek. By the time we passed town hall, the silhouette of the domed tower had emerged from the paling, early morning sky. I looked up at its tall, Spanish archway and thought I heard boys laughing...thought I saw a big, gas-filled balloon floating toward the heavens.

Meandering aimlessly along the creek, I listened to the taunting and name calling of yesteryear. Every bridge, every tunnel, every turn of the creek brought back a memory of growing up with Bedford, and following my older brother off to war. Could it really have been four decades since the last, great BB gun battle?

I thought back over the topsy-turvy script of Bedford's life. As a baby, he'd survived a near-fatal automobile accident, which was equally as ludicrous as the life he lived. Our mother was driving while a nurse held Bedford — wrapped snuggly in a blanket — in her arms. As they turned a corner, another auto broadsided their car and the little bundle that was Bedford went flying out the opposite window onto the pavement. Our mom's auto tipped over on its side. Miraculously, the vehicle landed with the open window directly over Bedford, and as the auto skidded along on its side, the warm bundle ended up unhurt, back in the arms of his startled nurse.

As the years went by, Bedford's path continued to twist and turn — often on the brink of disaster. But despite having survived several bizarre automobile and airplane crashes without a scratch, Bedford refused to admit to miraculous good luck, maintaining that he lived by his own wits and didn't intend to die in an accident or hospital.

"No, when I die it'll be at the Pierre Hotel in New York, leading the good life," he would say. And I knew he could do it, like any other prank, invention, or scheme he'd ever set his mind to. Hadn't he earned his MD by his 21st birthday, for instance, then become a best-selling author, and concocted a hand cream in his spare time that garnered him a half-million dollars?

As I threw a ball for the dogs to chase, I lamented the fact that Bedford and I had found little time to do things together lately. He'd been busy with his medical practice and successful writing career. I had been preoccupied with my architectural practice. That was a pity, I thought, for Bedford and I had grown up to genuinely enjoy being with each other and had a great mutual respect for each other's accomplishments.

During his college days, Bedford had introduced me to the wonderful world of Gilbert & Sullivan through his record albums of the comic operas he'd brought home from school. Now, these many years later, when I'd noticed that Gilbert & Sullivan's *Patience* was to be performed at a local theater, I felt a sudden compulsion to ask Bedford to go to supper, then to the opera since I hadn't seen him for some time.

We had sat there two nights ago in the darkened theater, basking in Sullivan's glorious music, Gilbert's clever words, and above all, in each other's company. Bedford would be off for New York the next day to sign a contract with the publisher for his third book. He told me that he hadn't been feeling well — his blood pressure was high again — but he promised to do something about it when he got back.

It was early this morning when I got that dreadful phone call — Bedford, at age 54, had died late last night of a heart attack in his room at the Pierre Hotel, following a contract-signing party for his new book, and supper at his favorite French restaurant. Now I was trying to come to grips with the awful, bitter reality that my brother was dead.

The rising sun began to break through the gloom as the dogs and I crossed the former no-man's land and continued to stroll along the creek bed. It cast long, darting shadows on the grass as the dogs chased their bouncing ball. I looked out over the parkway. It had the mystical appearance of the great battlefield we had imagined it to be in our youth. The rock retaining walls became the ramparts of Bunker Hill. The drainage pipes protruding from the embankments looked like the cannons of Fort Sumter. The grassy slopes rising up to the street appeared as the sorrowful hills of Gettysburg.

Suddenly, in the faraway distance, I heard the catcalls, the charges and retreats, the popping BB guns of bygone battles. Shadows became snipers hiding in the limbs of the giant cedars, and soldiers hiding behind rocks. I followed the stream under the old stone bridge and paused for a moment.

Why had Bedford left me again — this time forever, I wondered? Then I thought I saw a thin, tow-headed boy with skinny legs approaching through the shadows. He wore a fencing mask, a baseball catcher's protective chest guard, and carried a BB gun as he walked his mystic way.

"Bedford, why are you wearing all that stuff?" I asked. "Where are you going?"

"Wo, I've figured out this ultimate defense against the flying BB.

If they want to shoot their BB guns, let 'em fire away — they can't hurt me now. Victory will be ours today!"

"Take me along," I begged. "I won't be any trouble. I'll stay way behind and bring you a drink of water and give you a bandage when you're wounded."

"No," said my brother, adjusting the fencing mask. "Where I go you can't follow. I have to fight them alone."

"Please don't go...don't leave me, Bedford," I pleaded, holding tightly around his knobby knees, but he broke away, strode fearlessly down the creek, and disappeared into the morning haze.